Admiral Insubordinate
The life and times of Lord Beresford

Richard Freeman

Second edition © Richard Freeman 2015.

This print edition is published by the author. Printed by CreateSpace. Available from Amazon.com and other book stores. A Kindle version of the first edition of this book is published by Endeavour Press Ltd.

Acknowledgements

My thanks to Marion E Colthorpe, Professor Andrew Lambert and Carla Zipoli for their advice on the manuscript; to Peter Warburton for drawing my attention to the archives of the Central Committee for National Patriotic Organisations; and to Professor Jane Ridley for giving me access to her notes on the Lady Brooke affair.

This book could not have been written without the rich resources of: the British Library, Cambridge University Library, Churchill College Archives, Durham County Archives, Hansard online archive, *The Manchester Guardian* online archive, the McGill University Archives, the National Archives, the National Maritime Museum, *The Observer* online archive, the Parliamentary Archives, and *The Times* online archive.

Note on terminology

The First Lord was the political head of the Admiralty; he was also a member of the Cabinet.

The First Naval Lord – an admiral – was the professional head of the Admiralty. He was assisted by three junior naval lords. From October 1904 the term 'sea lord' replaced that of 'naval lord'.

Spelling

Place name spellings in quotations have been left as in the original documents.

Other books by Richard Freeman

The Great Edwardian Naval Feud. Pen and Sword, 2009.
Britain's Greatest Naval Battle. Endeavour Press, 2012. Kindle book.
Great Naval Commanders of the First World War. Endeavour Press, 2012. Kindle book.
The Dardanelles: Tragedy and Heroism. Endeavour Press, 2013. Kindle book.
'Unsinkable': Churchill and the First World War. History Press, 2013.

Contents

Contents	3
Preface	5
WILD YOUTH 1846-1871	6
Chapter 1 The wild youth from Curraghmore 1846-65	6
Chapter 2 First steps 1865-72	12
YEARS OF UNCERTAINTY 1872-1881	18
Chapter 3 Sailor or politician? 1872-76	18
Chapter 4 Marking time 1876-81	27
YEARS OF GLORY 1882-1885	37
Chapter 5 Triumph in Alexandria 1882	37
Chapter 6 Between wars 1882-84	44
Chapter 7 His finest hour 1884-85	48
WILDERNESS 1885-1899	63
Chapter 8 Fall from grace 1885-88	63
Chapter 9 Beached on the back benches 1888-89	73
Chapter 10 Back to sea 1890-93	82
Chapter 11 To be an admiral 1893-96	90
Chapter 12 Tub thumping 1896-98	94
Chapter 13 MP for York 1898	102
Chapter 14 MP for York 1899	108
UNEASY RECONCILIATION 1900-1905	113
Chapter 15 Giants at bay 1900-1902	113
Chapter 16 Hammering on the Parliamentary anvil 1902-03	124
Chapter 17 The Channel Fleet 1903-05	132
YEARS OF ANTAGONISM 1905-1910	144
Chapter 18 The Mediterranean command 1905-07	144
Chapter 19 The Channel Fleet 1907-08	158

Chapter 20 The Channel Fleet 1908-09	173
Chapter 21 Career's end 1909-10	187
BITTER HARVEST 1910-1919	191
Chapter 22 Return to the back benches 1910	191
Chapter 23 Member for the Navy 1911	197
Chapter 24 Home Rule 1912	202
Chapter 25 Slowing down 1913	210
Chapter 26 Last days of peace 1914	215
Chapter 27 The arrival of war 1914	222
Chapter 28 Goodbye to the Commons 1915	228
Chapter 29 In another place 1916	236
Chapter 30 Sniping from the sidelines 1917	246
Chapter 31 War's end 1918	253
Chapter 32 Last days 1919	257
Epilogue	261
Chronology	263
End notes	264
Bibliography	276
Index	280

Preface

Three times commander-in-chief, a member of Parliament for twenty years, and a public speaker who filled halls throughout the land – Lord Charles Beresford was all of these. Yet he was also a naval captain who had so little sea experience that he scrambled to qualify for flag rank. He endured long periods of unemployment when in disgrace with the Admiralty, while his one foray into ministerial life ended in resignation. He was also the most reprimanded naval officer of his time – perhaps of all time.

Few men have enjoyed such fascinating and adventure-packed lives as did Beresford. The first ten years of his naval career took him to every corner of the globe. He saw it all, from gold-mining to crucifixions, from the wild tribes of Terra del Fuego to the shadowy figure of the Emperor of Japan. When not recklessly throwing himself into perilous riding and wild hunting he could be found risking his life to rescue fellow sailors.

Yet, after a shaky start, Beresford's career changed when, at the bombardment of Alexandria in 1882, his tiny HMS *Condor* took on the guns of one of the massive Egyptian forts. He was an overnight hero and remained so until his death. Three years later his even more spectacular adventures in the Sudan made him the hero of the failed campaign to rescue General Gordon from Khartoum.

But his official life was marred by his persistent hostility to the Admiralty and government. He achieved the dubious honour of one Prime Minister (Lord Salisbury) vowing never to employ him again in a political capacity and one First Lord of the Admiralty (Reginald McKenna) vowing never to employ him again in the Navy. So antagonistic to authority did he become that his naval career was ignominiously ended by the curtailing of his final command. At the age of 64 all public appointments were closed to him. Never again did the Admiralty or government call on him for any purpose. He still, though, made his mark and, as an MP and then as a peer, he remained centre stage, speaking in Parliament up to a few weeks before his death and still writing letters on the day he died.

Like him or loath him, Beresford was a giant whom no one could ignore. His life, as I hope this book will show, was rarely dull and frequently astounding.

Richard Freeman

WILD YOUTH 1846-1871

Chapter 1
The wild youth from Curraghmore 1846-65

Charles William de la Poer Beresford was born into a minor branch of one of Ireland's wealthiest families on 10 February 1846. His ancestors numbered generals, bishops, archbishops and admirals. The family seat at Curraghmore boasted thousands of acres of forests and meadows. At the heart of the estate was the grand house with paintings by Gainsborough and Reynolds on the walls. Nearby was a private chapel and stabling for over 100 horses. The estate's owner, the third marquis of Waterford, was Beresford's uncle Henry, who was said to be the richest landlord in Ireland with an annual income of £27,000 (about £1.3m today).

Beresford's father was the Reverend John Beresford and his mother, Christiana, was the fourth daughter of Charles Leslie, MP. John Beresford was known as a 'wild Irish Rector', 'a savage kind of Christian' and a 'fox-hunting thug'. He possessed a temper so ferocious that one son (a VC winner) said he would rather 'meet an army of Zulus than his reverend father in a bad temper'. The whole Beresford clan had a reputation for undisciplined behaviour. Beresford's Uncle Henry had been expelled from Eton and removed from Christ Church Oxford for rowdy behaviour. Later he was described as 'the biggest bully and blackguard in London'. Several members of the family had died through reckless sporting activities. So wild was the family that it was said 'no Beresford ever died in his bed'.

John Beresford was the parson at Philipstown, part of the parish of Baronstown until, in 1859, his brother Henry broke his neck in a hunting accident and died. The Reverend John Beresford unexpectedly became the fourth marquis, while Charles took up his courtesy title of Lord Charles. The family installed themselves at Curraghmore, where the home life for the males centred around riotous hunting and hare-brained sporting activities.

As the second of five sons, Charles was not in line to become marquis. Despite this hereditary drawback, he was to outshine all his brothers. His elder brother John Henry (born 1844) had an undistinguished career, first in the Life Guards and then as an MP. After Charles came William (born 1847) who, despite winning a VC in the

Zulu War, led a dilettante existence and achieved nothing of note. Marcus (born 1848) did better as the manager of the racing stables of the Prince of Wales (later King Edward VII); his skill earned Edward a small fortune in prizes. Some distance behind came Delaval (born 1862), who was the black sheep of the family. After he emigrated to Mexico little was heard of him until his death in 1906. He appears to have returned to Ireland only for the funeral of his brother John in 1895.

Beresford was schooled at home until his father despaired of his waywardness and sent him to England. At Bayford School in Hertfordshire his fellow pupils included a future prime minister (Lord Rosebery) and a future First Lord of the Admiralty (Lord George Hamilton). It was Hamilton who later said of Beresford that 'a more unruly boy never defied the schoolmaster's birch'. Beresford himself claimed in the House of Commons in 1915 that he was 'more flogged than the whole of the rest of the boys put together'. From Bayford he was sent to school in Deal and, finally, to a naval crammers run by a Reverend William Foster.

Beresford entered the *Britannia* naval school in December 1859 despite failing to spell his name correctly in his examination. 'Book-work,' he admitted, 'did not interest me.' A fellow cadet later recalled that he never 'gave any clear indications of the greatness he was to attain'.

HMS Britannia where Beresford entered the Navy in 1859

It was at the naval school that Beresford first demonstrated his insubordinate nature. In his enthusiasm at being promoted to the rank of cadet captain, he emptied a bread-barge on top of a master-at-arms. He was derated the same day. When not being insubordinate Beresford could be reckless as when he borrowed a boat and was pushed out to sea without oars. He drifted helplessly to Spithead until he was finally rescued.

* * *

After completing his course at *Britannia,* Beresford was appointed as a naval cadet on the Mediterranean flagship HMS *Marlborough* in 1861. He adored the vessel, calling it the 'smartest and happiest ship that ever floated'. Her captain was Sir William Houston Stewart, who had captured revolutionaries in South America and fought in the Crimea and was just the sort of man whom Beresford admired.

HMS Marlborough on which Beresford joined as cadet in 1861

Once at sea Beresford encountered the raw side of Navy life. The food was atrocious, the hygiene poor, the work hard and rough. It was dangerous, too. A moment's inattention on the yard-arms could lead to death. Beresford escaped an early end when furling a sail. As he stood in his bare feet on a rope slung beneath a yard-arm a midshipman kicked the rope away. He was left high above the deck, holding on by just the grip of his fingers.

Later in life Beresford exaggerated the hardships of the *Marlborough.* In 1898, as a popular rear admiral, he gave a colourful account of the ship in an address to Harrow schoolboys. Drunkenness was rife, he said. Five hundred of the 1200 men 'could neither read nor write'. They were flogged 'for the slightest offence'. Within days a letter appeared in *The Times* from Rear Admiral Gillett, who had been first lieutenant in the *Marlborough* when Beresford served on her. He called Beresford's remarks on drunkenness 'ridiculous'; his comments on flogging were 'a very serious indictment' against Stewart; and he reckoned that no more than fifty men were illiterate. Twelve further officers wrote to support Gillett, all of them denouncing Beresford's fanciful memories.

Beresford's naval prowess was seasoned with a disobedient streak. He delighted in pranks and happily boasted of them in his memoirs. Whilst on the *Marlborough* he cheated in a sail contest, for which he was 'severely reprimanded' for 'staining the character of a ship'. He went on to paint '*Marlborough* Star of the Mediterranean' on the cliffs of Malta, only to be sent back to wash the words off. When his leave was stopped he simply swam ashore in the dark, changed his clothes, and returned at his leisure to the ship.

It was at Malta in 1862 that Beresford was introduced to the Navy's idea of target practice. He recalled in his memoirs that 'We used to practise firing at a cliff in Malta Harbour', although the ship's log book identifies the target as the uninhabited island of Filfla. He also learnt about the Admiralty's parsimonious attitude to ammunition, recalling: 'I used to be sent on shore to collect the round-shot and bring them on board for future use.'

In June 1862 Beresford was promoted to midshipman. A year later, on 25 June 1863, he was posted to the port ship *Hibernia* to await a passage home. While there he heard that the *Marlborough* had been sent to rescue a Turkish liner. Never one to miss a bit of excitement, he set off from Malta in a duck-punt – a vessel that was never designed to go to sea – and took part in the rescue. He recalled that 'Each British sailor took a Turkish sailor by the scruff of his neck, and ran with him from side to side of the ship, until she rolled herself into deep water.' At least that is the version in his memoirs. The truth was more mundane. The stricken ship (an Egyptian frigate, not a Turkish liner) ran aground on 25 June just outside Malta harbour. That day the *Marlborough* and other vessels secured the frigate with cables and, on the following day, the *Trafalgar* pulled her free. It seems doubtful that Beresford contributed much to the rescue.

* * *

On Beresford's return to England he was posted to HMS *Defence* in the Channel Squadron. Commanded by Captain Augustus Phillimore, she displaced over 6000 tons but had a mere 22 guns. Beresford detested the ship, calling her 'a slovenly, unhandy, tin kettle which could not sail without steam'. More to the point, he did not like the Channel with its 'cold skies and the dirty seas'.

Beresford's propensity for pranks continued. The most serious incident of this time resulted in a court appearance. He and some friends were in a cab and were taking pot-shots with pea-shooters at passers-by. In a penitent letter to his father Beresford confessed:

> 'I hit a lady who was leaning on a gentleman's arm in the face. The man chased us and with a good deal of difficulty, caught us; we were then taken to the stationhouse, and given into custody.'

Not only was Beresford fined £2 10s, but the story got into the papers. The Mayor of Plymouth accused the young men of 'sowing their "wild oats" ... in the public streets'. Another newspaper sententiously remarked that 'The days are gone ... when the pranks of a Waterford would be tolerated.' When news reached the Marquis, he responded with a diatribe that came near to disinheriting his son.

When it came to money Beresford never had enough. Although he became very wealthy at an early age he was always short of cash. In 1863, though, he was still living off his midshipman's pay (£31 a year, equivalent to about £1300 today) and £80 a year from his father. Unable to pay his debts following the pea-shooter fine he appealed to his father for help. All he received was a sharp rebuff: 'I ... tell you plainly that I will not pay your debts: if you run into debt you will be dishonoured and have to leave your profession.'

What with the debts and bad newspaper publicity the Marquis became concerned at the direction that his son's career was taking. He quietly arranged for his son to be transferred to HMS *Clio* in July 1864.

* * *

The *Clio*, a steam corvette of 1472 tons with 32 officers and 295 men, set sail for the Pacific three weeks after Beresford joined her. He was delighted to be back in a sailing ship. 'What,' he asked, 'can be more glorious than a ship getting under way? ... She quivers like a sentient thing.' He went on: 'Doctor, paymaster, idlers ... run up on deck to witness that magnificent spectacle, a full-rigged ship getting under sail.' (Idlers were men such as carpenters, who did not stand watches.) However he found the ship cramped and with a mess so small that the midshipmen had to walk across the table to cross the cabin. The rations were 'miserable'. As senior midshipman Beresford took charge of the shilling a day that each man contributed to a fund to supplement their diet. He accounted, he said, 'for every penny, with the most sedulous precision'. On the long voyage out they amused themselves by racing cockroaches and 'dropping lighted tallow' onto their tails.

The *Clio* crossed the Equator on 16 September, the log book recording that 'the usual ceremony' was performed. Beresford recalled 'being ducked and held under in the big tank' until 'insensible'.

From Ascension Island the *Clio* went on to the Falklands, where she stayed for just over a month. The ship's stay there offered the crew the macabre experience of volunteering as executioners. The Governor wanted to hang a man, but feared the local gauchos would rebel if he did so. He asked the *Clio* to oblige. When volunteers were called for there was no shortage of offers. The enterprising sailors built a scaffold, hanged the man, and disposed of the body at night. Whether Beresford participated he did not say.

While at the Falkland Islands Beresford witnessed scurvy at first hand when a merchant ship arrived with the crew in grave distress. He called it 'a most repulsive disease. The sufferer rots into putrid decay while he is yet alive.'

After the Falklands the *Clio* passed through the Straits of Magellan, with Tierra del Fuego along her port side. The natives 'totally naked … beat the sea in anger with their paddles'. A letter that he posted at the local convict settlement later reached his mother in Ireland.

In the Juan Fernández Islands the young officers found time for hunting. The quarry was goats, which were driven over a cliff edge by seamen while Beresford and his colleagues sat in boats ready to shoot them. The rough sea proved too much for the small boats and soon the waves were hurling Beresford towards perilous rocks. At the last moment a bluejacket came to his rescue.

In August Beresford made his first acquaintance with Canada, a country that would always be important to him; he thought it would 'become the centre of the British Empire'. There he formed part of a working party that was paid an extra shilling a day 'to cut a trail through the virgin forest'.

As Beresford transferred to his next ship, back home there was a ball at Curraghmore for 600 guests. Addressed by the Tory politician Lord Chelmsford, the guests heard him praise the absent son for exhibiting 'all the courage and generosity of his race'. Far flung as his travels were, Beresford's admirers had not forgotten him.

Chapter 2
First steps 1865-72

In October 1865 Beresford, still in the Pacific, was moved to HMS *Sutlej*, a steam frigate of 2066 tons. Five weeks later he was transferred to HMS *Tribune* for three months before returning to the *Sutlej*.

It was at this time that Beresford's wild behaviour came near to ending his career. Working at his sewing bench (sailors in those days made their own clothes) a sailor knocked it over. 'I took up the first thing which was handy, which happened to be a carpenter's chisel, and hurled it at the retreating figure. It stuck and quivered in a portion of his anatomy which is (or was) considered by schoolmasters as designed to receive punishment.' Had the chisel penetrated a more vital spot, Beresford's service might have been rapidly terminated.

HMS Sutlej gun deck

While on the *Tribune* Beresford was promoted to acting sub-lieutenant. On his certificate Captain Gilford noted that Beresford had shown 'sobriety, diligence, attention, and was always obedient to command'. This was about the last time that any commander found Beresford to be obedient.

Back on the *Sutlej* Beresford's service was brightened by a near-action at Valparaiso. Spain had been involved in a sporadic war with

First steps 1865-72

Peru and Chile since the previous year. When this war threatened the city of Valparaiso, ships of the Royal Navy were moved in to protect British interests. The *Sutlej* arrived on 26 January 1866 and *The Times* declared that 'the British naval force on this coast is now strong enough to protect foreign property'.

At the end of March the Spanish announced that they would bombard the city and the British ships prepared for action. In the *Sutlej* the cabins were dismantled and the guns run out. Shortly afterwards, the captain of the Spanish warship, the *Mendez Nundez*, declared that he had orders to sink both British and American ships if they intervened. So, on the morning of 31 March, as the Spanish moved in to attack, the British and American ships stood out to sea. So much for *The Times'* earlier assurance that British property would be protected. In fact, it suffered $20 million of damage. Beresford's first attempt to see war at first-hand had ended in retreat. He would have to wait another sixteen years before he could participate in the real thing.

* * *

Of the most notable event at this time, Beresford said not a word in his memoirs: the death of his father on 6 November 1866. Six days earlier he had been taken ill with 'retching of the stomach and gastric fever'. It is reasonable to assume that Beresford felt little grief at the death of his tyrannical father. The marquisate passed to Beresford's elder brother, John Henry.

* * *

During this period Beresford saved the lives of two men and was 'most strongly recommended for promotion' as a result. There was no promotion, though. He then had a brief posting to HMS *Research*, beginning on 29 January 1868. Stationed at Holyhead, the ship patrolled in the Irish Sea and barely spent more than a week at any one port. Nevertheless Beresford 'hunted a good deal from Holyhead' and even crossed over to Ireland to hunt. There was then a period of unemployment in the summer, which Beresford put to good use by attending a royal levée. Still only a sub-lieutenant, he was nevertheless presented to the Prince of Wales by the First Lord of the Admiralty. He then put in an appearance at a dancing party given by the Countess of Harrington. In July he was posted to the Royal Yacht *Victoria and Albert*. After a visit to the Royal Yacht Squadron Regatta in early August and assisting the passage of Queen Victoria to Cherbourg for a short trip to Paris Beresford's posting was unexpectedly truncated. An inspection of the yacht had revealed serious damage from a recent visit to the Baltic and she went into dock for major repairs. Ten days before leaving the yacht Beresford was promoted to lieutenant. He was now 22 years old.

* * *

Since serving on the *Clio*, Beresford had had short spells on six different ships in three years. Although promoted, he must have felt that his career was going nowhere. He was now to enjoy three years on HMS *Galatea,* which would take him to exotic climes and provide him with a fund of fantastic tales that would echo round London dinner tables for years to come. The ship was commanded by Prince Albert, Duke of Edinburgh (fourth child of Queen Victoria). Under his care Beresford was to enjoy the voyage of a lifetime.

Prince Albert, Duke of Edinburgh

The *Galatea* reached the Equator on 23 November, where the Duke had agreed that the usual ceremony could be observed, provided that those who did not wish to be shaved could remain below deck. 'The conditions of the agreement were [soon] forgotten,' noted *The Times*, with 'a rollicking disregard of social distinction'. Beresford fell into the spirit of the occasion, setting up a band under his direction.

There was a short stay in South Africa, where the Duke carried out various engagements and Beresford organized musical entertainments at Simon's Bay. The next stop was Australia where the Duke attended the swearing-in of Sir James Ferguson as Governor of South Australia. While in Australia, Beresford enthusiastically engaged with the locals, sometimes with surprising results. On one occasion he came across a man who had been transported for forgery and claimed to be related to him. Always a soft touch, Beresford gave him 'a small cheque', which the man promptly used to forge 'a bill of exchange for £50' – nearly £2300 today. On another occasion he began his lifelong association with freemasonry when he was admitted to the Australian Lodge as, he wrote, 'the most timid neophyte who had ever joined it'.

There was riding, too, even if it was nearly the death of him. Having bought a pair of horses, Beresford, with the commander at his side, was descending a hill when the Duke's horses bolted causing Beresford's mount to panic. They tore down the hill, heading straight for a train of carts. The road being blocked, Beresford frantically steered his tandem between a telegraph pole and a wall and came out unscathed.

It was then on to New Zealand, where Beresford witnessed Maori war dances, sampled hot springs and quizzed a reformed cannibal on his withdrawal symptoms – he was only tempted when he saw a plump woman, 'which ... was the prime delicacy'. Those pastimes being a little tame, Beresford leapt at the Governor's offer to hunt on his private island. Sir George Grey insisted that it was possible to hunt boar using only dogs and a knife. When Beresford took up the challenge, a sow got the better of him and he ended up badly cut.

In a typical Beresfordian fashion, a dog cart that he hired for two days to take him to the races resulted in his appearing in court. Having only used the cart on the second day, an argument broke out as to whether he should pay for one or two days. The local court found in his favour.

After New Zealand the *Galatea* set course for Japan, dropping in at various Pacific islands on the way. At Tahiti Beresford was intrigued by the locals who 'never seemed to do any work, with the single exception of carrying bananas'. He luxuriated in floating down the streams and courageously followed the young children in plunging down 40-50 feet waterfalls.

On arrival in Japan the *Galatea* was greeted by the Commander-in-Chief of the China Station, Sir Henry Keppel, under whom Beresford would serve when he returned to England. (They were to become lifelong friends.) Beresford threw himself into the local culture and was tattooed – much to the astonishment of the natives since 'in Japan none save the common people is tattooed'. He also witnessed six decapitations and a crucifixion at Yokohama.

First steps 1865-72

It was then on to China, which the *Galatea* reached in early September 1869. The Duke paid a formal visit to the Mikado (the Emperor of Japan), accompanied by Sir Harry Parkes (Minister to Japan), Keppel and Algernon Mitford of the British Legation, now better known as the father of the Mitford sisters. As they walked to the palace, all the upper windows of the houses were sealed – an honour usually reserved for sovereigns. Once the audience was over, six officers, Beresford amongst them, were admitted to the presence, which he recalled as a 'dim figure ... seated behind a screen'.

HMS Galatea arriving at Hong Kong 1869

It was at this time that Beresford 'bought' a servant called Fat Tom for £5. He entrusted him with his money and in due course found that Fat Tom had forged cheques to the value of £1200. The amount seems unbelievable (it would be £58,000 today) but *The Times* confirms that he was sentenced to five years in prison for the offences at the Winchester Assizes in 1878.

At Manila on the way to India Beresford found an 'extraordinary prevalence of cock-fighting'. After pausing at Ceylon (now Sri Lanka) the *Galatea* headed for Mauritius, where Beresford climbed the Pieter Both mountain.

On the *Galatea's* final leg home she called at the Falkland Islands. Here Beresford saved a man's life 'with much difficulty and at great risk'. This brought him a bronze clasp to his Royal Humane Society medal. On 19 May 1871 the long voyage ended with a 17-gun salute in Plymouth Sound. On the orders of the Prince there was no royal reception and he stepped off the ship as a captain, not a prince. If Beresford observed his captain's decorum, he felt no impulse to imitate it. Once he reached flag rank, each landing would be accompanied by as much pomp as he could muster.

Within three weeks of returning, Beresford had been appointed flag-lieutenant to Admiral Sir Henry Keppel, Commander-in-Chief at Plymouth. Immediately after this, he went on leave.

* * *

For seventeen months, Beresford almost disappeared from public view. His heady round of society events was capped in October 1872 with an invitation to Balmoral. As usual, Queen Victoria had few guests, so Beresford had ample opportunity to push himself forward in front of his sovereign and the Prince of Wales. (Not that the Queen ever took to him.)

Just a few days before he took up his post at Plymouth, Beresford joined the Prince of Wales in a visit to his friend the Earl of Aylesford at Packington Hall in Warwickshire – the ancestral home of Beresford's great rival Sir John Fisher. During his leave it is likely that he joined the Marlborough Club that the Prince had founded around 1868. It was to be the centre of Beresford's social life for the next twenty years.

It was now thirteen years since Beresford had joined the Navy. He had served on ten ships (including *Britannia*) and had reached the rank of lieutenant. Having been selected as a flag-lieutenant, his career looked set to flourish. It was a false promise. In the next eighteen years Beresford would serve on sea-going naval (as opposed to royal) ships for just two and a half years. His only significant sea-going postings were to be HMS *Thunderer* (May 1877 to June 1878) and HMS *Condor* (December 1881 to August 1882). It is hard to credit that a man who saw himself as the epitome of a naval officer would, from the age of 26 to 43, take almost no part in his profession.

YEARS OF UNCERTAINTY 1872-1881

Chapter 3
Sailor or politician? 1872-76

The Plymouth posting proved socially successful since Keppel, after having served at sea for the last time, treated his job as a sinecure, during which he indulged in sport and dining. It was said that every country house in the area was open to him and, Beresford recalled, 'We used to hunt a good deal with the Dartmoor hounds'; they even crossed the Irish Sea to hunt at Waterford. Keppel pandered to Beresford's high spirits and pranks and there is little evidence to support Beresford's claim that he did 'a good deal of hard work' at this time.

* * *

It was in June that Beresford had what he called 'my first independent command'. So proud was he of this posting that he refused to respond when Fat Tom called him 'Master' and insisted he was addressed as 'Captain of the *Goshawk*'. All this gives the impression that he now had a ship of his own but he had simply been asked to take the *Goshawk* – a gunboat of around 200 tons – from Plymouth to Spithead and back on the occasion of a visit of the Shah of Persia. This did not stop Beresford aggrandizing the event in his memoirs, writing 'The first thing I did in the *Goshawk* was to get from the flagship a big working party of a hundred men to work at holystoning the decks until they were as clean as a hound's tooth'. The only significant event of this command occurred when Beresford nearly ran the vessel onto a rock in Plymouth Sound, having passed on the wrong side of a buoy.

Three weeks later Beresford was back in London to dine at the house of the Marquis of Hertford. Naval business resumed in August 1873 when the Prince of Wales went to Holyhead to open a new harbour. On the day of the ceremony, Beresford and Lieutenant George King-Hall boarded the royal yacht before she steamed out to the breakwater, which was to be opened by the Prince. The ceremony was soon over and the there was a long day to fill so Beresford and Lord Suffield (a member of the Marlborough House set) organized a race. In his memoirs Beresford describes how he broke Lord Suffield's leg when he shoved him off the course. Suffield recalled the race years later but made no mention of the broken leg – it was one of the many examples of Beresford's capacity for embellishing a tale.

The Prince of Wales paid an official visit to Plymouth in late August, which resulted in an embarrassing moment for Beresford when he ran a yacht ashore under the gaze of Keppel and the royal party. The *Pall Mall Gazette* reported that it was 'with considerable difficulty' that 'a steam launch and several ships' boats' rescued him. As the yacht came free 'the Prince led the spectators in cheering the performance'.

Towards the end of the year Beresford was at Christ Church, Oxford to lunch with Dean Liddell, who was then Vice-Chancellor of the University but is now better known as the father of the Alice in *Alice in Wonderland*. One of the principal guests was the Prince of Wales; the others included the Duke of Marlborough and Benjamin Disraeli, the Leader of the Conservative Party. Rarely can a very junior naval lieutenant have dined in such company.

* * *

That Beresford's duties at Portsmouth were minimal is clear from his election to Parliament as the Unionist Member for Waterford in March 1874, ousting his Liberal predecessor by 1767 votes against 1390.

The election enabled Benjamin Disraeli to form his second administration. If Beresford can be believed, Disraeli took a fatherly interest in the new member and gave him some advice (which he never took). The story goes that Beresford announced that he was going to vote with a particular member because he agreed with him rather than with his own party. Disraeli remonstrated with Beresford, saying 'My boy, don't you know that it's your first duty to vote with your party?' Without such discipline, parties would collapse and 'Government could not be carried on.' Whether true in detail or not, the tale is true in spirit. Beresford was a hopeless party man, who always went his own way.

While at Devonport Beresford made few contributions to Commons' debates. In April 1874 he opposed a motion to repeal the *Gun Licence Act* 1870. The following month he opposed prohibiting the sale of alcohol on Sundays in Ireland. Drinkers, he argued, 'would lay in a stock of liquor on the Saturday night, and be certain to be more drunk than ever on Sunday' whereas, if they got drunk in a public house on a Sunday they would be ejected on 'the least sign of inebriation'. It was during this debate that *The Graphic* newspaper noted Beresford's 'exceedingly easy style of conversation' in debate. He had a capacity to 'tickle the fancy of the House'. Indeed, until he entered his pompous later years, he was one of the most popular speakers in the Commons.

In addition to his appearances in the Commons Beresford kept up with London society. Between May and July of 1874, he dined with the Prince of Wales, appeared at a levée, a state ball, a royal garden party and a royal fancy dress ball. He was then best man at his brother John Henry's wedding to Lady Blanche Somerset in July.

Beresford's Plymouth posting ended on 13 August, but since the Prince of Wales began a visit there that day, Beresford stayed on. He was present with the mayor, the corporation and Keppel to greet the Prince at the railway station.

It was just after the end of Beresford's Portsmouth posting that the newspapers began to circulate rumours that the First Lord of the Admiralty, Ward Hunt, had accused him of neglecting his naval duties. Hunt had told Beresford that his dual positions as MP and naval officer were incompatible and that he should choose between them. Beresford was reported as having replied: 'Oh, I'll give up the county [Waterford], and I know there are two Home Rulers who are anxiously awaiting the vacancy.' Under this threat, Hunt withdrew.

* * *

Beresford's next posting matched his peripheral attachment to the Navy. In December 1873 HMS *Bellerophon* had collided with a steamer, the *Flamsteed*, near Cape St Vincent. Although her crew and passengers were saved, the steamer had sunk. Eight months later the Admiralty recalled the *Bellerophon's* officers to London to attend an enquiry. Beresford was sent out to Halifax as one of the temporary officers to cover their absence. His appointment was made on 14 August and he set sail in the SS *Nova Scotia* around 26 August. The ship reached St John's, Newfoundland, on 4 September. Beresford waited at Halifax until the *Bellerophon* returned from sea on 5 October. Meanwhile he passed the time hunting with a local trapper 'camping out, and living upon what we could secure with our guns'. Since they shot 'bear and deer and prairie chicken' the living must have been substantial.

Beresford's account of joining the ship was pure imagination. He recalled that 'my old messmate in the *Marlborough*, Swinton C. Holland' had been put in command of the ship. He had obviously forgotten that the officers recalled to London were not only still on-board the *Bellerophon* when she docked at Halifax, but remained there until 3 November. He nevertheless Beresford remarked that leaving a second lieutenant in charge of a ship was 'a curious illustration of the incidents of naval life'.

HMS Bellerophon on which Beresford served for a few months in 1874-5

On 7 January 1875 the officers returned from England and took charge of the ship again. Beresford departed to begin a two-year period of half-pay.

* * *

For the next two years Beresford divided his time between the Commons and the Marlborough House Set. After a ball and a levée he joined the royal party for the launch of HMS *Alexandra*. *The Times* noted that 'launches of ironclads have been so rare in the last few years' that it merited "a special demonstration"' – a view that was shared by the 20,000 people who turned out to watch.

In April Beresford turned his mind to more serious matters by delivering a long speech in the Commons on the lack of barracks for Navy personnel. Through lack of proper accommodation, he argued, men not at sea were being left without access to training or suitable work. 'The men in the depots,' he said, 'were ... employed in dockyard work, and the time was thus wasted which might be turned to good account in re-qualifying them for service on-board ship.' They needed 'barracks, with accompanying frigates as drill ships, in which the men might be accommodated and trained for the Service during the time that they were in port'. In other countries, such as France, he added, 'there was better training accommodation for their sailors than this great maritime country had for its seamen'. (No action was taken over the neglect of seamen in depots until Sir John Fisher introduced his nuclear crew system in 1904. Despite what Beresford had said in this debate, in 1904 he condemned Fisher's sensible and economical solution to the problem.)

Just four days later Beresford was on his feet in the Commons again, this time denouncing the *Declaration of Paris* (1856). This agreement, made at the end of the Crimean War, had outlawed privateering but allowed, in war, neutral ships to carry an enemy's goods (other than contraband of war) and enemy ships to carry neutral goods (other than contraband of war). When the MP Baillie Cochrane proposed that Britain should withdraw from the *Declaration*, Beresford rose in support. He argued that in any future war, British merchant ships would be attacked and destroyed by an enemy. Then 'merchants would naturally put their goods in the vessels of other nations, and shipowners would have either to lock up their ships in harbours at home or sell them to foreigners'. Britain did not withdraw from the *Declaration* and Beresford was still decrying it when the First World War commenced.

In June Beresford took up another contentious naval issue: manning. The Admiralty perennially found manpower to be a nightmare. Either there was a huge surplus of officers or a worrying deficit, but never a sensible sufficiency. In 1870 Hugh Childers, then First Lord of the Admiralty, had inherited a colossal surplus of officers and had implemented a plan to ease the problem. In the Commons, Lord John Hay (an ex-Third Lord of the Admiralty) suggested that Childers' scheme had 'not met the hopes and anticipations' forecast for it. Beresford agreed, saying that the Childers' scheme 'had been excellent in theory; but, in practice, it had failed to give satisfaction to the Navy'. There were now so few promotions that 'no matter how much a young officer might distinguish himself, he got nothing by it. They promoted from the top of the tree, and there was therefore no inducement for young officers to work.' (Comments made with feeling by a lieutenant on half-pay.)

That same day Beresford took up a theme that he was to pursue until the First World War: a lack of cruisers. He was obsessed by the idea that a foreign power would launch a surprise attack on Britain and within 'a fortnight ... The enemy would send out three or four cruisers ... [and] ... would inflict a vast amount of damage on our commerce.' The only answer was 'a larger number of first-class cruisers ... possessing great speed, to be rigged as frigates, and able to keep at sea for a long time'. While he congratulated the Government on the nine cruisers under construction, 'he should have been greater pleased if the number had been 69'.

After a vigorous summer on the back-benches, Beresford was left without occupation when the House rose on 13 August. Fortunately for him, his Prince came to the rescue.

* * *

Earlier in the year Lord Salisbury, Secretary of State for India, had recommended that the Prince of Wales make a tour of India. The Queen took some persuading, not least because of the proposed inclusion of 'half a dozen of the gayest members of the Marlborough House Set'. In particular she was most unhappy about the presence of Beresford, Lord Carrington, the Duke of Sutherland and the Earl of Aylesford. Despite these objections, Beresford was appointed aide-de-camp to the Prince for the duration of the tour and Sutherland and Aylesford were included. The tour was to last from mid-October to mid-March, although the Prince did not return to England until mid-May since he undertook Egyptian and European engagements on the way home.

Edward Prince of Wales, Beresford's intimate friend until 1891

The Prince, with a few key staff and friends, left London to travel to Brindisi via Paris on 11 October. After a journey which the Prince described as 'somewhat monotonous' but relieved by Beresford who 'kept up our sprits', the party arrived at Brindisi to board HMS *Serapis* under the command of Captain H Carr Glyn.

HMS Serapis

On leaving Brindisi the *Serapis* ran into a gale. Beresford, along with all of the party bar Lord Suffield, succumbed to seasickness and was unable to face dinner. At Piraeus their bad luck continued as the ship lost both her anchors in the harbour and sheared off the bowsprit of a yacht belonging to the King of Greece. Continuing via the Suez Canal they reached Bombay on 8 November. For Beresford the journey had been enhanced by the news that he had been promoted to commander on 2 November.

Although Beresford appeared at the side of the Prince at the Bombay levée, along with the Duke of Sutherland and Lord Alfred Paget (a soldier and business man), his main role appears to have been as a hunting companion. This resulted in a stream of accidents. In November his horse was startled and threw him to the ground. As he fell, Suffield recalled, 'he came down heavily on the hilt [of his stick], which caught him in the middle, knocking his wind out' before he was knocked unconscious on the ground. Later, in the dark, the Prince's party was returning from a day's hunting when the carriage turned over while crossing a bridge. As the dust settled, the Prince, 'covered with *debris*', crawled out of the wreckage, along with an unharmed Beresford.

Just after Christmas Beresford and friends went off on that most dangerous of sports: boar hunting. He returned after breaking some teeth on a spear handle but, said Suffield, '[he] was happily not disfigured'. Only a week later Beresford was again the victim of the same boar when he and Suffield resumed their hunt. Beresford, who could never bear to be beaten, raced ahead of his rival, oblivious of the rough ground. After missing the animal, his spear struck the ground. Beresford was knocked from his horse and fell on his back. A few days later his brother, Lord William, had to rescue him from a charging boar. It is hard to disagree with Suffield's remark that Beresford was 'doomed to misadventure'. He was not, though, the only victim of pig-sticking. Lieutenant Prince Louis of Battenberg fractured his collar bone when 25 miles from camp and Beresford ministered first aid.

There were happier times as well. At the end of November the Prince gave a dinner on-board *Serapis* to celebrate Beresford's promotion. It was brought to a conclusion by a huge wave pouring through a porthole and sweeping a man in mid-toast off his feet.

Hunting over, the Prince returned to England via Egypt, landing in England on 11 May, 1876. Meanwhile Beresford had returned to England on mission of the utmost delicacy.

* * *

While at Cairo the Prince had heard that Lord Randolph Churchill, then a recently elected MP, was blackmailing him with the aid of letters that he, the Prince, had written to Lady Aylesford. Lady Aylesford was having an affair with Lord Blandford, Churchill's brother. In consequence, Lord Aylesford was seeking a divorce. The Prince was desperate to avoid a scandal but feared that Churchill's vehement support of his brother would soon lead to the affair being public knowledge. On hearing of Churchill's attempt to blackmail him, the Prince decided to challenge Churchill to a duel. He despatched Beresford to London to deliver the challenge, which he did on 9 April. Over the next few weeks, tempers calmed and Churchill slipped out of the country as soon as the Prince returned to England. Beresford left no comment on his role in this affair.

* * *

Parliament had been in session since 8 February but it was not until mid-June that Beresford next spoke in the Commons. A Mr Taylor had moved a resolution to abolish flogging in the Navy. Beresford spoke in vigorous defence of the punishment, saying that 'it was a good thing that captains of ships should have the power of flogging'. He declared that 'Seventeen years ago when he joined the Service as a Midshipman flogging was common ... [but] the Navy now tried to teach them instead of driving them.' Nevertheless, he continued, 'It was a great mistake to suppose that the abolition of flogging would stop desertion or induce more men to enter the Service ... what was wanted was a little more pay.'

Beresford had now been without employment for 15 months and was showing little interest in the Navy. At thirty years old it was time to take his career seriously. But he would remain an MP for three more years and, in doing so, leave his intentions in doubt.

Chapter 4
Marking time 1876-81

In December 1876 Beresford was despatched to the torpedo school at HMS *Vernon* for a training course, but still found time to attend the Commons. It was at this time that he made a speech which he liked to claim damaged his career. He talked about the new and fearsome weapon: the torpedo. Much of what he said would have delighted the Board of Admiralty, as when he argued that 'no economical consideration should tie the hands of the First Lord of the Admiralty and so prevent exhaustive experiments being carried out as to the best means of applying or resisting these terrible weapons ... which threatened to change the character of naval warfare.' The Board may have been less pleased when he pompously added that it was 'his duty to bring the question forward, and he should be pleased if, by calling attention to it, he strengthened the hands of the First Lord of the Admiralty'. In his memoirs Beresford claimed that the Board 'Took great exception to my speaking in the House upon naval subjects, and desired me to understand that I must choose between the career of a sailor and that of a politician.' In turn Beresford claimed that such a restraint was a 'breach of [Parliamentary] privilege'. He went on to say that he then appealed to Disraeli, who smoothed things over. On the other hand, perhaps the story is a total fabrication since Ward Hunt, the First Lord, spoke most warmly about Beresford's contribution, disagreeing only on minor points of interpretation. Whatever the Admiralty thought of the speech, *The Graphic* newspaper described Beresford's 'sailor-like' discourse as a 'pleasant interlude' in the debate. But it regretted that Beresford 'does not often favour the House' with his attendance.

* * *

A few weeks after speaking on torpedoes Beresford was appointed to HMS *Thunderer* in the Channel Squadron. He joined the ship on 3 May 1877, the day that she was commissioned by her captain, John Crawford Wilson.

From Beresford's point of view his time on the *Thunderer* began well with a visit from the Prince and Princess of Wales on 22 and 23 May. Dinner and breakfast were provided for the royal party by the local army chief, General Sir Hastings Doyle, and Beresford was invited on each occasion. Indeed, Beresford claimed to have been responsible for the visit in the first place. In the previous year the *Thunderer* had suffered a devastating boiler explosion. Fifteen men had been killed on the spot and a further fifty-six wounded, some mortally, were taken to hospital. Sailors saw such accidents as portents of ill-luck so, said Beresford, 'the Prince of Wales at my suggestion very kindly came on board' to show his confidence in the ship. Before leaving the vessel the Prince said that he had 'derived the greatest satisfaction from this inspection' and praised the 'excellent ... captain and commander'.

HMS Thunderer, which suffered a gun explosion in 1876

There was, though, some controversy surrounding the start of Beresford's command. When he first took the ship to sea, all sorts of technical problems arose and the speed trials had to be abandoned. The *Thunderer* ended up at Spithead where, it was reported, 'she is likely to be for some time'. The rumour went round that Beresford had rushed his ship to sea before it had been inspected by the port admiral. In naval circles, reported the *Freeman's Journal,* 'there is no little ridicule indulged in at the expense of the Commander'.

Service on the *Thunderer* must have been dull as she meandered round the British Isles, paying brief visits to Queenstown, Cowes and Yarmouth. However, after her voyage to Queenstown, Beresford was reported as saying that the ship had 'behaved admirably' and was 'an excellent seagoing vessel, very buoyant and comfortable'.

At the Cowes regatta in early August, Queen Victoria and her youngest daughter, Princess Beatrice, visited the *Thunderer*. After touring the ship and admiring the guns they enjoyed a dinner to which both Captain Wilson and Beresford were invited. The Queen inspected Beresford's cabin, 'which was very comfortably fitted up, and in which stood his Chinese servant'. On leaving, Her Majesty declared Beresford to be 'very funny ... but [a] clever and a good officer'.

Two days later the Prince of Wales was on-board for a more energetic visit when the ship went to sea to demonstrate her steering. The Prince fired two 38-ton and two 35-ton guns using an 'electric broadside' aimed at the easy target of some flags tied to barrels. They finished the day by ramming the target.

Unknown to Beresford, the *Thunderer* was being observed by the newly appointed First Lord (and bookseller), W H Smith, who was making his way to Osborne to kiss hands with the Queen. Beresford, though, had not omitted to drop him a letter of congratulation on his appointment. 'Don't think me rude,' he wrote, 'if I say I was enough Shipmates with you in the House to appreciate what a real good appointment the Prime Minister has made.' Doubtless Beresford was the only commander in the Fleet to have had the nerve to write such a condescending letter to his superior.

In November Beresford's transfer to the Queen's royal yacht was proposed, but Victoria forbade this on the grounds that Beresford was an MP. By the end of 1877 the *Thunderer* was laid up in a repairing basin at Portsmouth to save wear and tear in the winter months.

In March 1878 Wilson, Beresford and the officers of *Thunderer* invited a few friends in the Commons to visit Portsmouth and their ship. Before the visit took place so many MPs had signed up that a special train had to be laid on. It was the success of this impromptu event that led Beresford in later years to organize annual visits whenever he was an MP, to the point where they became part of the social life of the Commons. It all helped to emphasise his political status as 'member for the Navy'.

When there was not much call for Beresford's services on-board the *Thunderer* he turned his attention to Parliament. On 11 March Sir Charles Seely, MP for Lincoln, called for a select committee to enquire into the design of naval vessels such as the *Inflexible*. She had, he said, 'no stability' and was liable to capsize. Beresford denied the necessity for any investigation: 'The *Inflexible*,' he told the Commons, 'was one of the most indestructible fighting machines ever placed in the water.' With astounding exaggeration he declared that not even the guns of 'our most powerful iron-clads' could sink her. He did, though, agree with Thomas Brassey, MP for Hastings, that these ships were lacking in quick-firing guns: 'They could only fire once about every five minutes.'

Marking time 1876-81

Punch cartoon lampooning W H Smith's lack of interest in the Navy

In the following week Beresford gave his strong support in the Commons to the need for pensions for the widows of seamen and marines. These, he said, would 'benefit ... the men, and benefit ... the Service'. There would be fewer desertions and the Navy could expect to save 'not £150,000, but £300,000 a-year' given that desertions ran at 4 per cent per year. He claimed that the 'men would only be too glad' to contribute to such pensions. As to the Government's contribution, that would be no problem since 'If the First Lord were to come forward tomorrow and say he wanted £2,000,000 for the Navy, the country would give it.' W H Smith, speaking for the Government agreed, as ministers often do, 'to examine the question carefully'.

* * *

In March 1878 Beresford became engaged to Ellen Jeromina Josephine de Mandesloh Gardner (known as 'Mina' to her friends and as 'Dot' to Beresford), daughter of the deceased MP Richard Gardner and his wife Lucy Mandesloh. The journalist Raymond Blathwayt described Mina Gardner as 'a very pretty woman, with a very strong personality; very cynical, almost too much so at times, but with the kindliest manner and a wonderful sense of humour; well-read and *au courant du jour* to an almost uncanny degree, a brilliant musician and yet also with a great habit ... of needle and thread.' He called her 'exceedingly clever and a very outspoken woman'. According to the *New York Times*, she was said to be 'a good musician' and 'fond of art and drama'. Her house was 'the rendezvous of singers, artists, and literary people'. Mrs Patrick Campbell, the actress, was a great friend. Even when the Beresfords were living seven miles out of London in the 1890s Lady Charles 'frequently entertained large parties' on Sundays. These occasions were 'a feature of the London season'. These appreciations were all written for public consumption. As we shall see, over the course of the marriage, many observers were privately scathing in their assessment of Mina Gardner and her influence on her husband. Perhaps, though, the most important point for Beresford was Mina Gardner's wealth – she was widely reported to have £7000 a year.

Ellen Gardner, who married Beresford in 1878

As the *Thunderer* paraded along the Channel coast and acted as guard-ship to the Queen at Cowes in April, Beresford became more involved in parliamentary affairs. In May he opposed a bill to extend a railway in his constituency since the ratepayers were to be asked for a financial guarantee. Nevertheless, the bill passed by 222 votes to 76. In June he sought to promote denominational education in Ireland. On a motion 'to inquire into the condition, revenues, and management of the

Endowed Schools of Ireland' Beresford maintained that what was needed was 'not only a new system of endowments, but a new system altogether – a denominational system'. The problem was, he said, that 'the State did not like to make grants for educational purposes unless it had control over the manner in which that education was given'. What a surprise!

On 22 June, after a little over a year of service, Beresford left the *Thunderer*, to be replaced by Swinton Holland – the man whom he claimed had been left in sole charge of the *Bellerophon*. It would be three and a half years before the Admiralty saw fit to employ Beresford again.

Beresford and Mina Gardner were married at St Peter's Church, Eaton Square on 25 June 1878. In keeping with the bridegroom's status, the ceremony was conducted by the Archbishop of Armagh, Primate of All Ireland, and the wedding breakfast took place at the London home of the Waterfords. The presents included 'a most beautiful silver bowl' from the Prince of Wales' India suite of 1875. It remained, Beresford said, 'one of my most highly prized possessions'.

Of Lady Charles' influence on Beresford in the years to come, the verdict seems to have been universally negative. Totally lacking in judgement or reserve, she spurred him on when she should have held him back and talked in society about matters best not mentioned. Despite contemporary references to her intelligence, her letters suggest someone of wild opinions, profound prejudices and scatter-brain thinking.

Beresford and Lady Charles were city dwellers and set up home at 100 Eaton Square – Mina's mother lived at 101. They remained there for twelve years until their disastrous breach with the Prince of Wales. According to the author and relative of Beresford, Shane Leslie, they were known as 'the Red Admiral and the Painted Lady' or, less politely as 'the Windbag and the Ragbag'.

The rest of 1878 was taken up by Beresford's vigorous social life. He joined the visit of the Danish royal family in August and then took pleasure in some intensive hunting and shooting. With a party at Suffield's Gunton Hall in Norfolk he helped to shoot 'four hundred and nineteen hares and three hundred and eighty-three pheasants'. Meanwhile, in October Beresford received the welcome news that the Prince of Wales wished him to take command of his royal yacht, the *Osborne*.

Less welcome was the formal reprimand that Beresford received early in the new year. This followed the bursting of a 38-ton gun on the *Thunderer,* which had killed ten men. Without waiting to hear the details, Beresford had rushed into print, telling readers of *The Times* that he did not believe that any Woolwich gun could burst 'excepting under conditions unfair to the gun'. In this case, the cause was 'the shot not being home'. The Board reprimanded him for pre-empting the enquiry.

The Prince of Wales as admiral of the fleet on the Royal Yacht Osborne

The MP for Roscommon, Charles Connor, introduced a bill in May to establish a new university in Ireland. This found favour with Beresford but he 'would go even further than this Bill proposed to do, for he would support a Bill brought in for a Roman Catholic University'. Adding that he would 'support any Member who brought in such a Bill' he then undermined his case by saying that 'he did not think such a Bill would be of any use ... [since] it would have no chances of passing'.

Marking time 1876-81

* * *

On the 18 June 1879 Beresford took up command of the Royal Yacht *Osborne,* an event which in his memoirs he placed a year earlier in order to conceal the extent of his period on half-pay. His new post did not prevent him from attending the second meeting of the season of the Four in Hand Club in Hyde Park. He seems to have taken up this rich-man's hobby around this time and would continue to drive a coach to club meetings until around 1910, when he transferred his passion to yachting and motor cars. A few days after the club outing he won a first prize at the Alexandra Palace Horse Show – a further sign of his determination to remain centre-stage on the London social scene.

Painted dark blue with gold and white trimming, the *Osborne* was a 250 ft. long paddle-steamer. Inside there were comfortable lounges, scattered with deckchairs, staterooms with chintz decoration and watercolour drawings on the walls. She had, said one guest, 'a strange blending of the smartness of a man-o'-war with the luxury of a yacht'.

Commanding the *Osborne* was not a demanding post since the yacht was rarely used. Beresford's principal role was to accompany various royal parties during the vessel's rare outings. In 1879 the main events were the Cowes regatta in August and a royal trip to Copenhagen in September. There were also visits to naval establishments, where suitable entertainments were laid on. On one occasion he witnessed the royals being amused by a demonstration of throwing bombs at a floating cask, only to see a stave fly off between the Prince and the local commanding officer. 'Had it struck either of them he must have been killed.'

* * *

In August Beresford accompanied the Prince of Wales to an inspection of the naval schools at Greenwich, where the Prince distributed prizes. Later in the month he was with the Prince once more, this time for the opening of the new Eddystone Lighthouse. It was then on to Dunster Castle and back to the *Osborne* to welcome the return of Major General Lord Chelmsford, who had recently defeated the Zulus at the Battle of Ulundi. In October Beresford joined the Prince's party in Denmark for a pheasant shoot. The bag was disappointing after a wet summer. There was better shooting in the following month at Melton Constable. Just occasionally the odd parliamentary duty intervened in this round of royal pleasure, as when Beresford joined a delegation in December seeking a loan for a dry dock and waterworks at Waterford.

Disraeli dissolved Parliament in March 1880 and called a General Election. Beresford had already announced that he would stand again for Waterford and had begun campaigning ten days earlier. In his manifesto he reminded his electorate that he stood as a Conservative, but it was 'the claims of his family, who have proved their affection for their country by always residing in it' that he thought most spoke in his favour. As to policy, he desired to see denominational education, he approved of the *Intermediate Education Ac*t and thought the *University Act* was 'a step in the right direction'. He ended by reminding his family's tenants that 'he will always have their interests at heart'. His efforts were in vain – he lost his seat as did 104 other Tories.

The loss of his seat was bad enough, but the prospect of the new Prime Minister – William Ewart Gladstone – was even worse. Under Disraeli, Beresford had rejoiced in the acts of an imperial Prime Minister and found a sympathetic ear for his comments on naval policy. Now there were to be nearly five years of a distinctly anti-imperialist government, whose policies in Egypt and the Sudan would lead Beresford to outbursts of furious indignation.

* * *

From a biographer's point of view this period of Beresford's life is important since, for the first time, we discover something of his substantial wealth. Very little evidence of his finances remains. Amongst the few files to survive are two containing correspondence with his agent, a Mr Warhurst. It is here that we gain a first glimpse of his staggering financial position.

Aged 33 and still only a commander (pay £301 a year, or £14,500 today) Beresford wrote:

> 'What I want you to do is to pay off about 3000 of bills during the next two years from now without if I can help it reducing my establishment by a calculation now we can see; putting my income available at 5000 a year, as I do not want to touch my Caridan(?) estate income for some time ...'

So we learn that Beresford's annual income was £5000 (£240,000 today) – about seventeen times his naval pay. He also referred to some other estates, which were presumably in Ireland. He went on to give Warhurst instructions about renting out No. 2 Lowndes Street in London, a house only a short distance from his own home. By early 1880 Beresford was in Ireland bombarding Warhurst with instructions for staffing 100 Eaton Square. He was to ensure 'the plate is perfectly clean' and 'stop the draughts in the library window'. Meanwhile, Mrs

Grainger, the Housekeeper, was to 'be looking out for the new 1st housemaid'. There followed instructions for the appointment of a 'Scullery Maid & 2nd Housemaid at once', whilst the Butler was to engage a second footman, who had to be 'good looking' and would be paid £28 a year, or £30 'for a really smart one'.

In short, Beresford was wealthy and from an early age. This wealth, combined with his title, gave him easy access to every important personage in the land. It also contributed to his bloated sense of self-importance and his natural arrogance when dealing with anyone in authority. Then there was Lady Charles' income. Whether it was really £7000 a year as rumoured at the time of her marriage seems doubtful – the Beresfords don't seem to have been that wealthy. But what mattered was that Beresford himself was able to afford a life-style that his superior officers could never match.

* * *

Towards the end of his time on the *Osborne*, Beresford was elected as Worshipful Master of a new Masonic lodge in Portsmouth. He was installed in the presence of 'a thousand brethren from all parts of the country' and received a 'founder's jewel, consisting of 27 stones, the compass being formed of five diamonds, and the crown of diamonds and rubies'. An impressive achievement for one so young and still holding such a junior naval rank.

However, freemasonry and the House of Commons were no way to progress his career. It was time to get back to sea and prepare for promotion. No one could have foreseen that, in less than a year's time, Beresford was to be a national hero. He had been appointed commander of HMS *Condor*

YEARS OF GLORY 1882-1885

Chapter 5
Triumph in Alexandria 1882

Beresford joined the *Condor* on 30 January 1982 for what should have been a quiet supporting role in the Mediterranean fleet. Egypt intervened and gave Beresford his first taste of war.

The origin of the Egyptian crisis in 1882 went back several years and centred on a man called Arabi Pasha. An Egyptian, he had joined the army at the age of thirteen in 1854 and quickly gained promotion to the rank of colonel. Changes to service regulations led Arabi and other officers to suspect that the Khedive (the King of Egypt) intended to favour Turkish officers over Egyptian ones. This led to a petition for a Turkish minister of war. Arabi was arrested but released by sympathetic soldiers, so forcing the Khedive to back down. By February 1882 Arabi was Minister of War yet also the Khedive's implacable foe.

HMS Condor

On 11 May 1882 *The Times'* reported that Arabi's supporters were pressing the Khedive to accept him as President of the Council of Ministers. 'Egypt,' said the paper, 'is in a state of revolution.' By 13 May European families were fleeing Cairo. Four days later the first British ships arrived under the commander-in-chief Admiral Sir Beauchamp Seymour; *Condor* followed three days later. Arabi was not intimidated by this show of force and his refusal to back down gave Beresford the biggest career break of his life.

Admiral Sir Beauchamp Seymour

Seymour's orders were limited to showing the flag, so Beresford had time on his hands, which he used to shower British journalists with complaints about Britain's inaction in Egypt. Knowing that the Prince of Wales sympathised with his views, Beresford sent him copies of these letters. Unwisely, the Prince passed the letters on to the Foreign Secretary, Lord Granville, thinking that he would find the information useful. Granville was not pleased at the impudence of the young commander and made a formal complaint to Lord Northbrook, First Lord of the Admiralty, who, in turn, proposed to arrest Beresford and submit him to a court martial. The Prince begged Granville 'in justice to the great friendship and regard I feel for Beresford' to let the matter drop. Beresford was 'an Irishman', he added, which meant he was 'hasty and impetuous' yet 'I feel sure the Queen does not possess a more zealous and loyal officer than he'.

Meanwhile in Alexandria panic had taken hold amongst the 50,000 European residents. In their thousands they continued to head for the

Triumph in Alexandria 1882

quays to flee the city. By 26 June just about all of the tens of thousands of Europeans who wished to leave had departed. This had been achieved by the concerted efforts of various European powers, which had sent ships in vast numbers, and commercial shipping companies, which had laid on extra vessels. What part did Beresford play in all of this? We shall start with his own account:

> 'During the ensuing month there poured out of Alexandria an immense number of refugees of all nations and every class of society. These were placed on board various vessels and were dispatched to the ports of their several countries. I was placed in charge of these operations; which included the chartering of ships, their preparation for passengers, and the embarkation of the refugees.'

Since tens of thousands of refugees had been embarked in boats sent from many countries, Beresford's task seems staggering. But if we turn to *The Times* of 7 July, we find another story, where we learn that:

> 'The officer in charge of this service, under the orders of Lord Charles Beresford, is Lieutenant Wheeler, of the Condor, who lives on board the refugee ship, and is hourly, day and night, at his task.'

The operation described in the article concerned only the *British* refugees and not 'all nations and every class of society' as Beresford claimed in his memoirs. In fact, Beresford and Wheeler used just five steamers to evacuate 3319 people. It was a great achievement, realized with only one death (from a heart complaint) and one on-board birth. Beresford had no need to aggrandize it in his memoirs.

On 10 July the ships of Seymour's fleet received their orders to attack on the following day and the foreign ships moved out of the range of the Egyptian guns. At 4.00 am on the eleventh the *Condor* took up her battle station. On-board was Moberly Bell of *The Times,* who had been assigned to the ship by Seymour. Not surprisingly, *The Times* was to be full of the *Condor's* (and Beresford's) exploits, which in part explains the fame that he achieved on that day.

Firing was due to start at 7.00 am but before battle commenced the *Téméraire* ran aground. Seymour ordered the *Condor* to pull her free, which was soon done and by 7.50 am the *Condor* had returned to her station. Her crew had taken little satisfaction in this initial task since the battle had begun to rage around them before they could participate. Indeed, Bell noted their impatience when they heard the nearby *Cygnet* open fire at 7.30 am.

The *Condor*, along with the *Helicon,* was a repeater ship, that is, she was there to pass signals between other ships but not to fight. She was,

• 39

after all, tiny compared to Seymour's giant battleships and the Egyptian guns. Such a passive role did not appeal to Beresford so he said to his men: 'Now my lads, if you will rely on me to find the opportunity, I will rely on you to make the most of it when it occurs.' He did not have to wait long. Fort Marabout was directing shells at the *Monarch*, the *Invincible* and the *Penelope*, all of which were already engaged with other forts. Seeing his chance, Beresford moved the *Condor* in towards the shore and, as the log records 'Commenced action with Fort Marabout' at 8.15 am.

The naval bombardment of Alexandria 1882

To take on the huge guns of a fort with only the two 64-pounders and one 112-pounder of the *Condor* was perhaps reckless. Two things were in Beresford's favour though. First, his ship was close to the shore, so it presented a low and difficult angle for the fort's guns. Second, as Bell noted, '[we] are treated with contempt' with 'the three big ships [being] easier targets than one small gunboat'. The log book duly recorded the extraordinary success of the *Condor:* 'Silenced 3 of the enemy's guns.' In turn, this brought the famous accolade from Seymour that would for ever be associated with Beresford's name: 'Well done, *Condor*!' For the rest of his life, when he entered a crowded hall, as often as not, a voice would raise the cry 'Well done, *Condor*!' and cheers would follow. (In keeping with Beresford's habit of seizing all the glory for himself, he failed in his memoirs to record that, as soon as Seymour realised the success of the *Condor* he ordered the *Beacon, Bittern, Cygnet*, and *Decoy* to move in to support him.)

By mid-day the fighting had died down. Beresford was called over to the flagship, where, he remembered, 'the admiral's ship's company gave us three cheers, and he himself on the quarterdeck shook me warmly by the hand, and told me he was extremely pleased'.

The crowning moment of the day was Beresford's promotion to captain. Promotion, though, was a mixed blessing for a nineteenth-century naval officer since it meant leaving his post and going onto half-pay. Within weeks Beresford would begin a seven-year period without sea service – a strange reward for his masterful actions at Alexandria.

* * *

Events had now overtaken Seymour. After a trivial bombardment, which involved little risk to his ships and men, he faced a major land operation. Although troops were on their way from Malta and England he had to take action before the Khedive was murdered and the city destroyed. So on the morning of 13 July he landed 150 bluejackets and 450 marines to spike the Egyptian guns, secure the palace and begin to clear the streets. Under the command of Captain John Fisher of the *Inflexible* the men had taken control of all the key points in the city by dusk.

Having taken control of the city, Fisher appointed Beresford as Provost Marshal (Chief of Police) to deal with the still rampaging population. The immensity of his task is caught in a letter that Beresford sent to his wife at the time:

> 'I never saw anything so awful as the town on that Friday; streets, square[s], and blocks of buildings all on fire, roaring and crackling and tumbling about like a hell let loose, Arabs murdering each other for loot under my nose, wretches running about with fire-balls and torches to light up new places, all the main thoroughfares impassable from burning fallen houses, streets with many corpses in them, mostly murdered by the Arab soldiers for loot – these corpses were Arabs murdered by each other – in fact, a pandemonium of hell and its devils.'

It was not long before Beresford's work began to achieve results. When Bell toured the city on the fifteenth he found that the tribunals, churches, clubs and consulates were all being guarded and the fires were subsiding. He described the steps taken by Fisher and Beresford as 'ably executed'. Much of what Beresford achieved would not have been possible without the aid of sailors and others from the various nationalities in the city. For example, 120 Greek sailors saved, said

Bell, 'the Greek and Catholic churches, the European Hospital, and the Italian Consulate'.

By the eighteenth *The Times* reported that the fires were all extinguished, and 'The work of clearing the streets of the town is going on rapidly.' Beresford and a Captain Morrison were making 'energetic efforts ... to restore confidence and ensure public safety' although there were still some looters 'lurking about in odd corners'.

The following day *The Times* was eulogising Beresford and Fisher. A week ago Alexandria had been 'a town in ashes' with 'a hostile, looting, and incendiary population' but 'you may now walk or drive from one end of the city to the other in perfect safety'.

Beresford as Provost Marshal at Alexandria 1882

In a letter home Beresford said that he could not have restored order 'unless the admiral had trusted entirely to me, and given me absolute power of life and death, or to flog, or to blow down houses, or to do anything that I thought fit to restore law and order'. Bell told his readers that 'an Englishman like Lord Charles Beresford shrinks from ...

holding in his hands longer than is necessary the power of life and death'. There may have been some truth in that since Beresford had set up a court of one Egyptian general and four Egyptian colonels with himself as prosecutor. Bell described several cases, which give us an idea of what he called 'the humane means which have been adopted'.

In the first case, one of incitement to murder, Beresford pointed out to the court the serious discrepancies in the evidence of a witness and ordered his arrest. The witness was later sentenced to six years' penal servitude. In another of the cases cited by Bell the charge concerned firing on a marine. In addressing the court Beresford emphasised 'the absolute necessity of treating the firing on troops by natives as a capital offence'. Two days later Bell reported that two mosque-keepers were convicted of storing loot, whereupon Beresford demanded 'the infliction of severe punishment' in order to protect 'the inviolability of mosques'. The result was sentences of four and six years. By this time the court had pronounced two death sentences: one for incendiarism and one for the man who fired on a marine.

Beresford and his men had turned a city of murder, rape and pillage into an orderly state in just one week and, by 1 August, Beresford was transferred to other tasks. His police role brought him high praise from *The Times*, which said that he had done 'much to raise our reputation as administrators'. Seymour, too, was delighted: 'It would be impossible,' he wrote in a report to the Admiralty, 'to find an officer ... who could have carried out the duties with greater patience, energy, & tact.' Even his economy was commented on – he had done it all for less than £700 (about £34,000 today).

Around mid-September Beresford sailed for home to a hero's welcome and two years of half-pay.

One curious footnote to Beresford's work in Alexandria is that his account in his memoirs concludes 'It was after I had been placed in command of the police at Alexandria, in 1882, that I was offered the post of chief commissioner of police in the Metropolis.' True, but four years later.

Chapter 6
Between wars 1882-84

Soon after coming home Beresford was at Marlborough House to receive the formal thanks of the Prince and exchange less formal, but acerbic, comments on Egypt. In October he dined with the Queen at Balmoral, where propriety would have prevented him from commenting on Gladstone's handling of the Arabi uprising.

Beresford at Alexandria in 1882

In mid-October Beresford enjoyed the first fruits of 'Well done, *Condor!*' when he spoke at the Cutlers' Company dinner in London. He praised the Egyptians who had 'fought most gallantly' and whose conduct was 'astonishing'. Turning to the role of the Naval Brigade he described how 'From the 12th to the 16th of July 370 men held two miles of lines against an army of 9,000 men.' Not one of his bluejackets and marines 'took off his clothes during those four days'. After praising Fisher as 'about the best officer they had in the service' Beresford then fell back on jaunty and exaggerated stories. He told his audience how 'they had capital fun' at Alexandria when, eager for a scrap, 'he paid the Bedouins to come out and fight'.

Later that week the public were reminded of the reckless side of Beresford when one of his Egyptian souvenirs was in the news. He had brought back a shell which had fallen through the roof of the Marabout Fort, intending to present it to the Prince of Wales. It had been sent to the Nordenfelt works to be mounted. After filling the shell with water, a workman inserted a copper stirring rod and the 'empty' shell exploded. *The Times* reported that 'four or five men who were near were slightly hurt'. This was an understatement since one man lost a leg, although, in hospital, he was compensated by visits from both Prince Edward and Beresford.

As Beresford basked in the glory of his *Condor* exploits it is unlikely that he foresaw the seven years without a sea-going command that lay ahead. Ignoring his period on the *Osborne* (which was a royal, not a naval appointment) his one year on the *Condor* would be his total sea service from June 1878 to December 1889 – a gap of eleven and a half years. Almost half of those wilderness years would be spent in the Commons, creating the impression that Beresford was more a politician than a sailor. His indefinite status was well-captured by Rear Admiral Sir Percy Scott who recalled: 'In the Navy we knew he was not a sailor, but thought he was a politician; in the House of Commons, I have been told, they knew he was not a politician, but thought he was a sailor.'

* * *

It was in June 1883 that Beresford's passionate interest in machine guns first came to public attention at a lecture he gave to the United Services Institute. He could hardly have been in more exalted company as he spoke before both the Prince of Wales and the Commander-in-Chief of the Army, the Duke of Cambridge. He warned his audience of the 'danger to the ships of our fleet' from French machine guns; this 'could not be exaggerated'. He urged the development of 'machine-guns capable of throwing a pound shell' which 'should at once be added to the Navy'. Of course, he added, his views ... were shared by his brother officers' – a favourite claim of his whenever he wished to press a point. He went on to specify a design for a two-pound gun, saying: 'If the 2-pounder shell gun were supplied at once to our fleet, it would fill up a dangerous gap in our armament.'

A few weeks later in, front of numerous admirals, generals, colonels and MPs, Beresford unveiled a machine gun carriage of his own invention. It carried a five barrel gun and, to demonstrate its ease of use, he ran a course of two-thirds of a mile, with seven stations. At each, he stopped, reversed the gun and fired it, all in just under six minutes. A captain of months only, Beresford was determined to be noticed.

In July Beresford applied to the Admiralty to return a Turkish insignia that he had been awarded. Why he wished to return it is not clear but a possible explanation is that Arabi had received the same award. To the disgust of many, when Arabi was tried for treason in late 1882, the sentence was only exile. Perhaps Beresford found it abhorrent to hold the same insignia as a barely-punished enemy. Whatever his reason, the Admiralty firmly refused him permission to return the honour. Never one to accept 'No' for an answer, Beresford repeated his request a month later and was firmly told that 'my Lords cannot accept any [further] communication from him on this subject after their decision conveyed in letter of 7th Aug. 1883'.

It was around this time that Beresford was saved from an escapade that would have led to near certain death. The Egyptian government was still struggling with the aftermath of the Arabi revolution, but thought that Muhammad Ahmad, who claimed to be the Mahdi (or Islamic redeemer), was no longer much of a threat. It consequently hired Colonel William Hicks (known as Hicks Pasha) to lead a force of 10,000 Egyptians to retake Khartoum. Beresford applied to join this mission but, he recalled, 'my old friend Lord Dufferin was determined that I should not go upon that hazardous enterprise'. As British special commissioner in Egypt, Dufferin was in a good position to recognise that Hicks' expedition was most risky. So much so that, on 5 November, Hicks's force of 10,000 men was almost entirely wiped out in an ambush. Only about 300 men escaped.

* * *

The rest of 1883 was uneventful but 1884 opened with an early hint of the astonishing turn that Beresford's career was about to take. In February Beresford told Warhurst that 'I may have to go to Egypt shortly.' He hoped to join Rear Admiral Sir William Hewett with the Naval Brigade in Abyssinia, but the Admiralty turned down the suggestion. Not discouraged, by May Beresford was making efforts to join the military Gordon Relief Expedition. At the same time *The Times* announced that Beresford was to be one of the speakers at a meeting organized by the Gordon and Khartoum Patriotic Association to 'protest against the Abandonment of General Gordon'.

Just before departing for Egypt, Beresford was struggling to put his finances in order. In May he had found himself overdrawn by £1800 (about £87,000 today). Maybe part of the problem was that he and Lady Charles were overstretching themselves with their investments, since Lady Charles had lent her sister Lucy (Mrs Paget) £15,000 (about £725,000 today). No wonder their coffers were empty. Beresford decided to take things in hand. He sold three horses at Tattersalls, 'all very fast and splendid fencers' and then arranged with Coutts Bank to lend him £5000 at 5 per cent for 5 years. In the same letter he revealed the urgency of these arrangements since he had heard that 'there is to be an expedition to Khartoum & that we are to know all about it in 14 days'. The Beresfords, though, were hopeless at managing money. Within days of arranging the loan, Beresford lost £2000 on his racing bets 'so,' he told Warhurst, 'I shall have to borrow £7000 instead of £5000'. Like so many who fall into debt, he imagined that he and his wife could change their habits and be out of trouble in no time. All they had to do was 'allow us £400 a month to do everything'. With an annual income of £7500 (£362,000 today) 'we ought soon to pay off the principal and interest'. He would limit himself to 'only ... 3 houses ... [and] not entertain for a year'.

And so, finances sorted out, Beresford was ready to set off for Egypt, the Sudan and glory.

Chapter 7
His finest hour 1884-85

Although the bombardment and occupation of Alexandria in 1882 had succeeded in re-establishing the Khedive's authority in Egypt, the Sudan was still in a state of mayhem. Following his revolt of 1881, the Mahdi had steadily taken control of every significant town and outpost and, by early 1884, only Khartoum remained outside his control.

The British government had no wish to help the Egyptians retake the territory so in January 1884 a Cabinet Committee decided on evacuation. General Gordon, with his reputation for suppressing rebellion in China and experience as an ex-governor of a Sudan province, seemed the ideal man. Hurriedly appointed, he was seen off from Charing Cross Station on the 18 January by Wolseley (Adjutant-General at the War Office), Lord Hartington (Secretary of State for War) and the Duke of Cambridge. The Cabinet had acted with near criminal irresponsibility in sending a man like Gordon to Khartoum. Egotistical, maniacal and more inclined to take instructions from his God than from his government there was no possibility that he would produce an evacuation plan. Matters were made worse by his leaving England before the Cabinet had considered the terms of his employment and by Sir Evelyn Baring (Consul General in Cairo) making Gordon Governor General of the Sudan on his arrival in Egypt.

On reaching Khartoum Gordon abandoned any intention he might have had of evacuation and prepared the city for siege. By March it became clear that he was marooned in an ocean of the Mahdi's fanatical followers. Back in London Gladstone's Cabinet bowed to the public's demand that Gordon be rescued.

* * *

Just four days later Beresford's appointment as Naval ADC to General Wolseley appeared in *The Times*. That same day Wolseley boarded a train at Victoria Station in London to travel to Egypt.

On 2 September Beresford joined Colonel Sir Herbert Stewart (who would take command of the troops at Dongola) and other officers at Dover to set sail for Egypt. Meanwhile dockyards up and down the land received orders to manufacture 800 whalers – the boats to take the troops up the Nile. The plan was to despatch the whalers by sea to Alexandria. From there they were to be taken by train to Assiut. Next they were to go up river by barge to Elephantine Island and then be rowed by natives through the first cataract before being towed by steam launch to the foot of the second cataract, where the mighty task of hauling them over the rocks would begin.

Beresford and Stewart reached the expedition's headquarters in Cairo on 10 September and the first of the whalers was landed at Alexandria twelve days later. However, neither the whalers nor the various steamers on the Nile were under Beresford's direct command. As ADC to Wolseley Beresford could give orders to no one. Instead a Captain Boardman was in charge on the river. Bizarrely, Boardman along with 28 other naval officers and 190 men, was under the command of Rear Admiral Hay who was at Malta.

General Garnett Wolseley on the Nile in 1884

Beresford made his way to Aswan in an old steam launch which, he told Lady Charles, had 'the manners of a kangaroo: she bounds, she jumps, she creaks, she squeals, her boiler roars like a puffing billy'. From Aswan he moved up river to Wady Halfa, which was the base camp for the expedition. Beyond lay the terrible second cataract, which would occupy weeks of Beresford's time. When he reached Wady Halfa, the expedition received fearful news. On 12 September Gordon had sent one of his staff, Colonel Hamill Stewart (no relation of the Stewart in the relief force), and a journalist, Frank Powers, south in a steamer to make urgent contact with the British forces. The steamer had been wrecked and both Stewart and Powers were murdered. Physical contact with Khartoum was now cut.

Colonel Sir Herbert Stewart, commander of the Gordon rescue expedition 1884-1885

Bad news only spurred Beresford on and in an undated letter written at Wady Halfa he breathlessly told his wife about his reorganisation of the boat transport. By now he was Wolseley's staff officer and able to direct the men working on the boats. Every hour of daylight was used by the 6000 native labourers to bring the whalers and steamers through the nine miles of the second cataract, which was a mass of dangerous rocks and fearful rapids. Then there was the famous Bab-el-Kebir – a narrow gorge filled with a roaring torrent – which required the utmost skill to navigate. Appalled at the inefficiency of Boardman's methods – which included having twice as many men working as were actually able to grip the tow ropes – Beresford claimed to 'have got more boats forward in the last three days than they did in 13!' In addition to the whalers, Beresford was also hauling native nuggars (cargo boats), but their sails were frequently ripped to pieces and their bottoms holed.

Those working on the cataract lived away from the base camp. 'Fancy 9 officers Lieutenants Sub-lieutenants & a doctor living out in the desert 9 miles from here [Wady Halfa – see map on page 55] with their 70 blue jackets [and] have never had a servant all this time!' Beresford exclaimed to his wife. Hay had refused their request to hire natives, leaving them to wash their own clothes and cook their own food. This was no mere male grumble. They rose at 4.30 am, had breakfast, walked (or, if lucky, rode) up to ten miles across the desert to work, hauled boats all day and, at dark, walked all the way back to their camp. All they had to eat at midday was biscuit, washed down with river water. Major-General Buller (Wolseley's Chief of Staff) – 'a splendid fellow' – took pity on them and authorised them to take on native servants.

Whale boats on the Nile in 1884

Slowly Beresford's efforts brought success. The first whaler had passed through Bab-el-Kebir on 25 October. Two days later he again wrote to Lady Charles declaring that he 'never was so fit and well', in part because they had drunk 'nothing but Ginger ale, a great deal of Nile [and] sometimes claret cup in the evening'. He was riding thirty miles a day and was short of men, but his authority was increasing as 'Buller and Wolseley have insisted I am to give *orders* instead of requests & suggestions'. Everyone, he said, had opposed his portage scheme and his method of hauling but the former had 'got the boats through without a scratch, a bump, or an oar, pole or mast broken' and the latter had used far less manpower.

By 11 November, Beresford had brought 469 whalers through the second cataract to Gemai, of which 176 had departed upstream with soldiers on-board. Eleven days later 549 boats were through but Beresford was becoming increasingly worried at the rapid fall in the level of the Nile. 'The cataract,' he wrote 'is getting worse & worser'. On the previous day another man had drowned. 'Not one man who has fallen overboard & gone down has been saved' he told Lady Charles but 'I shall never go overboard if I can help it, without an oar or your lifebelt'. This inflatable lifebelt had been a gift from his wife and, when not protecting Beresford from the Nile, he used it as a pillow.

Two weeks later Beresford was still at the second cataract with 687 whalers through and just five more days needed to bring the last hundred or so to Gemai. His mind now turned to the Naval Brigade – a body of naval men who were to march with the soldiers. A Commander Hammill was to have taken charge of the Brigade, but Wolseley now opted for Beresford. *The Times* regretted that Hammill, who had 'rendered invaluable services in surveying the river cataracts' should be 'shelved'. Yet Wolseley's choice was to be the saving of the expedition.

So desperate was Gordon's plight that Wolseley now abandoned the original plan to take the whole force up the Nile. Instead, a small force – the Camel Corps – would race across the desert from Korti to Shendi, and then follow the Nile to Khartoum. The bulk of Wolseley's forces would continue slowly up the Nile for an unspecified rendezvous after Gordon's rescue.

On 8 January the camel corps moved off, as did the First Division of Beresford's Naval Brigade. He stayed behind to await the arrival of the Second Division and 'all the valuable stores [and] oil for the steamers'. With time on his hands, Beresford dined off two onions ('the best dinner I have had for several days') and found a moment to write to Warhurst to ask for news of progress in paying off his debts.

Beresford's reverie was broken by a frantic telegram from Buller, who wanted to know where he was. Had he received Wolseley's telegram 'to hurry up by shortest possible route'? Beresford had not, so he now had to seize whatever transport he could find to reach Korti. He left Dal at 6.00 am on 27 December and rode on camels for three days until he caught up with the pinnace of an Army officer, Captain Colvile, which he commandeered to go upstream. Slowed down by burning green wood, the boat crawled south until she met the steamer *Nasif-el-Kheir*, which took Beresford to Korti, where he arrived on 5 January 1885.

Here Beresford received his orders. His Brigade was to form part of Sir Herbert Stewart's column, which would cross the dessert to Metemmeh, setting out on 8 January. More importantly, the order described the crucial part that Wolseley expected Beresford to play in General Gordon's rescue:

> 'On arrival at Metemmeh, you will at once take over and man any steamer, or, if you can, steamers that are there or in the vicinity; and you will use every means in your power to put one or more of the steamers ... into an efficient state.'

His finest hour 1884-85

The steamers would then be used to convey a detachment to be sent to Khartoum.

* * *

And so began the march south. A long column comprising 1509 men, 98 officers, 304 natives, 2228 camels and 155 horses streamed from Korti at 2.00 pm on 8 January. It was, said *The Times,* 'a beautiful spectacle'. One man stood out: Beresford on his white donkey, County Waterford, specially sent up by boat from the second cataract.

Although the land through which they marched is termed 'desert', it was far from a sandy waste. Grass for camels and acacia and mimosa for firewood were abundant. At intervals there were large wells, between which ran a good road on which the going was generally firm. At that time of year the nights were cold and a breeze tempered the hot daytime sun.

The first nine days were uneventful but fatiguing. The column marched on into the night and halted at 3.30 am on 9 January. It set off again at 9.30 am. With halts, the march continued until the column reached El Howeiyat at 10.00 am the next day. On Sunday 11 January, the column arrived at the Abu Halfa wells after an overnight march. There they found 'one pond of dirty water, almost black with mud, and a few holes in the gravel with better water'. New holes were dug and soon a plentiful supply of water was found. The next day was a short march to the wells at Jakdul. These had previously been taken by the Guards, who had improved the wells and built two forts. So soundly dug in were the Guards that their commanding officer, Major (later Field Marshal) Herbert Kitchener, laid on a 'capital dinner' of gazelle and sand grouse. Tuesday was a rest day, giving time to water the animals and reorganize the column for the next day. There were only four hours marching on 14 January followed by a longer march on 15 January, which brought the column to Jebel Sergain, where it camped once more.

So far the march had been tough but not dangerous. On the 16 January the atmosphere suddenly changed. After an early morning march, the column stopped for breakfast around 10.30 am. Shortly afterwards, reports came in of enemy soldiers in the vicinity. Down the valley, towards the vital Abu Klea wells, a long line of banners could be seen, stretched across the path of the column. Tom-toms were sounding; soon bullets were whistling overhead. 'At first,' noted Colonel Sir Charles Wilson in his journal, they were 'few and far between, but they gradually increased until they got too numerous for the picket'. The column retreated into a zariba (an enclosure of grubbed-up thorn bushes). All night long bullets whistled overhead but the dark ensured that few found their mark.

Beresford's campaign map 1884-1885

The next morning it was obvious that the column would have to contest its way to the wells so it formed up as a fighting square. In the van were the infantry and the Guards. Beresford's Naval Brigade was at the rear, with the heavy camel regiment on either side of his men. The centre of the square was filled with the baggage camels. The lumbering column advanced across bumpy, scrub-covered ground towards the Arabs. The terrain which slowed down the animals and men helped the Arabs to conceal themselves in hollows. The cumbersome square was giving in places as the various elements tried to keep together – many men in the column had never marched in square formation before.

The attack, when it came, was so sudden, recalled Wilson, that 'our skirmishers had only just time to get into the square'. He continued: 'I remembered thinking, "By Jove, they will be into the square!" and almost the next moment I saw a fine old sheikh on horseback plant his banner in the centre of the square, behind the camels.'

Battle of Abu Klea 1885

As the Arabs were plunging towards the square Beresford had ordered his men to wheel the Gardner gun outside the square. There he laid it himself and began firing at the oncoming Arabs who were 'dropping like ninepins'. Not only were Beresford and his men outside the square (and making no attempt to close it up) but a Colonel Burnaby had actually ordered two companies of dragoons to wheel out of the square. The Arabs poured into the square behind Beresford and his gun. Whilst all this was happening, the gun jammed. Now Beresford and his men had Arabs in front and Arabs behind – the one thing a square was meant to prevent. As the Arabs fell upon them, all of Beresford's gun crew were slain; somehow he escaped with a spear-cut on one hand.

The whole attack lasted a mere five minutes during which time those on the outside of the square fired furiously at the oncoming Arabs, whilst those inside dealt with the Arabs who had penetrated the square. As the attackers retreated, 1100 Arabs were left dead. Of the camel corps, 83 officers and men had died, and a further 102 were wounded. Post-mortems continue to this day as to why the square broke and the role of Beresford and Burnaby. Whatever doubts there might be nowadays as to their role (and one recent account puts *all* the blame on to the two of them) at the time Beresford's action was seen as heroic. Sir Henry Newbolt had no doubt as to the heroic nature of the battle, writing:

> ...The sand of the desert is sodden red,
>
> Red with the wreck of a square that broke;
>
> The Gatling's jammed and the colonel dead,
>
> And the regiment blind with dust and smoke.
>
> The river of death has brimmed his banks,
>
> And England's far, and Honour a name,
>
> But the voice of the schoolboy rallies the ranks,
>
> "Play up! play up! and play the game!"

After fending off the last of the attackers, the square gathered itself together, collected the dead, tended the wounded and retrieved the animals. Beresford had lost his tobacco and field glasses and, more seriously, County Waterford had run off into the desert, never to be seen again.

The column then slowly moved on to the wells. With so many of his Brigade dead, Beresford had to take his turn on the drag-ropes to pull the Gardner gun across the sand and rocks. At the wells, despite the water having 'the consistency of cream' Beresford found it 'cool, sweet and delicious'. All that they had to eat that night was whatever biscuit they had in their pockets.

The next day, 18 January, was spent building a fort for the wounded and preparing to advance. With just 25 miles to the Nile the column set off in eager anticipation of fresh water. As night fell the tired men and camels marched on through scrub and bushes. The more they marched, the more disordered the column became as loads fell from camels, sleeping men dropped to the ground and camels wandered off in the dark.

His finest hour 1884-85

At dawn on the 19 January the exhausted column halted within six miles of the river. In no condition to move on, and surrounded by the enemy, the column retreated into a zariba. Here, recalled Beresford, 'The men breakfasted in a rain of bullets. So wearied were they, that some fell asleep over their food, bullets zinging all about them. Many of the men got no food at all. I saw two men shot while they slept.' A little later, Stewart received a serious bullet wound in the groin and command of the column fell on Colonel Wilson, who decided to leave a small force in the zariba and take the rest of the column on to the Nile. Beresford and the Naval Brigade stayed behind with the zariba party. There, with his Gardner gun and the help of two guns of the Royal Artillery, the detachment fended off the sporadic attackers. Meanwhile, the main column safely reached the Nile.

On the 20 January Wilson reorganized his forces, dismantled the zariba, brought all the men to the Nile, and buried the dead. The exhausted force was now at the village of Abu Kru, which, for unknown reasons, the British called Gubat. Beresford's own situation was somewhat desperate. He had lost all his officers other than a boatswain and a sub-lieutenant; his camels, he recorded, were 'hardly able to walk' and covered in 'ulcerating sores'; and he was far from fit. He was suffering from 'a horrid carbuncle' on his behind; sitting was painful and he could barely walk. Yet his carbuncle was to be the saving of the expedition.

The next day, 21 January, Wilson advanced towards the nearby town of Metemmeh to assess whether to take it. In the process his troops (including the Naval Brigade) were fired on both from the town and the surrounding area. (Beresford meanwhile remained on the sick list.) During the fighting, the flags of Gordon's steamers arriving from Khartoum came into view. Deciding that the cost of taking Metemmeh would not justify the result, Wilson withdrew and turned his attention to the steamers and the implication of their presence.

Wilson now had the means to send a force to Khartoum but rather than rush off in the steamers, he first carried out a downstream reconnaissance fearing that the enemy might be massing in his rear. He was later heavily criticised for this, but he always maintained that 'if I were again placed in similar circumstances I should act in the same way'. On the same day, at Beresford's request, Wilson appointed Mr Ingram, a journalist and soldier, as acting-lieutenant in the Naval Brigade.

Despite the criticism that Wilson received for not moving off to Khartoum immediately, he could not have done so even if had he wished to, since the steamers were in no condition for immediate action.

His finest hour 1884-85

Beresford busied himself on the following day in directing their overhaul and preparation for the expedition.

And so, at last, Wilson and a small detachment were able to set off on 24 January to rescue Gordon. It will be recalled that the principal reason for Beresford being appointed to the expedition was to take the steamers to Khartoum – yet he was too sick to move. This apparent disaster was to prove providential. The two steamers – the *Bordein* and the *Talahawiyeh* – left with a dozen or so officers, a few men and around 200 Sudanese soldiers. Mere Thames steamers, the boats were reinforced with heavy timber sides and armed.

Four days later, on 28 January, after an eventful and perilous voyage, during which Wilson's party heard reports that Khartoum had fallen, they sighted the city. One glimpse of its burned-out remains told all. Any hopes Wilson might have entertained about proceeding further were removed by the hail of fire directed at his boats. Ten months after Hartington had decided to rescue Gordon and five months after the force had arrived in Egypt, all was lost.

The assassination of General Charles Gordon 1885

Khartoum had fallen two days before. For the rest of his life (and, indeed, still today in many books) Wilson was castigated for his two days' delay at Gubat. If only he had left two days earlier, Gordon would have been saved. Except that that is utter nonsense. The Mahdi had had

His finest hour 1884-85

Khartoum totally surrounded for months. He hoped that the city would fall without a fight, but he had no intention of allowing the British to relieve it. Had Wilson set out two days earlier, the Mahdi would have simply sacked the city two days earlier.

Wilson could only turn the steamers round and return to Gubat. Four days later word reached Beresford that the steamers had both been wrecked and that Wilson's party was sheltering on an island upstream. It was time to rescue the rescuers. Thanks to his healed carbuncle Beresford was ready for the mission of his life.

At 2.00 pm on 1 February Beresford 'with 20 picked shots of the mounted infantry' and two Gardner guns set off upstream at 2.5 knots in the tiny *El Safieh*. Lieutenant Percival Marling, who had had command of the boat before Beresford took it over, said he had never seen 'a more disreputable craft' with its funnel 'riddled with bullet holes' and an engine that was 'a mass of scrap-iron'. The gun turrets were made of piled-up railway sleepers and surplus boiler plate. Perhaps the most terrifying part of the enterprise was the Arab pilot. These pilots were widely suspected of deliberately driving the steamers onto rocks to thwart the expedition's success. True or not, Beresford took no risks. He told the pilot that 'if he took us safely up and down he would be rewarded, but that upon any indication of treachery he would be shot at once'. He then handcuffed him to a stanchion and placed a guard at his side.

El Safieh sailed steadily upstream on Sunday and Monday, mooring for the night a few miles short of the fort at Wad Habeshi, where there were 3000 of the enemy. On Friday 3 February Beresford set off to pass the fort. In his official report he said that *El Safieh* opened fire first at a range of 1200 yards and that the response was 'heavy rifle fire from 600 or 800 rifles'. He continued: 'Owing to the depth of water, the steamer had to pass about 80 yards from the fort; but the machine gun and marksmen's fire ... was so accurate that the enemy were unable to fire their two guns.' Further upstream, with the boat's stern retreating from the fort, the Arab rifles began to tell and a bullet went straight through the boiler. The stokers and the engine-room artificers were seriously scalded as the pressurised water shot out, leaving a foot of water in the hold.

The crew panicked but Beresford calmly took charge of the situation. He ordered his men to bring the ammunition and stores on deck before turning his attention to the boiler. The fires had to be drawn and the boiler cooled before Chief Engineer Henry Benbow could survey the damage: a three-inch diameter hole in the boiler, edges bent inwards. Benbow, like Beresford, kept his head and set about the long task of repairing the boiler. It was a complex job, including cutting the threads of the new nuts and bolts for the plate that was to cover the hole, but Benbow kept at it in the stifling heat of the hold, accompanied by the pings of the bullets striking the hull. Up on deck the men worked the guns while further reinforcing their casements.

El Safieh under fire on her way to Khartoum 1885

While the desperate repair was going on, Wilson had sent a man downstream to make contact with Beresford. Wilson's party then moved downstream until they were on the bank opposite *El Safieh*. With difficulty, signals were exchanged until Wilson understood the boiler situation. He was to go downstream below the fort, where Beresford would pick him up the next day.

Benbow mending the boiler below and Wilson moving downstream were signs of progress, but Beresford could do nothing to quell the rain of gunfire from the fort. All he had left was deception. *El Safieh* had been towing four boats to bring back Wilson's men. He hauled these alongside and openly disembarked his men, who floated off. The Arabs were fooled into thinking that *El Safieh* had been abandoned and they ceased firing. Meanwhile Benbow worked on in the stifling heat and at 9.00 pm, after ten hours' work, the boiler was repaired.

The next day, Friday 4 February, Benbow lit the boiler at 5.00 am, taking care that no sparks shot from the funnel. Fifty minutes later there was enough steam pressure to move off. Just ten minutes of darkness remained as *El Safieh* weighed anchor and moved upstream for three-quarters of a mile, turned, and came downstream past the fort once more. Although the furious Arabs fired for the last time, no further damage was suffered.

But the day was not quite over. Wilson's wounded had been floated downstream in a nuggar, which had run aground within sight of the fort. *El Safieh* halted once again while Sir Henry Keppel's son, Sub-Lieutenant Keppel, freed the boat – three hours of work under fire from the fort. Once the nuggar was clear, the two boats sailed two miles north to pick up Wilson's party from the bank. After that the men were clear of danger and *El Safieh* arrived back at Gubat at 5.30 pm with just one stop to collect wood.

The news of the failure of Wilson's expedition sped down the Nile to Wolseley, but it was tempered by that of Beresford's triumph. There was universal recognition that he had saved the column.

The return march was not without its hazards. At one point the Naval Brigade occupied a redoubt with two Gardner guns in order to provide a rear-guard for the baggage train. Once more they came under fire, although no one was wounded. That same night the camp was attacked. Beresford recalled there were two men killed and thirteen wounded, but the official history states that the enemy were 'driven away without loss'. Beresford's false memory must also throw into doubt his claim that, the next morning, stepping out of the redoubt, he was struck in the back by a ricochet and thrown to the ground. More important for the column was the news that Sir Herbert Stewart had finally died from the wound he had received back in January.

On leaving the Abu Klea wells on 23 February the column found itself once more facing 8000 Arabs. Buller, in a desperate situation with parched men and a serious lack of camels, abandoned his plan to destroy the forts and instead filled the wells with stones. His men marched on, harassed by shots from scouts, but without any further engagement and arrived at Jakdul on 26 February. From there an uneventful march brought the Naval Brigade to Korti on 5 March.

In early March Wolseley inspected the Naval Brigade at Korti and, said *The Times*, 'praised the conduct of Lord Charles and his men in the highest terms'. Benbow was called out to the front, where Wolseley presented him with his cigarette case. (In fact, it was probably Gordon's cigarette case since, when Wolseley waved Gordon off on 18 January 1884, they had exchanged cases.)

Coming on top of 'Well done, *Condor*!' Beresford's exploits in the Sudan renewed his status as a national hero. The nation's shame at the failure to save Gordon was tempered by its pride in the *El Safieh* rescue. Yet Wolseley's plea to the Admiralty that Beresford's 'excellent conduct' should not go unnoticed was in vain. It was to be four years before he received another ship and he was never to persuade the Board to recognise his time in the Sudan as sea-service.

At home there was fulsome praise for Beresford. In the Commons the Chancellor of the Exchequer, Sir Michael Hicks Beach, said, to loud cheers, that he was sure 'there are none who will withhold their admiration from that most gallant feat of arms performed by Lord Charles Beresford'. In the Lords Salisbury declared that 'Possibly there is no incident which has taken so much hold of the popular imagination as that of Lord Charles Beresford and his gallant sailors mending their boilers under the fire of the enemy's guns.'

A few days later Beresford and Boardman were made Companions of the Bath, an honour qualified by a letter from the Admiralty admonishing Beresford for his unsatisfactory 'statement of reasons for relinquishing command of the Naval Brigade, Soudan'. The details of this incident are now unclear.

* * *

Beresford was now 39 years old with a public reputation that must have been the envy of every officer in the Navy. It would take just under two years for him to severely damage it.

WILDERNESS 1885-1899

Chapter 8
Fall from grace 1885-88

No sooner had Beresford returned from the Sudan than he began to attack the government over the state of the Navy. In a speech at the Mansion House he alleged that 'if war was to be declared so many tasks would be thrown upon the Navy that it would be utterly impossible ... to perform those duties'. He demanded an immediate £20 million loan to build cruisers and defend coaling stations. Although he had not presented any evidence for his claims, he was rewarded with loud cheers – quite a success given that he was only responding to a toast. Whatever his motives, Beresford had taken a first step towards his future role as the Admiralty's number one critic – a role that only death would force him to relinquish.

Beresford always presented his shipbuilding campaign as a one-man fight against reluctant politicians. In fact this was not. In the autumn of the previous year the Board had surreptitiously leaked details of ship deficiencies to the journalist W T Stead, who published these in a series of high-profile articles in *The Pall Mall Gazette.* His *The Truth About the Navy* campaign resulted in Lord Northbrook (then First Lord) announcing additional expenditure of £5,525,000 in December of the same year. Indeed, in 1893, Lord Salisbury had singled out Northbrook – not Beresford – as 'the first person who awoke Parliament and the country from the torpor into which we had fallen in respect to Naval construction'. Far from Beresford being faced with an indifferent Board, he was simply following a lead that it had already taken.

* * *

Gladstone's government had fallen and in June and the Tories had taken office under Lord Salisbury. Salisbury had attempted to govern without calling a general election, but in November went to the polls. Beresford's prevarication over his career ended when he accepted the nomination for the Marylebone East constituency. Two weeks later he beat his rival candidate, a Mr Grant, by 3130 to 2186 votes. Polling in those days was spread over a three-week period; his own seat secured, Beresford went off to support other Conservative candidates. In Norfolk, when aiding Lord Henry Bentinck's campaign, he repeated his

£20 million demand, this time suggesting that the cost should be met by suspending payments on the National Debt.

Lord Northbrook, First Lord of the Admiralty 1880-1885

Back in March Beresford's brother John Henry, the Fifth Marquis of Waterford, had suffered a fearful hunting accident that left him crippled and in chronic pain. He had still not recovered when the hunting season began so in November Beresford took his brother's place in charge of the Queen's staghounds and began to hunt regularly with them. In fact, the Marquis never recovered and shot himself ten years later.

* * *

The general election of late 1885 brought in a short-lived minority Conservative government, which left office in January 1886 after losing a vote on the Queen's speech. So, when Beresford challenged the Navy estimates on 15 March 1886 his old foe Gladstone was back on the front bench. He opened his attack by suggesting that the 80,000 unemployed ship-workers in the country and 'the cheapness of material for shipbuilding' had created an opportunity 'to put the Royal Navy in that state of efficiency which is necessary for the safety of the Empire, at the least possible expense'. He then plunged into a welter of figures which, he claimed, showed the comparative weakness of the British Fleet. Singling out the French Fleet (then Britain's main rival) as an example he said that its ships were newer, heavier and had thicker armour. He called for 20 more cruisers, three new torpedo depot ships and 21 more torpedo boats. All this would cost £5,577,000 – rather less than the £20 million he had declared necessary the previous December.

* * *

Around this time Hugh Childers, the Home Secretary, offered Beresford the post of Chief Commissioner of the London Police. It had already been turned down by Major General Sir Redvers Buller. Beresford, too, showed no interest. (He was rumoured to be under consideration for the position for a second time in November 1888 but was not then thought to be ideal for the post.)

* * *

In June Beresford organized another of his MPs' visits to Portsmouth, where Fisher, now Captain of the gunnery school, HMS *Excellent*, laid on various displays. Around 150 MPs turned up to see mock attacks and the latest guns and rockets. They also had a chance to roam over the mighty HMS *Colossus*, where, under the direction of Lieutenant (later Admiral of the Fleet) John Jellicoe, they saw the loading of a 714 lb shell. Firing this with a 250 lb charge had, though, been ruled off-limits by the Admiralty. Beresford repeated the visit in the following year.

On 8 June Gladstone's first *Home Rule Bill* for Ireland was defeated in the Commons, precipitating yet another general election. With the Liberal Party split over Home Rule, Lord Salisbury had little difficulty in leading his Conservative Party to victory with 376 seats in a chamber of 670. Beresford had voted against the bill and in his election speeches he explained why he had opposed a measure favoured by 'a majority of his countrymen'. Home Rule, he said would result in civil war – north against south: 'England would have to reconquer the whole country.' When accused of saying that he would fight on the side of Ulster if Home Rule were imposed he denied this, remarking that he was 'a Queen's officer'. (But when the crunch came in 1914 Beresford sided with the rebels and even signed up to a role in the illegal provisional Ulster government.) He was swept back to Westminster on the Conservative tide and with an increased majority.

Beresford expected Salisbury to appoint him Chief Secretary for Ireland in the new government – a preposterous suggestion for a man with no ministerial experience. The Prince of Wales more realistically suggested that he was better suited to be head of the Irish Police Force. In fact, Salisbury gave him the post of Junior (Fourth) Naval Lord. His task was to look after naval transport, medical services, victualing, chaplains and naval intelligence. It was a humiliation for a man who thought he knew better than anyone how to run the Navy.

Beresford was very much the subordinate in a department of four naval lords. Both the First Naval Lord (Sir Arthur Hood) and the Second (Sir Anthony Hoskins) were admirals, while the Third (Sir William Graham) was a vice admiral. They were overseen by the civilian First Lord, Lord George Hamilton (Beresford's fellow pupil of thirty years ago), whose ministerial career dated back to 1874. Alongside this impressive team a captain of just four years' standing was clearly the junior, yet Beresford was to behave as if he were superior to them all.

Hamilton later wrote that Beresford was 'the weak spot in my team'. Not only did he 'not like his post of subordination' but he was 'neither by instinct nor training an office man'. It was not just Beresford's meagre administrative powers that distressed Hamilton. What riled him was Beresford's tongue. So voluble was he that he attracted shoals of reporters to the Commons' lobby, where he regaled them with the wonders of the changes *he* was effecting at the Admiralty. Changes and reforms being handled by other naval lords appeared in the press as his work. Hood's labours on the Naval Reserve were so reported, as was Graham's design for a new cruiser. All this, said Hamilton, generated 'an atmosphere of friction'.

* * *

The trouble started within weeks of Beresford taking office when he wrote a hard-hitting paper criticising the Admiralty: 'The perilous absence of any plan or preparation for war,' wrote Beresford, 'and the gravity and imminence of the danger which may result to this country from such a state of affairs, has induced me to write this paper'. Referring to 'the scare of 1885' (when war with Russia seemed imminent) which had showed 'what we should actually require' if war were to break out he said it was 'inexplicable' that 'no steps have been taken to organize or prepare any method or plan for showing how or where these absolutely necessary requirements are'. He described how the headquarters staff of 'France, Germany, Russia, Austria, and Italy' drew up 'elaborate descriptions for war preparations'. Yet, 'in England, no similar plan or system exists'.

Turning to Britain's weak points, he said that 'our foreign stations' were vulnerable to pre-emptive attack 'from the total want of ordinary foresight' at the Admiralty. It was 'indispensable' that the Board immediately recognize 'the gravity of the present state of affairs'. And why had there been such neglect? Because, he said 'there is not a single reference to preparation for war' and 'mobilisation of the Fleet' in the list of tasks allocated to the naval lords. The solution, he said, was to set up an Intelligence Department to replace the existing Foreign Intelligence Committee. This should have a staff of 'an Admiral, junior captains, two lieutenants or commanders, two marine officers, one higher division clerk, three lower division clerks, and two writers'. After noting that 'the captains could be readily procured, as they are generally on compulsory half-pay for three to four years after their promotion' he also asked that they receive additional pay. As to the lieutenants '[they] should receive their full-pay, in addition to salaries named, because, owing to our being so short of these officers, they would be actually on full-pay, if not employed in the way indicated'. These few sentences were to bring about the end of Beresford's ministerial career.

The Admiralty secretary, Sir Evan McGregor, had circulated the paper to Board members by 6 October, with a strong recommendation in its favour. He told his colleagues that it was a matter of 'extreme importance'. Even before that date it seems that Admiral Hood had set up a group to work on Beresford's proposal and McGregor was suggesting weekly Board meetings to progress Beresford's ideas. Beresford was delighted at the reception that his paper had received, telling Randolph Churchill that 'the Board have accepted it & I am driving away at it'. In view of this ready response to his paper, what happened next is baffling.

A week or so after McGregor had written so enthusiastically about the paper, a draft copy appeared under Beresford's name in *The Pall Mall Gazette*. Hamilton was curious to know how this paper had reached the press. When challenged, Beresford said he had thrown a 'rough copy into a waste-paper basket' and someone had taken it to the press. In public Hamilton accepted this explanation telling the Commons that 'It became public by means by which a great many other documents have become known – through the waste paper basket.' Beresford later claimed that 'It was stolen from the Admiralty by an Admiralty messenger' who 'was arrested, brought to trial, and sentenced'.

Hamilton pressed the Board to agree quickly to an enlarged Naval Intelligence Department (NID). By the end of November a committee (with Beresford as a member) had reported in favour of the proposal. It was, they said 'of the utmost importance' and should be pursued 'without delay'. There followed a list of proposed staff, their duties and their salaries. By mid-December the Admiralty had requested permission from the Treasury to spend £900 in the current financial year to cover the additional costs of the NID before they could be included in the next annual estimates.

At this point in the story we need to insert a piece of fiction from Beresford's memoirs. A short time after writing his proposal, he claimed, the Board rejected it. Beresford then went to see Salisbury who 'very kindly read the document' and commented (astutely) that 'I lacked the experience required to give force to my representations'. On this occasion Salisbury declined to overrule Hamilton. Beresford begged him to consult the other three naval lords. A week later he met Salisbury again. Beresford was right, said Salisbury and 'the Board of Admiralty had decided to form a new department upon the lines I had suggested'. As is clear from the above account of the origins of the proposal, there is not a word of truth in this story. His proposals received solid support from the moment his colleagues first read them.

Lord Randolph Churchill

Progress on the NID was rapid. The Treasury approved the additional costs until the end of the financial year and staff had been appointed by mid-February. At the end of the month, details of the new

Fall from grace 1885-88

department were announced. It was to be 'purely advisory' and was 'to collect and sift ... all information likely to be of use in time of war'. It was also 'to propose and keep plans of mobilization of naval forces'. Some of its tasks echoed past Beresfordian demands, such as the requirement to keep records of 'the state of the defences of all British coaling stations' and to note 'the number of British vessels of war that could be got ready in a given time'.

The new department was a fine achievement. Rarely can a fourth naval lord have had such a triumph. It is not surprising therefore that Beresford told Randolph Churchill 'We are getting on capitally at the Admiralty & with a thorough good overhaul and a business organisation which has never existed up to date.' Yet the new NID was to bring about Beresford's fall within a year of its starting work.

Emboldened by his success in persuading the naval lords to accept his plans for the NID Beresford launched a public attack on the First Lord in a speech at Grantham on 5 January 1887. He was received with 'much cheering' when he rose to respond to a toast to the Navy. Departing from his line of blaming a succession of naval lords for the dire state of the Navy, he now attacked 'the system under which they worked'. The real culprits were 'First Lords of the Admiralty with a party programme' – a thinly disguised reference to Hamilton. In his usual muddled way he admitted that 'the old system existed at the present moment' and he praised Hamilton for asking the naval lords for their opinions. Nevertheless 'he might use the despotic power he possessed and overrule the whole Board'. Such language gives the impression that Hamilton was a tyrant, which he was not. He listened attentively to his naval staff and gave due weight to their opinions. In the end, though, he had to decide policy, which in turn he had to defend in Parliament. For Beresford, the fact that the naval lords could not overrule the civilian First Lord was enough to constitute a dictatorship.

***

Beresford's capacity for causing trouble found new outlets at the Queen's Jubilee Review at Spithead in July. Righting his actions that day was to need the intervention of the Queen, the Prime Minister, the Prince of Wales and the First Lord. Just before the Royal Yacht departed at the end of the day on 23 July, observers were surprised to see a lengthy signal emanating from the vessel. 'Some further change in the programme was feared,' wrote *The Times* but 'anxiety was immediately allayed' when it turned out to be no more than a message from Beresford to his wife, which read: 'Tell Lady Charles to go at once on-board the yacht *Lancashire Witch*, where I will join her.' The message was innocuous but it had been made without authority from a ship bearing the flag of the Lord High Admiral and Sovereign – a serious breach of etiquette. In making this signal Beresford must have assumed that no journalist would be able to read it but a seaman had mischievously passed it on to a *Times* journalist.

As soon as the signal appeared in the paper, Beresford sent in his resignation to Salisbury. He had committed, he said, '[a] tremendous breach of discipline' and shown 'grave want of respect' to the Queen. Salisbury replied the same day, refusing to accept the resignation but agreeing to forward Beresford's letter to the Queen 'but I am quite sure she will decline to receive it'. Beresford had copied his correspondence to the Prince of Wales who replied saying that he thought an apology would have been sufficient. Neatly summarising Beresford's problem he added: 'you have always acted all your life (like an Irishman would) on the impulse of the moment'. On the following day Salisbury was able to tell Beresford that the Queen had refused to accept his resignation.

* * *

Five months later Beresford was once more in resigning mode. The new cause was the special NID salary scale temporarily accepted by the Treasury when the NID had been established. In March, after further correspondence with the Admiralty, the Treasury declared that it was 'still unreconciled to the scale of salaries proposed'. Hamilton accepted this ruling and Beresford promptly resigned.

Given the myths that Beresford was to create around his resignation, it is important to note that Salisbury acknowledged the unvarnished truth in a letter to Beresford. Salisbury told him that he had resigned 'on the ground that the Treasury had refused to continue the additional pay provisionally assigned to the officers who constitute the Intelligence' and that 'you contended that the First Lord had no right to take such a step without previous consultation with his colleagues on the Board.' Salisbury would not intervene because 'It appears to me to be a matter which is entirely within his [Hamilton's] province to decide: and that he cannot be made responsible to Parliament for the satisfactory conduct of his department if his discretion in such matters is overruled.' Salisbury commented to the Queen that Beresford had 'great ability afloat' but was 'too greedy of popular applause' to be able to function in a department.

At the end of January 1888 Beresford took his first steps to create the myth behind his resignation. He told his constituents that he had resigned because 'outside the Admiralty administration he could better assist in resisting the civilian influences at the Admiralty'. Clearly 'civilian' was code for Hamilton. Then he turned to his paper – the one he had previously said he had to go to Salisbury about to get accepted. Now the story was 'my colleagues took it up at once'. The committee which had been set up 'were unanimous on the question of the department [NID]'. As to the salaries: 'The First Lord objected' which was 'the only power that could prevent these reforms being carried out'. (This was nonsense since the reforms, which Hamilton supported, *had* been carried out; Hamilton had only overruled Beresford on the salaries.) Then, backtracking on what he had said earlier, he added 'I resigned on the question of the £960 ... great principles were involved.' As time went by Beresford embroidered his resignation story more and more. By the time he wrote to Emperor Wilhelm in October 1889 he claimed that 'the formation of the Intelligence Department ... cost me my seat in the Government before I could get it carried'. This brazen untruth is breath-taking. By 1909 the reason that he gave to the Cabinet Enquiry for his resignation was 'on question of Strength of Fleet'.

It was now time for Hamilton to defend his department, which he did in a speech to his constituents at Ealing on 3 February 1888. Referring to his decision to bow to the Treasury's view on salaries, he said 'I will show you that the question was not naval, that it did not affect efficiency, that the naval lords were not unanimous, and that considerations of economy hardly entered into the controversy.' The key to Hamilton's defence, though, lay in the fact that, since the date of the Treasury ruling on the salaries, he had had to replace two NID officers. 'In both instances we have obtained the services of the exact officer we wanted.' The lower salaries had not, as Beresford claimed, prevented 'efficiency'. He added that 'Lord Charles Beresford's minute, by agreeing to it [the salary change] as regards the future but protesting to it as regards the present holders of office, practically came to the same conclusion.' As to his dictatorship, 'Every Naval Lord was opposed to Lord Charles reviving the question.' Before some closing remarks in praise of Beresford, Hamilton re-emphasised the fundamental point at issue: 'Neither Parliament nor the country would ever tolerate a system under which four naval men not in Parliament were empowered to dictate the policy to be pursued.'

Despite Beresford's remarkable achievement in setting up the NID, his period as Junior Naval Lord was essentially a disaster. He had leaked documents, claimed credit for the work of others, upset the naval lords and driven Hamilton to distraction. He was never asked to serve again in the Admiralty.

In the same period, even his Commons attendance was lacklustre. In September 1887 a Mr Kelly computed the attendance of office holders for the recent Parliamentary session. The worst attendee (who had been ill for much of the time) was Lord John Manners, MP for Melton. Next came Beresford who had attended on 311 of the 485 divisions.

Chapter 9
Beached on the back benches 1888-89

At 42 years old Beresford had not commanded a vessel for five years. More recently, despite his success in re-establishing the NID, he had severely damaged his political career by a pointless and petty resignation. It would seem that neither his naval nor his political career had much future. Although urged by the Prince of Wales to return to sea, he retired to the back benches to seek revenge against the man whom he said had abused his dictatorial powers.

When in March the Government agreed to a Royal Commission on the administration of the War Office and Admiralty, the terms of reference were limited to 'the civil and professional administration of the Naval and Military Departments' and how these could be changed to improve efficiency. In the Commons Beresford found this remit tame and demanded that the Government admit 'the dangerous weakness and inefficiency of both Services'. W H Smith, First Lord of the Treasury, refused to argue the point.

During the next five months Beresford hassled the Government over the Commission's membership. In March he asked when the membership would be announced but only received a temporising reply. In July he wanted to know who were to be the military members. He was most dissatisfied when he heard that the Government had changed its mind: there were to be no additional members. Towards the end of the year he asked when the Commission would report. Forgetting Commons' procedure, he addressed his question to the commission's chairman, the Marquess of Hartington, who happened to be an MP. As Hartington pointed out, it was a question for the Government to answer. (It was two years before the Commission reported, by which time Beresford was at sea. Had he still been in the Commons he would no doubt have shared the view of *The Times* that the report 'had fallen flat'.)

* * *

It was around this time that Beresford gave the name 'The Souls' to that famous social group of the Victorian and Edwardian era. According to Lady Desborough, a leading soul, Beresford had said 'You all sit and talk about each other's souls. I shall call you the souls.' This occurred at a dinner party at Lady Brownlow's house, but despite Beresford's presence, there is no indication that he was ever a 'soul' himself.

* * *

It was time for another shipbuilding campaign. Beresford always presented the campaign of 1888-89 as his and his alone, referring to it as 'my shipbuilding programme'. While it is true that his was the loudest voice, he was far from alone, being joined by Admiral of the Fleet Sir Thomas Symonds, and Admirals Sir Geoffrey Hornby, Lord Alcester, Sir Edward Fanshawe, Algernon de Horsey and others.

Admiral of the Fleet Sir Geoffrey Hornby

An early indication of Beresford's own intentions to start a new shipbuilding campaign came when he spoke at a Primrose League meeting at Welbeck Abbey in front of 2000 people in May. The League had been set up in 1883 by Lord Randolph Churchill and others to encourage grass-roots participation in the Conservative Party. Beresford, who always lacked influence in the higher reaches of the Party, was ever ready to speak at League meetings. On this occasion he moved a resolution on 'the unsettled state of affairs in Europe' and the need to keep Britain's naval and military forces 'in a full state of efficiency'. He repeated much the same line of argument at a meeting of the select committee on the estimates in June, when he made an extraordinarily muddled demand for more ships. He began by saying that he and his fellow campaigners 'did not ask for increased expenditure for itself; they wanted a better naval administration and a definite standard of defence to be laid down'. Gone were any calls to spend £20 million. His listeners, however, might have wondered how he squared this comment with that of his closest fellow-campaigner, Hornby, who only a week earlier had called for a fleet of 186 cruisers.

Despite this bizarre beginning to the campaign, and despite the fact that Beresford had not requested a particular sum or number of ships, he was clearly wanting more vessels. He described how in 1814 Britain had 489 cruisers to protect 24,411 merchant-ships but now had 42 cruisers to protect 36,725 vessels. Such a critique only made sense if he wanted more cruisers now, yet he 'did not ask for increased expenditure'. Never flummoxed by his own incoherence, he went on to ask for £7m from the Sinking Fund to be spent on ships. And then he came clean: he wanted five battleships and 24 cruisers – 'the minimum required to make us safe'.

Hamilton made a strong defence of the Government's strategy. He attacked Admiral Hornby for his recent demand for £20m for cruisers. If Hornby was right, argued Hamilton, Britain would have eight times as many cruisers as France. 'Does anyone believe that the taxation necessary for that would be borne by the nation, or that such a system of defence would be maintained for any time?'

Lord George Hamilton also sought to show that differing naval experts gave wildly varying advice. A short while back, he said, 'I was then urged to rush into a wholesale expenditure on torpedo boats and torpedo boat catchers'; now the same advisers 'advocate this enormous expenditure upon cruisers'. Then there was the ill-advised suggestion of suddenly building a vast number of similar ships: 'There is no single instance in which ships laid down by the dozen have not shown defects common to all of them, which would have been avoided if they had been laid down gradually and continuously over a series of years.'

Beresford's confused demands and his failure to agree a policy with his fellow campaigners had made things easy for Hamilton. So disunited was the shipbuilding lobby that, just the day after the committee discussion, Beresford attacked Hornby in public at a City National Defence meeting in the Cannon Street Hotel. Hornby, he said, should never have mentioned £20m since, in the debate, 'The First Lord and the Secretary of State for War had pounced upon that statement at once'. (Beresford seemed oblivious to the fact that it was he who had first mentioned the £20m target.)

In the following month Beresford received support from an odd quarter – an official report. Three admirals (Sir William Dowell, Sir Richard Vesey Hamilton and Sir Frederick Richards) had been asked to analyse the results of the 1888 manoeuvres to determine whether, in the event of a hostile attack by France, the Channel Fleet would be capable of blockading the French Fleet. Blockade was found to be impracticable but the crux of the report was its conclusion that 'Great Britain ... is very far from being as strong as she should be on the seas in "personnel" or "*matériel*"'. There was a need for 'a resumption and steady continuance of ironclad building' to place '[the] Navy beyond comparison with that of any two Powers'. Time would tell whether Lord George Hamilton would take from his three admirals the advice that he had rejected from Captain Beresford.

* * *

June saw another Portsmouth jamboree for MPs. Beresford, noted *The Times*, had 'established himself as the mentor and guide of his Parliamentary colleagues in respect of naval matters'. The visits were now 'a necessary part of Parliamentary training'. The special train from London carried 190 people, many of whom had been present on previous occasions. It was a problem to find a fresh programme, so the afternoon session offered demonstrations of mining and torpedo boat evolutions. The day was rounded off by a tour of Nelson's *Victory,* where members were able to inspect 'the spot where the hero fell'. They returned to London clutching chips of oak from the ship's beams, while Beresford received a paperknife and a walking stick, the latter also fashioned from the ship's timbers.

With Parliament in recess from early August to early November, Beresford was out of the public eye. Then, in December he was thrown from a horse while riding in Rotten Row. A stranger helped him up and took a stunned, mud-covered Beresford into Knightsbridge Barracks. Although bruised and bleeding, he merely wiped his face, walked out and rode away. Just four days later he was well enough to return to the attack in the Commons.

Having criticised Hornby for calling for £20m to be spent on shipbuilding and having said that he 'did not ask for increased expenditure', Beresford asked for £20.1m on 13 December – slightly above his figure of three years earlier. Speaking in the House he said he was now ready to 'put a definite shipbuilding policy before the House of Commons'. He first went into great and baffling detail of the comparative strengths of the British and French navies. Taking account of the greater range of tasks that the Royal Navy had, its 49 battleships (built and building) gave an insufficient margin over the 30 that France possessed. A momentary 'oversight, or a Fleet escaping from a port' might lead to 'the total destruction of the British Fleet'.

Beresford asked his listeners to see the cost of the Navy as an insurance premium for the protection of trade. From that viewpoint the current estimates of £11.9m to protect £660m of trade compared badly to the 1860 estimates where £12.3m protected only £375m of trade. Then came the shopping list. He wanted four first-class ironclads, ten second-class ironclads, ten first-class cruisers, ten Thames class cruisers, twenty Medeas class and twenty Sharpshooters. At this point, humour stepped in. Beresford was making this speech on a vote to approve £1,606,200 for shipbuilding, repairs, maintenance and personnel. Parliamentary procedure dictated that those who objected to this sum could only reduce it, so the chairman was puzzled:

> *Chairman*: 'Does the noble and gallant Lord move to reduce the Vote?'
>
> *Beresford*: 'I do not understand, Mr Courtney. I rather wish to add £20,000,000 to the Vote.'
>
> *Chairman*: 'That is inadmissible.'

(Beresford was always weak on Parliamentary procedures.)

In response, Hamilton did his best to demonstrate that the Royal Navy was a better match for the French than Beresford made out: 'my noble and gallant Friend takes an exaggerated view of the power of France' and 'exaggerates the effect of a few hostile cruisers in their depredations on commerce.' As to shipbuilding, 'the average expenditure, including this year, has been £3,100,000, whereas the French expenditure was only £1,600,000 ... The Committee will see that, whereas the difference six years ago was only £200,000, our expenditure now is nearly double that of France.'

* * *

At the end of January 1889 Beresford left for Berlin. According to *The Times* he was to visit shipbuilders and gun manufacturers. Three weeks later the paper had decided that he was there to arrange the programme for the Emperor's visit to England later that year. The latter seems an unlikely task, being the domain of an ADC or a diplomat. Presumably he was researching his shipbuilding campaign.

Beresford was royally welcomed by Emperor Wilhelm and his entourage. There was an audience and lunch on 2 February and then dinner four days later. There he met Count Waldersee (Chief of the

General Staff), Vice Admiral Baron von der Goltz (Chief of the Admiralty) and Rear Admiral Heusner, along with other senior military people – quite a feat for a mere captain, who had commanded a ship at that rank for just six weeks in 1882. *The Times* correspondent remarked, 'I do not remember the case of an Englishman who has been treated here with more distinction than the sailor hero of Alexandria and the Soudan.' For all his faults, Beresford was becoming a man of international renown. How to treat an officer who was feted by emperors was to be a headache for the Admiralty for the next 20 years

Wilhelm II, German Emperor 1888-1918

While Beresford was abroad on his fact-finding expedition, Hamilton and his colleagues had been rethinking the Navy's shipbuilding requirements. On 7 March the First Lord announced a major new programme. Hamilton recalled that the Northbrook programme of 1884 would be all but complete by April 1890. It was, he told the Commons, 'our duty to submit a new shipbuilding programme to the House'. That would not have been a surprise to members, but the scale of what he suggested surely was: 70 ships, of which ten were to be battleships and 60 were to be cruisers, all to be built within four-and-a-half years. The cost was to be £21.5m of which

£11.5m would come from funds allocated to the Navy and £10m from the Consolidated Fund. This represented new expenditure of about £10m.

It all sounded very much like Beresford's programme, so recently rejected by Hamilton and his colleagues. Not according to Hamilton, though, who told the House that this was a programme based on 'a full survey ... of the requirements of the Navy and of the country' as suggested by the select committee of the previous year. Admittedly Beresford had been a member of that committee but Hamilton could not bring himself to mention his name in connection with the new expenditure. Nor was Beresford grateful in victory. He regretted that Hamilton's programme was 'a phantom' for which he had given no 'clear and definite reason'. He naively added that 'I wish to make the House responsible for the standard of the Fleet, so that we may avoid these periodical scares and panics.' He forgot that the wild fluctuations in the Navy's size were caused by politicians, who had other priorities than to pay out vast sums for ships when times were peaceful.

The Times welcomed Hamilton's proposals which were 'eminently satisfactory'. As for Beresford, his remarks had been 'hasty and ungenerous'. This was too much for Beresford, who complained that the comments showed 'how extremely difficult it is for a politician' not to be misunderstood. He made no reference as to how difficult he made it for newspapers when he criticised Hamilton's programme in such an incoherent manner. The programme that he had condemned in the House the day before was now 'almost identical with the one I submitted ... though better as including more formidable battleships'. His complaint was that Hamilton had not produced a paper 'giving definite reasons for his proposal'. Few can have been deceived by this hair-splitting. The truth was that he and Hamilton were in close accord yet neither would acknowledge the other's contribution to the new programme.

When the estimates came up for debate in April Beresford remained incoherent. He first said 'we agree entirely'. This was, after all, the programme which he had so carefully calculated as matching the nation's needs. Suddenly, he changed tack: 'Well, I am not going to acquiesce in everything. I know that £21,000,000 is not half enough to spend on the Navy.' Gradually Beresford was adopting the style that he would assume for the rest of his life: he would say anything, contradict himself any number of times to avoid agreeing with the Board.

Another, more ominous trait was developing. Although the Parliamentary sketch writer Henry Lucy noted that 'When news went round that "Charlie" Beresford was on his legs, the House filled as if by magic', it was filled by those expecting entertainment. Those in search of serious debate took another view, as the Prince of Wales noted when he commiserated with Beresford on 'how empty the Government Bench was' during his speech. The long decline of Beresford's political influence had begun.

One example of Beresford's lack of influence was his attempt to persuade Hamilton to conduct trials to find out whether battleships with un-armoured ends could be easily put out of action by small gun fire. In reply, Hamilton said he knew of no 'distinguished naval officer with a knowledge of modern ordnance' who held this view and, in any case, 'there is no ship afloat ... of the same date ... that has not an inherent weakness of some kind'. There would be no trials.

In May the estimates were back in the Commons for their second reading. The interval had given Beresford time to think up new reasons to oppose Hamilton's proposals. There were insufficient battleships, he argued, since the 65 to be available in 1894 included 13 coastal defence vessels. The remaining 52 were not enough to 'watch and destroy combined fleets such as those of France and Russia', which he added, 'make a total of 59 armoured battle ships'. These criticisms were 'somewhat hostile' retorted Hamilton. As to Beresford declaring that this was not his scheme, Hamilton agreed since 'it is a scheme prepared by my naval advisers ... of whom the noble Lord, the Member for Marylebone is not one'. He astutely added that 'and I am convinced that, if my noble Friend had scrutinized the list of foreign vessels with the same keenness as he has scrutinized those of Great Britain, at least half of them might have been knocked out of the list.' This was all too true. In 1909 at the Cabinet Enquiry into the fleets in home waters, Beresford would be ruthlessly exposed for the way in which he compared worst possible cases for British ships against best possible cases for foreign ones.

* * *

Beresford's need for a sea-going command to rejuvenate his career did not stop him from picking another needless quarrel with the Admiralty. The German Emperor was due to make a private visit to Britain in August. Even a private visit needed a bevy of courtiers and officers to minister to his needs. Determined to be of that number, Beresford lobbied the Admiralty to be appointed as an ADC to the Queen. When the Admiralty refused, it fell to Hamilton to explain to the Prince of Wales why protocol and precedent had blocked Beresford's request. It must have been with some glee that he told the

Prince that Beresford 'is a junior Captain and neither in War Service experience, or sea service is he superior to those of his standing'. In any case, the Queen 'has a number of ADCs ... all of whom are senior to him'. Then came a cruel dig at Beresford's claim to social privilege: 'The social and personal qualities which he possesses hardly justify such a priority being given to him, and his selection under the circumstances would give great umbrage and offence to the service generally and would be without precedent.' In Beresford's long career this is one of the few occasions when the Admiralty refused to cower before his aristocratic standing.

Presumably Hamilton never expected the Prince to show Beresford his letter – but he did. A torrent of abuse was heaped on Hamilton in Beresford's next letter to Edward. Hamilton and his secretary (Captain Walter Kerr) had completely misunderstood the situation, he told the Prince; he had never asked for nor expected to be made an ADC. We can safely dismiss this as bunkum. To accept otherwise is to suggest that Kerr, Hamilton and Prince Edward had all misunderstood him – and all in the same sense. So let us turn to the anger that Hamilton's letter aroused in Beresford. The letter was 'offensive'. Hamilton did not know how fortunate he had been in the self-restraint that Beresford had shown all these years. Did he not realise 'how often, if not always, I could have held him up to ridicule and contempt for his want of knowledge?' He was livid that Hamilton had written about his 'want of war service' and his 'social and personal qualities'. As to the actual visit, it would seem that Beresford chose to shun the British side since his only appearance seems to have been on-board the Emperor's yacht on 4 August.

* * *

And so Beresford's second stint as a member of Parliament came to an end. In December 1889 the public learnt that he was to command HMS *Undaunted* in the Mediterranean. Before he could take command he needed Fisher's help in finding officers since 'I have been so long away I am sad to say from the Service that I do not know the best men of the junior ranks.' Fisher was to find him 'the best commander you know available' and 'a good navigator'. 'Do this for me Jack', he added 'and I shall be eternally grateful to you.'

Such an appointment was normally for three years. How would Beresford fare away from the Prince of Wales, the Commons and the press?

Chapter 10
Back to sea 1890-93

Beresford boarded *Undaunted,* an Orlando class cruiser, on 18 February 1890 and took command of her 461 officers and men, and 72 marines.

Two weeks after assuming command Beresford took *Undaunted* to sea for trials. The ship was loaded with dignitaries, including Lady Charles. *The Times* reported that the trials had been a great success and that the engines had 'worked splendidly'. On 7 March *Undaunted* set sail from Plymouth to join the Mediterranean Fleet.

HMS Undaunted, Beresford's command 1890-1893

In August Beresford's mind was still on politics when he invited Randolph Churchill MP to visit him 'whenever you like to come'. He was already planning his own election address, which would centre on the 'reform of [the] administration of the services'. What he aspired to, though, was to be 'Minister of Defence for 8 months', during which time he would 'draw up a programme which I am satisfied would meet the unanimous approval of both Services'.

Beresford had told Arthur Balfour, Chief Secretary for Ireland, that 'I am so innocent and good out here', but his agitations behind the scenes had not gone unnoticed in high places. Queen Victoria learnt about them from her secretary, Henry Ponsonby. He told her that Beresford and Vice Admiral George Tryon (Superintendent of Reserves) were agitating for increased naval expenditure – not the done thing for serving officers. In October Beresford again tried to persuade Churchill to visit the Mediterranean since he was keen to consult him about his manifesto for the next election. Beresford was certain that the two of them together 'could form a definite Policy of Defence in which both the Services could work together as one'. A few weeks later he confided his ambitions to George King-Hall (commander of the *Melita)*, telling him that he wished to be 'Minister of Public Defence'. When King-Hall warned him that 'the politicians would simply use him' and then discard him, Beresford boasted that he intended setting up a new party with Churchill 'and he did not mean to let R.C. use him, rather the reverse'. Beresford was proving to be a most reluctant sea-going captain.

* * *

On the whole Beresford's time in the Mediterranean was uneventful but when a French armoured cruiser, the *Seignelay* parted with her anchors and was carried onto the rocks at Jaffa, Beresford found the excitement that he always craved. King-Hall was one of the first to hear of the incident on Monday 27 April 1891; he promptly steamed off to the site of the wreck. The *Melita* reached the *Seignelay* at 11.00 am on the Tuesday, a day earlier than the *Undaunted*. Three merchant ships were already at the scene, but none was powerful enough to pull the *Seignelay* clear. Meanwhile the *Undaunted* had left Alexandria to steam the 270 miles to Jaffa.

When the *Undaunted* arrived on the Wednesday, King-Hall and Beresford boarded the *Seignelay* where, Beresford recalled '[we] found her captain seated in his cabin, profoundly dejected at the disaster'. The two visitors immediately took charge of the situation and soon 140 men were relieving the *Seignelay* of 450 tons of coal and other items.

On the Thursday there was great drama as the *Melita* and a Turkish vessel attempted to pull the *Seignelay* off the rocks. The *Melita's* screw fouled on the *Seignelay*'s 3.5-inch anchor cable. In shallow water, held only by her kedge anchor, the *Melita* was now in danger of running onto the rocks. With the aid of a tug from a Turkish paddle boat and the rapid making of sail, King-Hall managed to yank his ship away from the rocks, trailing 60 fathoms of heavy cable behind him. Beresford, watching from *Undaunted* signalled his congratulations to King-Hall as the *Melita* escaped disaster.

The ships worked on through the night of Thursday/Friday and, by 3.00 am, the *Seignelay* had been moved 15 yards. Then the hawser broke free. King-Hall sent the rescue parties off to rest, while a 6-inch hawser was put in place, aided by shackles from the *Undaunted*. Once more, at 11.00 am, the ships pulled on the hawsers, but the *Seignelay* did not respond. Nor did she move when a further attempt was made at 4.00 pm. Then, as the tide rose, *Undaunted* pulled yet again and King-Hall saw *Seignelay* 'come off with a swish'. He had just enough time to free the cable connecting the two ships before the *Melita* shot off towards open sea. The *Seignelay,* minus her rudder, was free and floating.

On the Sunday Beresford arranged a dinner on *Undaunted* for the captain and two officers from the *Seignelay*, and a Turkish captain. King-Hall, who had already attended divine service, lunch and tea on Beresford's ship, and was no doubt exhausted by his endeavours, showed some reluctance at the prolonged stay, but gave way when Beresford seemed offended.

* * *

It was at this time that Beresford's past relationship with Lady (Daisy) Brooke (later Countess of Warwick) brought about the greatest crisis of his life. Lady Brooke had been born Frances Evelyn Maynard in 1861 and, when just four years old, had inherited estates at Easton Lodge in Essex with an annual income of £20,000 (just under £1m today). In 1881 she married Lord Brooke (later fifth Earl of Warwick). Lady Brooke was rich, beautiful and an exuberant socialite, so it is not surprising that she was drawn to the dashing and heroic young Beresford. Their affair began in 1883 and resulted in Beresford being the father of her second child, Marjorie, born in 1884. Their relationship then cooled and their intimacy came to an end.

Early 1889 Lady Brooke sought to re-establish the relationship. She wrote a long and passionate letter (now lost) to Beresford. He was at sea, so the letter fell into Lady Charles' hands thus revealing to her the existence of her husband's love-child. The two women fell upon each other as they fought over the absent Lord Charles. Relations became so fraught that Lady Charles turned to the society solicitor, George Lewis, to restrain Lady Brooke. His letter to Lady Brooke sent her running to the Prince of Wales for his aid.

At 2.00 am one morning the Prince took a cab to Lewis' house and demanded to see the letter. Lewis, breaking his duty of client confidentiality to Lady Charles, showed him the letter. The Prince immediately recognized how damaging it would be to his own reputation were it to become public so he went off to Eaton Square to demand that Lady Charles hand over the original copy. Lady Charles refused. Some sort of a truce followed, although the Prince stopped speaking to Lady Charles.

Frances Evelyn 'Daisy' Greville, Countess of Warwick

By the middle of 1891 it was clear to Beresford that his wife was being systematically ostracised by the Prince's circle over the Lady Brooke affair. From the *Undaunted* at Alexandria he wrote a wild and furious letter to the Prince of Wales. In a torrent of abuse he told the Prince that 'you have instituted a species of society boycotting against [my wife]' and 'people have actually apologised to her for not asking her to certain parties on account of YRH known antipathy'. Turning to the Prince's attempts to get his hands on the letter, Beresford declared 'Your interference as nearly as possible caused a separation between myself and my wife.' Beresford finished with a peroration in which he called the Prince 'a blackguard and a coward'. Salisbury persuaded Beresford to withhold the letter but hostilities continued to rage between the parties. By December Lady Charles could take no more. She telegraphed to her husband asking him to return home immediately.

Beresford reached England on 16 December. Two days later he wrote to the Prince of Wales accusing him of 'openly slighting and ignoring' his wife and compelling her 'to sell her house and announce her intention ... that ... she would rather live abroad'. He demanded an apology. Were that not to be forthcoming, 'I shall no longer intervene to prevent these matters becoming public.'

Frantic efforts were now made by the Palace and Downing Street to bring the quarrel to a conclusion. Beresford insisted on an apology from the Prince for his treatment of his wife. In his turn, the Prince declared that he was at 'a loss to understand how Lady Charles can imagine that I have in any way slighted or ignored her during your absence abroad'. Under Salisbury's insistent pressure the Prince produced a mealy-mouthed apology to Beresford in which he declared:

> 'I regret to find from your letter of 23rd instant that circumstances have occurred which have led Lady Charles Beresford to believe that it was my intention publicly to wound her feelings.
>
> 'I have never had any such intentions, and I regret that she should have been led to conceive an erroneous impression upon the point.'

But the truth was that the Prince had cut Lady Charles and was now to cut Beresford as well. The couple moved out of town to settle in Park Gate House in Richmond. Never at a loss as to how to present himself in a good light, Beresford described his enforced move in romantic terms. There 'I had a model farm, producing milk, eggs and poultry, which were readily sold in Richmond, whose streets and thoroughfares were greatly enlivened by the daily procession of my large and shining brass milk-cans.' The move may also explain why 'a small collection of the property of Captain Lord Charles Beresford' was put up for sale at Christies in June.

The long-term consequences for the Beresfords were dire. The Prince of Wales told Waterford in April 1892 that 'I can never forget, and shall never forgive, the conduct of your brother and his wife.' And he never did. The Beresfords were cut out of the Prince's social world. There were no more visits to Marlborough House, no more cosy suppers, no more yachting and hunting together. Even when he became King, Edward only invited Beresford to formal state occasions where his attendance *ex officio* was unavoidable. As to the effect of the rupture on Beresford's career, we can only speculate that the loss of the Prince's support cost him dear in his rivalry with Fisher.

* * *

Having now disposed of the Lady Brooke affair, we need to backtrack to August 1891 when Beresford received a pleasing piece of news. His friend (and collaborator in agitations against the Admiralty)

Vice Admiral George Tryon was to be the new commander-in-chief in the Mediterranean.

Vice Admiral George Tryon

Notwithstanding their friendship one of Tryon's first acts was to pass on to Beresford a rebuke from the previous commander-in-chief, Admiral Sir Anthony Hoskins, who had just become First Naval Lord. This concerned some extraneous comments that Beresford had inserted into a report. 'Whatever his [Beresford's] parliamentary experience,' wrote Hoskins, 'it is a subject that has no proper place in official correspondence.' In due course this led to another black mark on Beresford's Admiralty record. Some of his remarks, the Board said, were 'of a disciplinary nature which they cannot pass over without notice'. 'Reports shall be confined to the subject to which they purport to relate' and not stray into 'personal, political, or extraneous matter.'

* * *

In the autumn, torpedo exercises at Volo in the Aegean Sea in 1892 led to some controversy. Beresford, with two cruisers and torpedo boats, led a night attack on a force under Captain A K Wilson of the *Sans Pareil*, moored at Port Surbi. This took place before the days of camouflage, so Wilson's white ships would have been easily picked up by searchlights. To hide his ships as best he could, Wilson moored them stern-to-shore and then piled up bushes and olive branches to disguise their outlines. To further confuse the enemy he sent some men with bells, bugles and searchlights along the shore, so disguising the location of the ships. Beresford claims to have sent a man ashore to cut the searchlight cable, though Wilson makes no mention of this in his record. Despite these deceptions Beresford located Wilson's ships and ran in at high speed, launching torpedoes on the fly. He aimed his torpedoes at the *Sans Pareil* but came dangerously near to colliding with *Dreadnought*.

When Tryon came to write his report on these experiments he found himself torn between supporting a captain whom he greatly admired and giving an honest assessment of what had happened. The truth was that Beresford had taken a grave risk in running *Undaunted* so hard up an unknown creek in the dark. Tryon felt he had to tell Beresford that his report to the Admiralty showed that such a risk was 'not justifiable in peace'. He continued, '[you] only escaped a catastrophe by a fluke'. In an effort to lighten this rebuke, Tryon added that he was sure that Beresford had taken 'good care of *Undaunted*' even if this did not show in the report.

* * *

In January 1893 Tryon decided that the port of Alexandria in Egypt had been lately neglected by the fleet, so he asked Beresford to take *Undaunted* there. He hoped this arrangement was to Beresford's liking. It probably was since Beresford always preferred an independent command. *Undaunted* arrived in Alexandria at 6 January 1893 and remained there until 24 March.

One of the privileges of being on detached duty was the chance to influence British government policy in Egypt. In January 1892, the Khedive Tewfik Pasha had died, being succeeded by his eighteen year old son, Abbas. It was not long before Abbas showed his hostility to British influence in Egypt. When Beresford visited him in February, he quickly picked up the gathering tensions, which he reported back to Salisbury. The young Khedive, he said, was 'A boy with a man's head and the determination of a thirty-year-old.' In this, Britain faced a problem since, although 'For the last ten years we have been telling Europe that the Khedive was the real ruler' the truth was that 'the real pharaoh was [Lord] Cromer', the Consul General. Firm action was needed by the British to assert their role in the governance of

Egypt. 'If we drift here,' he told Salisbury, 'we shall have 1882 and the Sudan over again.'

***

The Volo torpedo practice was not the only occasion on which Beresford was charged with hazarding his vessel in the Mediterranean. In April 1893 he and his staff-commander faced a court martial after *Undaunted* had touched the bottom when leaving Alexandria harbour. Evidence was presented to show that Beresford was aware of the difficulties of the passage and had taken special precautions when passing through it. He was 'honourably acquitted' but Richards, his Staff-Commander, was 'reprimanded and cautioned'.

After returning from Alexandria the *Undaunted* remained in Malta harbour until 26 May, when she set sail for Plymouth where she was paid off on 19 June. Tryon expressed his sorrow at losing 'a ship that was always ready and cheerful to undertake anything she was called on to do' and asked Beresford for a copy of his photo. Less than a month later he was dead.

The story of Tryon's death is too well-known to repeat in detail here. Suffice it to say that on 22 June (just after Beresford had left the Mediterranean) the Tryon's fleet was cruising off Tripoli. In a routine manoeuvre, the *Camperdown* rammed the *Victoria*, which sank with the loss of 358 lives, of which one was Tryon's. There was one sole cause of the accident: a fatal signal from Tryon.

Naturally, when Beresford heard of the disaster he knew what had caused the collision without making the least enquiries. *The Times* reported that he had declared that 'he was confident that when they got to the bottom of the matter it would be found that the collision ... was not the result of a mistake ... but something had happened to the helm'. He could not accept that his beloved Tryon was the cause of it all. The most likely explanation is that Tryon had some form of brain disease. Some of his 1893 letters to Beresford are incoherent, suggesting that his mind was in a very deranged state.

Chapter 11
To be an admiral 1893-96

Despite Beresford's attempts to return to Parliament while he was with *Undaunted*, on arriving back in England he accepted the post of Captain of the Steam Reserve at Chatham, which he took up on 18 July 1893. It is doubtful whether he wanted the appointment although it was better than being at sea, which would have kept him away from his political agitations. He took it because he still needed to make up his sea-service in order to qualify for flag rank, but this acceptance was not before making a further request to have his time in the Sudan recognized for sea-service. Once more the Admiralty refused.

With just a few days to go before his command would officially silence him, Beresford slipped in a speech to the London Chamber of Commerce. Much of what he said reiterated his usual complaints as to the insufficiency of cruisers, of which Britain needed fifty-two if trade via blue-water routes were to be protected. If the Suez route were used, even more would be needed because the Mediterranean was 'so cleverly studded with torpedo bases'. France, he said, was the only power that could challenge Britain's sovereignty of the seas. She had 80 torpedo boats in the Mediterranean against Britain's twenty-one. In the Channel, British torpedo boats were outnumbered 62 to 131. He also demanded the lengthening of the mole at Gibraltar to 1800 feet, which was an 'immediate necessity' before money was spent on any other base. Nothing had yet been done with the £5000 voted for this construction in the previous year he complained.

* * *

As Captain of the Steam Reserve Beresford's role was to supervise the construction, repair and trials of all the ships in the Chatham dockyard. The fact that this required him to take 36 ships to sea for trials of a few days enabled him to boast at the 1909 Enquiry that 'I commanded more ships at sea than any man.' It was a spurious claim and he was fortunate that the Enquiry never pursued it.

In his memoirs Beresford illustrated the nature of his work by recounting some of the problems thrown up by trials. There was the ship that ran out all its anchor cable in deep water and then found that its capstan was too weak to raise it. Then there was the torpedo boat with the helm that jammed when travelling at full speed. Just as alarming was the destroyer that, on his last day in post, had a coal bunker that caught fire. The men sought to extinguish it with hoses, but the trial had to be abandoned and the boat was still on fire when it came into port. The work was not without its hazards for Beresford. On one occasion when fire broke out in a galvanizing workshop, he was showered with falling tiles and rafters, but escaped unhurt. On another occasion he was in a punt in the basin when it capsized, throwing all the occupants into the water. Beresford set off to swim to the landing stage but when a rescue boat appeared he swam to it and climbed in unaided.

Chain testing at the Chatham Steam Reserve

In December Beresford was unwell with influenza and asked for special leave, which was granted. He then went off to Egypt (apparently without Lady Charles) for a stay of over seven weeks. Given the length of his stay it is likely that he was troubled by more than influenza. At only 47 years of age Beresford was experiencing the first of what would be many bouts of illness.

***

The start of 1894 saw the beginnings of an organisation that was to play an important part in Beresford's sparring with the Government and the Admiralty: the Navy League. Although the League did not hold its first public meeting until the following year, the preparatory work of setting it up began now. A letter in *The Times* called for 'a permanent "Navy League"' which should be 'independent of ordinary party organizations'. It was to seek 'the maintenance of a permanent standard of naval security' and would 'annually examine the Navy Estimates' to ensure the League's aims were met. Whether Beresford had been consulted at this stage is not known, but he was to be one of the League's founder members and had an on-off relationship with it for many years. (His rival, 'Jacky' Fisher would have nothing to do with the League.)

* * *

After keeping a low-profile on disciplinary matters for some time, Beresford provoked trouble in February 1895 on two occasions. First, he made one further attempt to convince Their Lordships that they should recognise his Sudan duties as sea-time. He cannot have been surprised to be told that their Lordships could 'only refer him to the answer given on 22 July 1893'. Then he complained about being passed over for his expected appointment as ADC to Queen Victoria and of his non-receipt of a good service pension. The Lordships expressed surprise at this letter and declined to meet either request.

The sea-service, the ADC appointment and the pension were all discussed in the Commons on 7 March when the MP for Deptford, C J Darling, asked about the first of these and Thomas Bowles, MP for King's Lynn raised the other two. The two members were particularly concerned as to whether Beresford was being unfairly treated in comparison with other officers of similar seniority. It fell to Edmund Robertson MP (Civil Lord of the Admiralty) to defend the decisions. As to the ADC appointment, 'the First Lord asks me to say that he must decline to give reasons for his submitting or not submitting' to the Queen recommendations for ADC appointments. He pointed out that no officer had a right to assume he would receive such an appointment.

The answer to the good service pension question must have been particularly painful to Beresford. Yes, five captains junior to Beresford *had* received these pensions. But the most junior of these had four and a half more years' service than he did; the most senior, ten years' more. To emphasise the point Robertson added, 'Lord Charles would undoubtedly have received the Good Service Pension, had he served for the usual qualifying time.'

Finally there was the question of sea-service. The Admiralty had already granted his time in the Sudan as service, 'but not as service in command of a ship of war at sea'. It was essential that 'a Captain should serve the first three years of his qualifying sea-service in command of a ship of war at sea'. Harbour ships did not count, no more than service in the Sudan. As to whether Beresford was being treated differently from others, Robertson pointed out that the one other comparable officer with Sudan service – Captain Boardman – had had his request refused as well. Robertson's final words were an indictment of Beresford's endless attempts at special pleading:

> 'This refusal to allow Lord Charles Beresford to count this time in Egypt as in command of a ship of war at sea affects neither his seniority, his pay, or his retirement. It simply means that the Admiralty expect Lord Charles to continue serving until he has completed the minimum service required by the Regulations to qualify for the high position of British Admiral, a minimum which few officers are content not to greatly exceed.'

Beresford was to do the bare minimum to the very day.

* * *

In March Beresford lost one of his most influential naval allies with the death of Admiral of the Fleet Sir Geoffrey Hornby. A determined battler for a stronger Navy and only recently elected as President of the Navy League, Hornby had joined forces with Beresford in many campaigns for larger fleets, better guns and more reserves. His death was to be a great blow for Beresford since, for all the latter's claims to speak for his brother-officers, Beresford found few other leading naval men who would side with him in public.

The last significant event of the year was the death in October of Beresford's elder brother, John Henry, who was found lying in a pool of blood in his study with the top of his head blown off. Only a few minutes before he had been seen calmly walking in his dressing gown, a cigarette in his mouth. But after ten years of chronic pain and permanent disablement he could take no more. The inquest returned a verdict of suicide while temporarily insane. *The Times* regretted the loss to Ireland of a man 'so able, zealous and influential'. Had it not been for his accident he would have become the Unionist leader in Ireland, the paper said. He was succeeded by his son Henry de la Poer Beresford.

Although the Admiralty never relented over the question of Beresford's time in the Sudan (and Beresford never forgave them for their intransigence) they did accede to his request to leave Chatham as soon as he had qualified for flag rank. This meant he could leave four months early. There was loud cheering for Beresford as he left the Dockyard on 13 March 1896.

Chapter 12
Tub thumping 1896-98

Whether by intention or not, Beresford now faced nearly two years with no obvious occupation. Having relinquished the Steam Reserve, he made no serious attempts to enter Parliament. Adrift at the age of fifty Beresford filled in his time as best he could, mostly by making public pronouncements.

With naval expenditure now high enough to satisfy even Beresford, he renewed his attacks on what he called 'the system'. Speaking at the Birmingham Conservative Club on the 19 March he approved of the naval programme 'as far as it went' and welcomed the fact that, for the first time, 'naval defence had been made out upon business-like principles'. At last the government had the men, the ships, and barracks for the marines. This was not, though, enough to satisfy him. Only 'a statesman and a politician' could run the services. In his view the current ministers did not run their services since they 'were never told anything about the requirements of defence'. He compounded this ridiculous exaggeration of the relationship between ministers and service chiefs by failing to elaborate on how he proposed to reform the system. The one item of interest in his speech was a public confession about his 1888 resignation. He had not resigned, as he said at the time, 'on the cost of this department [the NID]'. That, he said, 'was just an excuse'.

Beresford's next big speech was to the Navy League in April. It was little more than a year old yet Beresford felt ready to assess its 'past work' as well as its 'future usefulness'. To the League's agitations he attributed the recent increases in fleet size and the fact that the public were better educated about the Navy. He thought that a civilian organisation like the League was more likely to be listened to than the professionals who might be suspected of self-interest. It is hard to see this remark as anything more than polite flattery of his audience since no one worked harder than Beresford to push the professional view. Nevertheless he concluded that the Navy League had 'a very great future before it'.

* * *

Despite his apparent satisfaction with manning levels when in Birmingham, the change of air to Sheffield a month later found Beresford declaring that there were 'not enough men to man our ships'.

Manning became his new obsession. At the Civil Service dinner in May, he claimed that the First Lord's reaction to his Sheffield speech had been to describe him as 'irresponsible'; but drew comfort from the flood of telegrams, letters and invitations to speak which he had received. The public saw him as responsible and, in any case, he was only trying to 'help authority'. It was, he said, George Goschen, the First Lord, who was irresponsible when he had declared that the Navy was only 11,000 men short. He had taken no account of the ships now building and was 'a very grave danger'.

George Goschen, First Lord of the Admiralty 1871–1874 and 1895-1900

In July Beresford told the Liverpool Chamber of Commerce that the reserve was 'useless', given its lack of training. And, reflecting what was to be a growing problem, the once all-British mercantile marine was now 40 per cent manned by foreigners. In war, he predicted, once Goschen had extracted 11,000 reservists for the Admiralty, the foreigners in the merchant fleet would 'put captains in irons' and sail off to foreign powers. Roused by Beresford's graphic forecasts of imminent treachery, the meeting declared its 'sense of grave danger' and called for an immediate enquiry into manning. This drew a response from Goschen in a letter to *The Times*. The Commons had accepted 'without division' his manning proposals, he wrote. As to numbers, these were increasing steadily, with an increase of 31,350 since 1889.

He gave the increase for the current year as nearly 5000 men. Beresford refused to be put off, declaring that these increases were 'a myth' being made up of 'clerks, boys and cadets'.

Vice Admiral Phillip Colomb, a prolific writer on naval matters, now came to Goshen's support. Admiring the 'fine personal character' of Beresford he feared that 'he is losing his touch'. With regret he declared that 'It is the easiest thing in the world to declaim against the Admiralty'. Closer examination of the facts showed a more subtle picture. True, the Admiralty did not have enough hands but if the number were increased too rapidly, it would be impossible to give them enough sea experience. Rapid expansion would reduce the standard of the men and so reduce efficiency. There it is was: 'efficiency' – Beresford's favourite word. Anything that increased efficiency was good; what decreased it was bad. Yet his own proposals, if implemented, would reduce efficiency said Colomb.

Meanwhile Goschen seems to have taken little notice of the fracas, adding a further 6000 men in his estimates of March 1897. The average increase for the past three years had been 5693, so there is no evidence that Beresford's insistence on vast increases had affected government thinking in any way.

* * *

In June the Institute of Naval Architects met in Berlin, Beresford being one of the British party. They were greeted by the Emperor 'who chatted pleasantly' but whether the Kaiser was still on such friendly terms with Beresford as he had been is not clear – they seem not to have corresponded since 1894. But at least the Emperor invited Beresford to attend some army manoeuvres in which he personally commanded the troops.

As to the purpose of the visit, Beresford was happy to present himself as an expert on naval architecture when he spoke on watertight doors at the Institute's meeting. He wanted to abolish most of the doors, condemning the Navy's 'vogue' for closing them. Sir William White, one of the most respected ship designers of the day, challenged Beresford. He had spent a week with the Channel Squadron, from which he had learnt that 'his brother officers' did not share his view. He admired Beresford 'as a naval officer' but 'had not so high opinion of him as a mechanical engineer'.

Although more or less in a state of perpetual war with the Admiralty Beresford had not yet completely lost his sense of tact. When in September the Board declined his request to attend the steam trials of two ships, there was press comment to the effect that he had been snubbed. Writing to the *Manchester Guardian* he declared 'there was no snub whatsoever'. The Admiralty had been 'most courteous' and explained that 'the trials were contractors'' trials so they were not in a position to invite officers to attend.

There was something nearer to a snub in October when George Goschen, refused to accept Beresford as a member of a delegation to the Admiralty organized by the Association of Chambers of Commerce on the subject of the strength of the Navy. The refusal was compounded by Beresford only finding this out from the association. This, said an unknown interviewee, 'was not a nice thing'. It only emphasised the refusal to recognise his service. Once more returning to the ADC question, the interviewee remarked that 'out of the fourteen senior captains in the Navy list, he alone, being eighth in seniority, has been deprived of the good service pension or the post of A.D.C. to the Queen'.

* * *

Between October 1896 and April 1897 Beresford seems to have retreated to private interests. Then, in the spring, he paused to consider other possible employment. He told one correspondent in 1897 that he would 'be disposed to accept' a suitable Parliamentary seat if it was offered. He also informed Salisbury that since he could not hope for a sea-posting 'for three or four years' he would like to join a Nile expedition in the autumn. He was confident that the Army would call on him since 'the success ... of such an expedition must depend upon the Nile'. He made a further attempt in November to be considered 'for the future governorship of the Sudan'. For the moment, though, the only concrete recognition of his public standing was the award at the end of March of his long-awaited appointment as ADC to the Queen.

After his passion for manning in 1896, Beresford turned his attention to ships and guns in 1897. In a major speech to the Institute of Naval Architects he called for the rearming of 17 of the 45 vessels that still had muzzle-loading guns. 'Either the ships mentioned should be rearmed and made effective, or they should be wiped off the list of the fighting strength.' To Beresford anything he said was self-evidently true so he may have been surprised at the opposition he received. Admiral Bowden-Smith declared that some of these ships did not have sufficiently powerful engines to be rearmed: 'it would be a waste of money'. An Admiral Boyes could not accept that a ship was obsolete merely because she carried muzzle-loading guns. Admiral Penrose

Fitzgerald, meanwhile, did not agree that 'these ships were useless'. Although Beresford received 'a hearty vote of thanks' no one had spoken in his support. This did not stop him from writing to the MP Charles Dilke to tell him that the Admiralty should either build twenty battleships or rearm obsolete ones.

Naval promotion and pay were of much interest to Beresford. On the whole he took a sympathetic and disinterested concern in the welfare of the ratings and the more junior ranks. At times he strayed into self-pity when he reflected on his own stalled career. In April, in a speech at Newbury, he reflected that 'the life, pay, and prospects of the executive officers in the Navy were such that they drove every independent man out of the service'. Warming to his own situation he declared that 'the Navy was the only profession in the world where a man ... could not rise to the top by his own ability, energy [and] hard work'. In his own case he was sure 'that had he entered any other profession he had sufficient ability or go-ahead spirit to have got to the top'.

Having disposed of his personal gripes Beresford then turned to the situations of others. He accepted that the admirals and captains were fairly paid. Commanders were another matter. Their pay of £30-£36 a month, out of which it was customary to buy paint for the ship, 'did not go very far'. Some admirals were in debt 'never having got over their period as commanders owing to the cost of the paint'. Lieutenants, 'the backbone of the service' were paid £15 a month. The worst part of all was the half-pay system. Captains 'often got four years' compulsory half-pay' on promotion.

* * *

It was at Ascot races in June 1897 that Lord Marcus Beresford attempted a reconciliation between his brother and the Prince of Wales. The Prince told Lady Brooke how Lord Marcus 'said he had a great favour to ask me'. Only after signalling his agreement did the Prince discover the nature of the favour: to permit Beresford to approach him to congratulate him on his horse Persimmon winning the Gold Cup. Cornered, the Prince reluctantly received his estranged friend. They shook hands, chatted for a while about racing, and parted. If Lord Marcus had hoped for more he must have been disappointed. Never would the Prince go back on his determination to banish Beresford from his social circle. (Earlier in the year the Prince's brother, the Duke of York, had actually refused to shake hands with Beresford when he was presented to him.)

Tub thumping 1896-98

That same month saw the Queen's jubilee and the accompanying massive naval review. As one of the major contributors to the *Navy League Guide to the Naval Review* Beresford benefited from the prominence of the League at this time. The League also gained from his forthright support in a speech that he made in Oxford. He praised its role in assisting the public 'to set the authority right'. But 'the public had to pay the piper'. All this was routine Beresford rant, but he then showed a progressive streak, quite out of tune with naval tradition, when he called for the Royal Naval College at Greenwich to be closed down and the officers sent to Oxford University. Greenwich cost £40,000 for just 245 students a year whereas the whole of the University of Oxford cost £67,000 a year, he declared.

Naval Review 1897

Beresford must have revelled as he rode along the processional route as one of the nine naval and military ADCs. *The Times* noted that 'Lord Charles Beresford came in for a marked share of attention.' He was also a guest at the Buckingham Palace garden party and the banquet for colonial premiers in the following week.

In the early autumn Beresford received the news that he had been promoted to rear admiral, effective from 16 December. All those tedious years of putting in the absolute minimum of sea service had finally been rewarded with the rank he had so coveted. It stretches credulity that, possibly on the very day he was promoted, Beresford swept regulations aside by inspecting a Royal Navy Reserve Battery without permission. An Admiralty minute noted that 'It is very bad form' but also added that this was all that could be expected from 'a Naval Officer who on about the very day he completed the qualifying service for Flag Rank resigned an appointment ... for the avowed object of stumping the Country as a political talker on naval subjects'. This

Tub thumping 1896-98

latter remark shows that, though the Admiralty agreed to Beresford's early departure from Chatham, they had taken a dim view of his fickle behaviour.

Beresford's last major speech before returning to Parliament was made at the New Vagabonds' Club Christmas dinner in December. The Chairman's introduction emphasised Beresford's high standing with the public. Not only had he been a Lord of the Admiralty, but 'his many medals, distinctions, and mentions, the thanks of both Houses, and even once of the French Government ... showed that he had done all that might become a seaman'. In a speech that initially left his listeners aghast, Beresford attacked those people who thought money was 'the only thing worth possessing'. 'Any vulgarian,' he said, 'could buy his way among those who were described as the best and proudest in the land.' This should not be allowed. People must go back to the times of chivalry and patriotism, abhorring 'all that was sordid and selfish'. Truly an odd speech from so wealthy a man.

* * *

After two years of aimless activity Beresford turned his back on the Navy and accepted the nomination for the York Parliamentary seat. At a speech in that city he declared that he was standing because the state of the country was 'very black'. Only an 'independent-minded man ... could put his views clearly and strongly before the people'. He spoke about Britain's defences (inadequate); the manning of the mercantile marine ('a most serious question'); foreign policy (should be firm and consistent); Home Rule (must be opposed); disendowment of the Church (must also be opposed); education of the people (must be promoted 'in every way'); and defence administration (must be reformed). There was not much there to appeal to York – an inland constituency with no naval connections, and far from the Home Rule controversies. On the one issue that at the time most concerned the citizens of York – a serious local engineering labour dispute – he had little to say other than that 'the State could not interfere between the two people without disturbing the liberty of the subject'. As to arbitration, he supported it but opposed compulsion. Whatever its merits, the speech won Beresford the nomination.

No sooner had Beresford given his speech than he heard that his mother was seriously ill. He broke off his campaigning and departed for Ireland, accompanied by Lady Charles. Despite this interruption to his campaign, he quickly established himself as a popular candidate. *The Times* saw his 'growing popularity' as 'the most striking feature of the election'. He was 'winning golden opinions' wherever he went. His election would be a certainty 'if he had time to canvass the whole electorate in person'. But he had not, so his opponent still had a chance. Sir Christopher Furness was an immensely wealthy shipping magnate. Like Beresford he had previously been an MP (1891-96) but was now without a seat. He appears to have been a run-of-the-mill member and had made very few contributions in the Commons. It was no surprise that he made little impact, while the city was 'ringing with his [Beresford's] praises'. Furness was also strongly behind the employers in the engineering dispute, a fact that *The Times* thought might push some radicals to vote for Beresford.

Sir Christopher Furness, MP in 1902

On the day of the poll – 12 January 1898 – Beresford's campaign suffered a setback with the death of Sir Joseph Terry, his election committee chairman. Terry (son of the founder of the confectioners Terry's of York) was the second biggest employer in York and, despite his 70 years, had taken an active part in the campaign. Whether Terry's death affected events either way we can never know. Beresford scraped home by 11 votes on a second recount at 25 minutes past 12 on 13 January. He was now MP for York – or was he?

Chapter 13
MP for York 1898

Beresford's election was warmly welcomed by the Navy League, which described him as 'a critic and expert of the first water' who was much needed in the Commons. But when he walked into the House on 8 February to be sworn in he was not aware that his right to his seat was to be challenged. Three days later Furness's solicitors presented a petition for a recount. Arrangements were made for the formal scrutiny of the votes at the Royal Courts of Justice. Furness was out of the country and was most upset when he returned to discover how formal and cumbersome the procedure was. He called his petition 'a mere question of arithmetic' and described the petition law as 'absurd'. All he wanted was an accurate count of the legal votes.

When the recount began on 1 March the court was inundated with newspaper reporters and Beresford's supporters. Soon they were all ejected, but not before someone had noted that 20 ballot papers had already been rejected. After three days of counting and discussion of dubious cases, the result (ignoring disputed votes) was announced: a tie. Questioned by the press as to what would happen next, the Returning Officer was struck dumb. The officials were saved the bother of determining the case by a surprise letter from Furness in which he declared he was abandoning his petition. All that remained was for the technicalities of his application to be completed. The whole affair had cost him his lost petition deposit of £1000 (about £57,000 today). Beresford was at last the undisputed holder of the seat.

***

Not long after Beresford's return to the Commons the naval estimates came up for approval. Beresford threw himself enthusiastically into the debate on 10 March. He declared the under-spend of £2.27m in the previous year to be 'a very serious question'. With his ally, the Tory MP Charles Dilke, he maintained that the fleet was not keeping pace with that of foreign powers. In a lengthy and spirited reply, the First Lord, George Goschen, declared that 'we have maintained the standard which has been laid down by the House'. Rather than building masses of ships – which he would do if there were an emergency – it was better to 'concentrate our efforts on completing … the ships we have in hand'. As to accusations that the 'system' was at fault, Goschen maintained that for 'all technical matters … I am the spokesman of the views of those most able professional officers who are at the Admiralty'. (Which was exactly how Beresford said he wanted the Admiralty to be run.) The under-spend, he added, was largely due to industrial disputes outside the government's control.

Sir Charles Dilke MP – a Beresford ally in calling for higher defence spending

As to the contentions of Beresford and Dilke that the government was neglecting Britain's defences, a few figures demonstrate the monumental efforts that the government was making. Before the *Naval Defence Act* of 1889, naval expenditure was £13m (14.1 per cent of government spending). In the last three years the average expenditure had been double this figure and now consumed around 20 per cent of government expenditure. Hardly neglect, by any standards.

Having made no progress with his attacks on the government's shipbuilding programme Beresford turned his attention to naval pay a few days later. Speaking of commanders he said that they frequently 'shrink from being promoted to be captains' since promotion meant going on half-pay. Promotion to admiral occurred too late, when a man 'is long past his prime'. In his own case he had not reached the rank until he was 52 and 'I may think I am as good a man as I was at 40, but, I am not.' Then there was the iniquity of leave: 'an officer coming home is entitled to six weeks' leave, but if he gets ill on the way ... and goes into hospital ... the period is [taken] out of his leave.' It was to the credit of the Service, he argued, that the Commons had never heard this before – officers did not like to agitate – but he hoped his speaking out would lead to the government putting things right. It was a powerful, well-argued speech, only spoilt by his never knowing when to stop. He even managed to talk about his 1888 resignation at one point.

Whether aided by Beresford's prodding or not, the Admiralty announced their amended rules on pay and sick leave in June. From then on captains and commanders would have the full-pay leave that lieutenants had. Also full-pay sick leave would be provided for up to three months at the discretion of the Admiralty.

The day after his speech on pay Beresford was at Harrow School, where he gave his address about life on the *Marlborough* in the early 1860s that caused him so much trouble. His remarks were reported in *The Times* on 21 March and Rear Admiral Gillett's rebuttal appeared in the same paper on 4 April (see Chapter 1 for the details of this episode).

* * *

The estimates in March gave Beresford a chance to pursue other pet interests. Having failed to gain any support at the Institute of Naval Architects' meeting in the previous year for his plan for rearming muzzle-loading ships, he turned to the Commons. How many muzzle-loaders were in the 'A' division of the fleet, and how did this compare with foreign powers, he asked in March. In reply the Secretary of the Admiralty said that Britain had ten such ships and 'there are some vessels similarly armed in European navies'. In the British case they were ships of no importance. Again, there was no enthusiasm for Beresford's idea of rearming old ships. (Later in the year Goschen explained the Admiralty's objections to such rearming. The shipyards were working at maximum capacity; rearming old ships would mean delaying work on the new ships voted by Parliament. Undertaking the work recommended by Beresford would put 'six good fighting ships *hors de combât* for a year'.)

Now confidently back in public life, Beresford was pestered with requests for his signature. He announced that he would no longer provide these free of charge. In future, applicants would be asked to make a donation to the Royal Naval Benevolent Society. He suggested half-a-crown (about £7 today).

In July, in the midst of a debate on the Navy estimates, a sharp dispute erupted between Beresford and Goschen on the subject of the *Naval Defence Act* of 1889. Goschen had declared that he did not allow

MP for York 1898

public opinion to influence his shipbuilding programme. He must, responded Beresford, '[be] about the only man in this House that public opinion does not affect'. It was public opinion, he said, that brought forward the Act. Goschen retorted 'that is not so', maintaining that many other people also claimed to be its author. Stung by this remark Beresford disingenuously declared 'I do not claim the authorship of that Act, and I do not ask for credit on that score.' (Hardly a week went by when he had not declared ownership of the Act.) As the exchange heated up Beresford foolishly let slip that he had 'suffered very much' for having acted 'from purely patriotic motives', adding 'I was treated with ignominy over my A.D.C.-ship to her Majesty, and I had my time stopped in the Soudan when no other officer had it stopped who was engaged in the campaign of war service.' Finally losing all control he accused Goschen of having dragged these issues up. Goschen, of course, had not said a word on the matter.

* * *

For the next two years Beresford's primary concern would be China. There is no obvious reason why he developed this interest. His last service in the region had been in 1871 as a lieutenant and he never seems to have made any special study of it until 1898. Beresford was convinced that Britain had a great commercial future in China, but only if only the Russians could be kept out. In a letter to *The Times* in March he addressed the need to protect British commercial activity in China. Britain, he said, had to 'control the "belly" of China', by which he meant the Yangtze waterway and its hinterland. If this zone was 'kept free and untouched by any other Power' Britain would have no need of open ports since 'It would be an impossible task for other countries to keep our goods out of their spheres of influence.'

This letter implied that Beresford was not happy with the assurances that the Under Secretary for Foreign Affairs, George Curzon, had given him in February when he had asked what concessions the Chinese government had made to British trading interests. Curzon explained that Peking now permitted British steamers to use China's internal waterways and that, in the Yangtze region, no territory would be 'leased or ceded to another Power'. Additionally the post of Inspector General of Maritime Customs would be held by a British officer as long as Britain was the largest trading nation in the area.

Not content with talking about China, Beresford decided on a grand expedition to the country. He gave Arthur Balfour, now Leader in the Commons, the impression that he wanted the Chinese government to take him on, rather as the Egyptian government had made use of General Gordon, and was still making use of Lord Cromer. The Prime Minister Lord Salisbury thought that Beresford could be useful in China if he reported on China's military organisation but he was adamant that he would travel without any endorsement from the British government. Beresford overcame these difficulties by suggesting to the Association of Chambers of Commerce that he go on its behalf. Its chairman, Henry Northcote, accepted the offer since the Association was keen 'to obtain accurate information as to how security is to be insured to commercial men' in China. He requested that Beresford produce 'a comprehensive report' on the subject.

Ignoring the strictly fact-finding nature of the visit, three days after Northcote had sent Beresford his commission, he was again telling Salisbury of his military ambitions. Capital would 'pour into the country' if only the Chinese government would allow him 'to organize their forces in the Yangtze Valley'. Salisbury, too, seemed to be warming to the military aspect when he next wrote to Beresford. Echoing the latter's letter in *The Times* of the previous March, Salisbury was of the opinion that 'The only power we have of acting in China is through our ships.' He wanted Beresford to find out 'how many of our present gunboats could destroy or threaten how many of their important towns? How many could we threaten if we had gunboats [armed with] two 6-inch guns?'

Beresford left for China on 24 August. His journey took in Hong Kong, Shanghai, Peking, Niu-Chwang, Chifu, Han-Kau, Nanking, and Fu-Chau between 1 October and 6 December. His main purpose was to interview European traders on their concerns about the security of their operations. In Manchuria he found his worst fears confirmed when he observed Russian commercial and military activity in the area. There was 'great Russian railway activity' there and Russian cargoes were being landed 'without customs supervision or payment'. The railway in particular was 'securing positions of [military] advantage' for the Russians.

It was inevitable that Beresford would stray from his remit. In early November he was reported as having said that he had obtained permission 'to place a body of 2,000 Chinese troops under the command of a British officer in the Yangtze Valley'. Yielding to the consequent displeasure of the Chinese authorities he denied ever having made this statement and claimed that he had merely said that 'unless China did something to help herself, he would be obliged to use all his influence towards persuading the British public to demand a partition of China'. Meanwhile, Beresford had upset the Empress, who had heard that he had visited Yuan Shik Kai (later, the last Emperor of China), whom she suspected of plotting a *coup d'état* against her.

Shanghai street scene, c 1900

During his trip Beresford was received as a high dignitary wherever he went and welcomed by enthusiastic Europeans at every stopping place. Consuls and viceroys turned out to greet him and arranged for interpreters and introductions to local communities. The Chinese gave him every opportunity to inspect their military activities. He saw troops drilling at Wuchang, visited arsenals and ironworks, and inspected gun batteries. All he saw left him with a conviction that the Chinese army was of poor quality, supported by run-down armaments factories. As for transport, Beresford was treated like a head of state with a cruiser being put at his disposal at one point; and the forts saluting him as he returned to Shanghai from Nanking.

Stopping at Hong Kong on his way home Beresford offered some preliminary thoughts on what he had seen. The Chinese government was, he said, effete and 'there was no security for trade'. The British therefore had 'to assist in establishing security'. 'Commercial enterprises were already interfered with', which was worse than imposing tariffs. As to the Russians, they were constructing strategic railways, which were not there 'to develop trade'. Soon British trade could be 'excluded from a Chinese province'. He called for the reorganisation of the Chinese Army – preferably by the British – reform of tariffs, residence rights and 'the proper opening of waterways'.

Chapter 14
MP for York 1899

Back home, it was not long before Beresford made use of his new-found knowledge of China. In March 1898 the British government had leased a naval base at Wei-hai-wei on the opposite side of the bay where the Russians had leased Port Arthur. In the estimates debate in April 1899 Beresford rather pompously gave his approval. It was, he said, 'as good a naval base as we could have anywhere – that is to say, if it is made into a proper and efficient naval base'. He praised 'the capabilities of the harbour' which was 'the only harbour, with the exception of Hong Kong, where a battleship can lie close to the shore'. Having praised the potential of the base he went on to say 'I do not think that the Government would be wise to incur a very large expenditure of money upon Wei-hai-wei'. This was too much for Ughtred Shuttleworth (an ex-Secretary to the Admiralty) who could not resist the temptation to puncture Beresford's self-important contribution. He was so glad to see Beresford back in the House since without him 'we were rather in the dark before as to what is going to be done with Wei-hai-wei, or what in the future we should wish to be done'. Regrettably, he added, 'we are not very much more enlightened after his speech'.

Beresford again raised the issue of Wei-hai-wei in the Army estimates on 21 April when he asked when the construction work would be done. He recalled a conversation with a German admiral who commented on the contrast between the Russians (frantically fortifying their base), the Germans (making a parade ground at their base) and the British ('employed with great industry in making a cricket ground' at their base). The First Lord admitted that '[we] proceed more leisurely' but pointed out that Wei-hai-wei was only an 'accessory' to Hong Kong. For the Russians and the Germans, these bases were their only bases.

By June Beresford had stood his argument on its head. In the Commons he attacked the plan to spend £130,000 on barracks at Wei-hai-wei: 'I shall oppose the proposal in every way I can.' In case his listeners thought this a change of view he declared 'It may be said I am altering my opinion as to Wei-hai-wei. Not at all.' The barracks, he declared, showed that the government were 'drifting into a sphere-of-influence policy as against the open-door policy'. Since 'Wei-hai-wei is in the German sphere of influence the place would become a great danger to us and to our Fleet'.

MP for York 1899

* * *

In May Beresford's massive tome, *The Break-up of China,* was published. The title came from his conviction that China's policy of allowing European nations 'spheres of influence' in the country would lead to a weakening of the central government and, eventually, to its collapse. Without a central government, war would then break out between the other powers. This could be avoided, he argued, if the European powers acted together to protect their interests and if China adopted an open door policy with no geographical limits on where each foreign power could trade.

The book basically consists of Beresford's notes of his meetings with Europeans in commercial centres in China. From these notes he drew his conclusions as to what the future might hold and how Britain could best protect her interests there. His overall conclusion was gloomy: 'no security at present exists for the future development of British trade in China'. He ended with eleven recommendations for the Chinese authorities, including introducing an imperial coinage; tax and monopoly reforms; residence rights for traders; protection of copyright and trademarks; and a host of regulatory reforms.

The Times was impressed by the speed with which Beresford had produced 'so elaborate and comprehensive a report' but disappointed in the title, which seemed to presuppose that China must break-up. This was at odds with the book in which Beresford argued that there was no need for it to break-up. For the paper, 'the value and importance' of the book was less in Beresford's opinions than in 'the information he has so diligently collected'.

While *The Times* gave little warning of what readers would find in the book the *Manchester Guardian* cautioned its readers that it was not 'light reading'. It was 'solid' and 'deserving of praise' and 'as free from literary pretensions as a consular report'. As to the style, 'Lord Charles, as it were, hurls his notebooks bodily at the reader's head and tells him almost angrily that these are his views'. It continued: 'The armchair reader will be tempted to give up the book in pique … As literature it is not to be recommended.' For 'the hardier student' it would have its rewards.

There was no need for a formal government response to Beresford's report since it was addressed to the Association. However, by chance, William Brodrick, the Under-Secretary of State for Foreign Affairs, made some interesting points during the discussion of the Foreign Office estimates. Beresford had criticised the First Sea Lord who had sent ships to defend British trade with China. 'Very big words' had been used, he said, but 'we have seen them followed by very small deeds.' In tit-for-tat mode Brodrick responded that while Beresford had 'received magnificent receptions' in China 'the results which have come from it have hitherto been almost nil'. He then went on to explain why he thought little would ever come of Beresford's proposals. He concluded 'I think he has not grasped the greatness of the problem with which he has to deal.'

* * *

Beresford was now 53 years old. Already there were clear signs of deterioration in the quality of his speeches. His discourses were to become ever more rambling and repetitive, endlessly recalling the glories of 'my building programme' of 1888.

Beresford's tendency to talk first and think afterwards got him into trouble again in June when he made some remarks (no longer traceable) 'to a stranger', which had got into the press. He had given the impression that Britain should go to war over the increasingly heated dispute in the Transvaal over the rights of the Uitlanders. (These were migrant workers – many of them British – who were working in the Boer-controlled Transvaal goldmines.) In fact he did not regard this as a question 'upon which we could go to war'. Nevertheless, unless Kruger, the President of the South African Republic, 'saw the true wisdom ... the existing irritating ... circumstances might drive us into a conflict'. Public men needed to be 'extremely careful in their utterances' since 'any chance expression' could lead to trouble. It was a typical Beresford explanation in that it explained nothing. He clearly thought Britain should go to war, but squirmed as to how to phrase that sentiment. He need not, though, have been so apologetic. In September the British government issued an ultimatum to the Transvaal, demanding equality for British citizens resident there. The Transvaal's rejection of this demand led to the South African War (now known as the Boer War).

* * *

Despite the detailed and apparently final explanation that Beresford had received in 1895 to his dispute over his sea-service, he raised the matter yet again in July. This time he wanted to know 'the conditions under which British Military officers were employed in the Soudan'. In particular he wanted to know 'whether the officers referred to were allowed to count the time employed in the Soudan towards their time for promotion and towards their time for pension'. The answer was 'Yes' to both.

President Kruger announcing a fourteeen-year residency requirment for Uitlanders to qualify as voters

By mid-October conflicting reports of a sea appointment for Beresford were circulating. *The New York Times* declared that 'it is now certain that Admiral Lord Charles Beresford will become second in command of the British Mediterranean fleet'. He had, the paper said, already 'selected his staff' and would fly his flag in the *Revenge*. On the same day *The Observer* declared that there was 'no truth in this report'. In fact 'Lord Charles Beresford will be compulsorily retired'. He had gained 'the ill-will of the old gang at the Admiralty', which had not appreciated 'the sacrifice of his career for the sake of the Navy and the nation' when he resigned in 1888. The article was an obvious Beresford plant, but it is also telling that the paper willingly printed as a fact Beresford's utterly fictitious account of his resignation.

It was not until the 20 December that the appointment was confirmed. Shortly before Beresford was politically silenced by his Mediterranean appointment, he made several remarks on the progress of the Boer War. On 6 November, responding to complaints that the government had not sent enough troops, he wrote 'The very fact that we had not our troops there early showed our earnest desire to maintain peace.' In Sunderland he again defended the current troop levels. Yet in his memoirs he claimed that 'I most emphatically advocated the dispatch of a much larger force ... in the fire brigade, if an officer thought a fire needed four engines to put it out, he would send eight.'

UNEASY RECONCILIATION 1900-1905

Chapter 15
Giants at bay 1900-1902

Seven years after stepping off the *Undaunted*, Beresford was about to go to sea once more. His uncertain naval career was to be crowned with nine years of flag appointments and flawed by his accelerating crusade against the Admiralty. What should have been a period of triumph proved a period of ever increasing turmoil, caused by his uncontrollable jealousy of Sir John Fisher.

* * *

In early January 1900 Beresford was the chief guest at a banquet given by the London Chamber of Commerce to honour his departure. In return he gave the diners a knock-about speech with little serious content but one prescient remark, when he noted that he was not yet on the active list so he could 'say what he liked'. Soon 'his duty would be to his commanding officer ... and he would know nothing whatever about politics'. Amused laughter greeted this comment but Beresford's failure to accept this discipline would lead him into a sea of troubles.

Beresford was still an MP at the time of his speech so on 18 January he travelled north to York to enjoy some final festivities with the Mayor and other dignitaries before formally renouncing his seat on 26 January.

It was on the last day of January 1900 that Beresford boarded the Continental express from Victoria to Genoa. For once there was no grand farewell: he was seen off by Lady Charles and his brothers Lord Marcus and Lord William. At Genoa HMS *Venus* was ready to take him to Malta, which he reached on 3 February.

When Beresford joined the Mediterranean Fleet Sir John Fisher had been its commander-in-chief for six months. Fisher had found a sleepy, self-satisfied fleet that exercised in stately formations, neglected gunnery practice and was unprepared for war. He had begun to train his officers to manoeuvre at speed, to fire guns at long-range targets and to take the initiative. Meanwhile he harangued the Admiralty about his lack of ships and warned it of the threat to the Mediterranean Fleet from French torpedo boats.

On arrival Beresford found his flagship, HMS *Ramillies*, was in the Malta dockyard, where it was undergoing extensive repairs. He had to wait until 14 April before he could take her to sea. It was a delay that vexed him, particularly since '[I] had to take a house in Valletta at £180 a year'. But it was the clashes with his new commander-in-chief that were to become the hallmark of this posting.

HMS Ramillies, Beresford's flag ship 1900-1902

The first clash between Fisher and Beresford took place around the end of March. Beresford had taken a group of men to the naval parade ground on the Corradino Heights above Malta. There he sought to teach them signalling using the men to represent individual ships. As he described the exercise the men were 'linked together with a tack-line, in order to keep them in station'. In this way they were to perform 'the evolutions of a fleet in obedience to signals'. The exercise was interrupted by a signal from Fisher, which peremptorily ordered him to return his men to their ship and explain in writing why he had landed them without permission. The signal was greeted with incredulity by the rest of the fleet and was much discussed in the cafés and bars that evening.

There were early signs in March that Beresford had no intention of accepting his subordinate role when, in a conversation with Fisher's Chief of Staff, Captain George King-Hall, he expressed his concern about the coal stocks at Malta. King-Hall noted in his diary that Beresford was 'anxious to stir everyone up at home on this and other matters'. His judgement was quickly confirmed when Beresford secretly wrote to both Arthur Balfour and Balfour's secretary, John Sandars. He was sufficiently aware of the enormity of what he was doing to send the letters to Lady Charles, who was to deliver them by hand to Sandars.

The Corradino Heights, scene of Beresford's first clash with Fisher

Although Beresford had been in the Mediterranean for just two months, his letter to Balfour betrays his sense of isolation from the political scene. He desperately wanted to address the British public but it would not be 'in the interest of discipline if I were to write a public letter'. Beresford debated whether he should 'go home and warn the country of the state of affairs'. And what were these 'affairs'? There followed a list of eight immediate needs of the fleet: bigger coal stores at Malta and Gibraltar; a school for captains of torpedo boats and destroyers; colliers; cold storage for food; distilling ships; telegraph ships; and more signals training for officers. But, if he could not come home, he could at least invite Balfour 'as the only possible future Prime Minister' who was surely in want of 'a rest and change' to visit the Mediterranean. If only he would come he would quickly see that 'the Fleet is not ready to fight or nearly ready to fight'. He admitted to Sandars that Fisher was 'sending home strong representations' on these same points but bemoaned that 'I can do nothing ... as I am only second in command.' One excuse for this extraordinary correspondence was his conviction that Fisher's appeals to the Admiralty would achieve nothing. He was mistaken in this belief as we shall shortly see.

Beresford's initial frustrations came to an end with the release of *Ramillies*. Her trials started on 10 April and on the fourteenth he was finally able to take charge of his ship. It was at this time that he first began to confide to his notebook his gripes about his role. He recorded that 'from 5th February to 13th April [I] had nothing to do of any sort'. He complained that he had not been consulted on the fleet, on war organization or anything else. What would happen, he wondered, 'if anything were to happen suddenly to CinC'. Beresford would be in command yet all the fleet's plans were in Fisher's head. In his view the second-in-command should have been in charge of manoeuvres and drills rather than having to wait for orders. He understood that his lack of a role was not really Fisher's fault since, as he told Balfour, it was 'the *Custom* of the Service [that] prevents his communicating with me'. Indeed, when Beresford became a commander-in-chief, he treated his second-in-command in just the same way, including withholding war plans from him.

* * *

By June Beresford was feeling bold enough to let Fisher know about his political lobbying. In a twenty-one page typed document he set out 'an official letter on the strength of the present Fleet under your command' which he admitted he should not write but excused himself on the grounds of his 'being a public man outside my naval profession'. Not satisfied with this effrontery he then told Fisher that he was sending a copy of the letter to the Prime Minister and Balfour. Fisher has been much maligned for his treatment of Beresford but this extraordinary episode so early in Beresford's posting illustrates the depths of the latter's provocations. From the earliest days of their conflict, it was Beresford who determinedly played the part of the agitator and Fisher that of the restrained sufferer.

In the summer Beresford invited members of the Navy League to visit the Mediterranean. Little evidence of this visit remains but we do know that, on their return, the recently ennobled Viscount Goschen detected what he called a 'strong Mediterranean flavour' in the writings of Arnold White, the *Daily Mail* journalist. But it was the fleet manoeuvres of 1900 that best illustrate the underlying relationship between Beresford and Fisher. After a mock battle in late September, Fisher told his wife that Beresford had done 'uncommonly well' in what had been a 'most exciting' clash, which was 'as near war as it well could be'. So pleased was Fisher with Beresford's manoeuvring that he happily passed over the near collision between *Ramillies* and *Royal Oak* as they came within 70 feet of each other. Nor did it matter that *Ramillies* had been captured and Beresford had had to abandon his ship and 'pull for his life' to reach the safety of *Royal Sovereign*. It had all been great – but serious – fun with no sleep for 48 hours and four days of nerve-wracking tension.

Of all the outcomes of the exercises perhaps the most surprising was their impact on Beresford. As soon as the fighting was over he called on Fisher to tell him that he had abandoned his plan to return to Parliament and would now stay with the fleet for the full period of his posting. He had, he told Fisher, 'learnt more in the last week than in the last 40 years'. Any doubts that Fisher had exaggerated Beresford's satisfaction are removed by similar private thoughts in Beresford's ledger. He noted that 'I have never seen any exercises carried out with a view to practising Officers and Men in work that they will have to do in war time, until this year'. Fisher, he said, was the first man to introduce such training methods.

Beresford was not above attempting to get his own back on Fisher when he felt slighted. In a story that his first biographer received from a private source, he neatly turned an oversight of Fisher's to his advantage. It occurred at the annual regatta at Lemnos. The fleet mail needed to be collected from a Turkish port and Fisher gave the task to the *Theseus*. By custom he should have sent a more junior vessel. In response Beresford sent the open signal: 'I regret that after the good work *Theseus* has done under my command during the recent exercises, she is not to be allowed to take part in the regatta.' This alerted Fisher to his error and he rescinded the order. Another signal followed from Beresford: 'I am glad that after the good work *Theseus* has done under my command, the Commander-in-Chief has seen fit to allow her to take part in the regatta.'

* * *

At the end of the year Beresford's brother Lord William died from an attack of peritonitis. After recounting his dramatic winning of a VC by his rescue of a Sergeant Fitzwilliam under close fire from Zulus in 1878, *The Times* described his work as military secretary to three viceroys of India and his life on the turf. Referring to his talents the paper remarked that '[he] did not employ them in the most productive way'.

At almost exactly the same time as Lord William died, R H Macdonald, Beresford's secretary in London, committed suicide after incurring gambling debts of £300 (about £17,000 today). Discreetly reporting his death 'in tragic circumstances' the *Manchester Guardian* lauded his 'mastery of naval questions' and his value to Beresford. Beresford turned to his friend Carlyon Bellairs for help. (Bellairs was an ex-naval commander and an MP from 1906-10 and then from 1915-1931.) Would he be willing to take over the secretarial post? The fact that Bellairs was then a Radical (he was later a Tory) was an advantage since, Beresford said, it would help him to 'see both sides of the question'. Bellairs declined but quickly engaged a replacement for Macdonald.

At the end of Beresford's first year in the Mediterranean he told Bellairs of his admiration for Fisher. Of all his correspondents at this time, Bellairs was his most trusted. He confided his most secret and scurrilous ambitions to his friend, so we have no reason to doubt that the opinions he expressed in these letters are genuine. 'I get on,' he said 'quite exceptionally' with Fisher and 'I admire his ability immensely.' As to his earlier view that Fisher could not wrench concessions from the Admiralty, Beresford now admitted that 'he has succeeded in some particulars'.

* * *

At this stage of his career Beresford was a determined trainer of men and rightly saw that captains needed help in the transition from commanding a single ship to commanding a squadron. On several occasions he gave the impression that Fisher and the Admiralty opposed this approach. Closer examination of his correspondence with Bellairs and Beresford's Mediterranean notebook shows a different story.

An entry in this notebook for March 1901 almost certainly represents the truth when he wrote: '[I] was told I should not have exercised Captains at taking charge of Squadron during manoeuvres without CinC's permission'. This entry makes clear that the offence was not one of putting captains in charge of squadrons but doing so *without permission.* But when writing to Bellairs, he claimed that he had received a 'severe reprimand' for 'proceedings so contrary to the customs and usage of the Service'. In case we are in any doubt as to this interpretation we only have to turn to press reports nearly a year later when we find that Beresford was described as having introduced 'a complete innovation in the usual methods of command ... Night and day for a week the division under his command has been manoeuvred by the various Captains.' Whilst it is obvious from the fulsomeness of the article that it was planted by Beresford, it is also clear that Fisher in no way opposed this innovation.

* * *

Almost since his arrival in the Mediterranean in July 1899 Fisher had been bombarding the Admiralty with complaints about the weakness of his fleet, the need for more ships and the lack of harbour defences. By early 1901 the Board had had enough and decided to visit the Mediterranean to settle the argument. Lady Charles' interpretation of the impending visit was typically bizarre. She told Arnold White that 'Lord C. is not going to tell them *anything'* – a degree of self-effacement that Beresford could never have achieved. Somehow (in a manner that Lady Charles did not explain) this would lead to a rapprochement between Beresford and the King and then there would be '<u>nothing</u> to prevent the admiral coming straight to the top'.

On 13 April, the new First Lord, Lord Selborne (appointed November 1900), together with the First Naval Lord, Lord Walter Kerr, and other staff arrived at Malta. Whatever Beresford and his wife thought about the visit, it was a triumph for Fisher. Selborne listened to his arguments and concluded that he had a strong case. Overriding Kerr, he conceded many points to Fisher, in particular the need for more cruisers. It was all 'more urgent than I had previously thought', he wrote.

* * *

No sooner was the Board visit over than Beresford began to search for other ways to promote his views of the fleet. He turned to the *Daily Mail* journalist Arnold White and in May invited him to come at any time and to stay as long as he wished. In addition to his journalism, White was a member of the Executive Committee of the Navy League. The League had been looking for new ways to attack the government over the weakness of the Navy, so Beresford's invitation proved opportune. White accepted both as journalist and provocateur.

White arrived in early June, accompanied by the League's President, Robert Yerburgh. One of their first meetings was with Fisher, who found the two League members just as concerned about his fleet's strength as he was. King-Hall noted that White was 'very strong … on the necessity of strengthening [the] Navy'. Fisher knew how to manipulate White to his own ends and, within days, there was a *Daily Mail* leader praising Fisher and Beresford who 'have made efficiency their cult' and had trained the fleet and had developed the fleet 'to a point of excellence never before reached in time of peace'. But, added the paper 'the Mediterranean Fleet is weak' and should be augmented by 'a division of the Channel Squadron with half a dozen cruisers'.

After he had returned to England, White worked on an article for the *National Review* that was to encapsulate Fisher's case. Under the title *A Message From the Mediterranean*, White detailed the fleet's weaknesses and declared 'we no longer possess supremacy at sea because we stint our fleets'. It was strong stuff but Fisher's stage-management of White ensured that White spoke on his behalf. Thus when the League sent a copy of the article to every member of Parliament, Fisher's fingerprints were nowhere to be seen.

Malta harbour c 1900

Beresford could never match Fisher's skill with the press; his handling of White was to prove a disaster that came near to ending his command. Above his name, on 21 June 1901, a letter appeared in the *Daily Mail* in which he said 'It would be most improper and prejudicial to discipline if I were to give you details as to why I am so extremely anxious when considering the want of strength and the want of proper War Organisation of the British Fleet in the Mediterranean.' He added that he had repeatedly warned 'the constituted authorities' of this 'in as strong and clear Anglo-Saxon language as I can command'. The letter was addressed to 'Dear ___' but it was White who had placed it in the paper. (Its true origins were to remain a mystery until revealed to Parliament in the summer of 1902.)

A few days later the paper reinforced Beresford's letter with a leader headed *Before it is too late* which described him as 'a great naval authority' and called for immediate action on his letter. Next day questions were asked in the Commons as to how a serving officer had come to publish a letter about naval matters, contrary to *King's Regulations*. On behalf of the Government, Hugh Arnold-Forster, Secretary to the Admiralty, said that 'there is nothing to show that the letter was intended for publication' and made clear that no further action would be taken. This was not the last that the Commons would hear of this troublesome letter.

* * *

At Fisher's request, the Channel Fleet under Vice Admiral A K Wilson had joined the Mediterranean manoeuvres in order to replicate the coordinated working of the fleets in war. King-Hall acted as an umpire and enjoyed watching Beresford and Wilson in battle together. Both Beresford and Wilson were accomplished fleet-handlers so the battles were close-fought. On 6 September King-Hall commented that 'Wilson in A fleet had the worst of it, at the commencement of the action and the best of it at the end.' On 10 September Beresford had more and faster ships than Wilson. As King-Hall observed the fight from his vantage point in the fore top he noted that Beresford 'had decidedly the best of the action'.

Admiral Sir John Fisher in his cabin on Renown c 1900

Fisher was pleased with the outcome, telling Selborne that 'Both Wilson and Beresford handled their own Squadrons most admirably when working independently against each other.' Beresford, too, was content. According to Lady Charles he was 'in the best of spirits' because 'at last he has been able to prove that his reputation has been sustained as regards practical handling of the fleet'. (This is an odd comment since, for all his faults, no one ever accused Beresford of not being able to handle a fleet.)

The summer cruise ended with the most notorious of the Fisher-Beresford clashes in the Mediterranean. The fleet was returning to Malta on 9 November. Fisher, in *Renown*, had entered the harbour first, landed, and walked up to the Barrakka – a promenade high above the harbour – from where he was to watch his fleet come home. As *Ramillies* came into the mouth of the harbour her captain misjudged the narrow entrance with its awkward turn and the ship became jammed across the waterway. Although his staff tried to restrain him, an enraged Fisher issued the open signal 'Your flagship is to proceed to sea and come in again in a seamanlike manner.' Lieutenant Chatfield, who observed this, recalled that 'news of it spread throughout the Service'. Beresford obeyed and, for the moment, said nothing.

How much the fleet and its workings mattered to Beresford is unclear. As early as July 1901 he had let it be known that he wanted to return to politics so as to have 'a free hand in criticizing recent developments'. His self-assurance in what he would be able to achieve was unbounded. He told Bellairs in October: 'I feel confident that my time will shortly come in which I may be of use to the Empire & rouse our people up to look at things as they are.'

***

Much has been written about the Fisher-Beresford relationship during this period. Often the frictions between the two men have been cited as the origin of their quarrel. The picture is more complex than that. We don't have to look far to find the harsh side to Fisher. He refused to let Beresford have information on coal stocks; he refused to let him take ships out on occasions; and he issued peremptory open signals. King-Hall found the communications between the two men to be so acerbic that he held back some of Fisher's memos to Beresford and, at the same time, listened to 'C.B. abusing Fisher to me'. And yet something is missing in this interpretation of their relationship; something that could account for this jolly note that Beresford sent to Fisher:

> 'I have a children's party 4.30 to 6.30 Saturday here. Do come
> and help me: they would like to see you. You put your head on
> the block on this naval question and you will win ... I hope to
> send you some fish tonight ... Meet you Sat.'

Here we have two men who were easy in each other's company and, in their own writings at this time, there is not a hint of animus. For example, writing in his notebook, Beresford recorded his high opinion of the prize essays that Fisher had introduced to the fleet. Fisher, he said, deserved 'the lasting gratitude of the country for instituting these essays'. The two men also shared near to identical opinions on the Mediterranean Fleet. When Beresford sent Fisher his views on the outcomes of the exercises of mid-1901 Fisher annotated the document with remarks such as 'concur' and 'fully concur'. In turn, Beresford's conclusion was that 'it is quite impossible to overrate the value and utility of such manoeuvres ... which hitherto have been totally neglected in Her Majesty's Fleet.' When Beresford's time in the Mediterranean was almost up he was fulsome in his praise of Fisher's methods. In his notebook, he recorded that he had been in the service for 43 years and only just found 'the proper position for an Admiral in his Fleet in action'. He called the 'practical manoeuvring of one Fleet against another' and added: 'Simply incredible!!!'

Fisher in his turn was full of praise for Beresford in March 1902, telling Lord Spencer (First Lord, 1892-1895) that 'He is a first-rate officer afloat, no better exists in my opinion ... and in the two years he has been under my command he has never failed once to do everything he has been ordered, cheerfully and zealously, and *has always done it well*.'

We can only conclude that the much reported animosity between the two men was just not there. Their stature accounts for this: they were both men big in spirit, who were used to dominating others. They were both plain speakers and intolerant of anything but the best; it was easy for them to brush off a brusque remark or a harsh judgement.

In the case of Beresford his attacks during this period were exclusively aimed at the Admiralty and the Government. In addition to the letters that he wrote to the First Lord and Balfour, his notebook overflows with notes for speeches, decrying one failure after another in naval administration. We are forced to conclude that up to early 1902 Beresford and Fisher enjoyed a positive and productive working relationship.

In early November Rear Admiral Burges Watson was appointed to succeed Beresford in the Mediterranean, bringing to an end the speculation as to his future. There was to be no naval posting so his return to politics seemed certain. On 1 February there was a farewell dinner for Beresford in Malta, attended by all the captains in the fleet. After a leisurely return to England the formal seal on Beresford's sea service came when he was received by the King on 26 February. Now he was free to speak out.

Chapter 16
Hammering on the Parliamentary anvil
1902-03

While in the Mediterranean Beresford had made arrangements to make a major speech to the London Chamber of Commerce on his return to England. Fisher saw this as an opportunity to press home some of his demands for improvements to the Mediterranean Fleet and, in a letter dated 27 February 1902, he urged Beresford 'to call for a fleet so strong that [it] *would cause three powers to pause before they attacked England*'. Then there was the building programme: 'Can anyone say that 2 battleships and 2 armoured cruisers is a sufficient building programme?' It was no use waiting until a war occurred to start building: the ships had to be 'ordered 4 or 5 years before … war was declared'. Fisher next turned to the Admiralty's failure to prepare for war:

> 'What we want is an additional naval member of the Board of Admiralty absolutely disassociated from all administrative and executive work and solely concerned in the "*preparation of the fleet for war*" Battenberg has invented a magnificent name for this – "the war lord"'

In writing to Beresford Fisher had recommended that he ask *The Times'* journalist James Thursfield to 'revise your speech'. On the same day he wrote to Thursfield sending him a copy of his letter to Beresford. He asked Thursfield not to reveal this and begged him to keep Beresford's 'head straight'.

And so the day arrived when Beresford was to re-launch his political career. On 14 March, after a fulsome welcome from the chairman of the London Chamber of Commerce, he rose to 'prolonged cheers' and spoke on 'the lack of efficiency in the administration of both services'. For once he was reasonably satisfied with the strength of the fleet, which was 'strong enough for the money they paid for it'. Although the country was 'outside the margin of extreme danger' it 'had not yet arrived inside the margin of that security which they ought to have'. He even went so far as to say that if he were First Lord, he would 'accept the 31 millions as all they could reasonably ask from the people'. Beresford concluded with a surprising announcement: he did not want to go into Parliament: 'Parliament was moribund.' One month later the *Manchester Guardian* would delight in throwing these words back at him.

However, Beresford's speech was to be remembered for three indiscretions. First he claimed that, when in the Mediterranean Fleet, he had written 'a most respectful letter' about the deficient coal stocks in the Mediterranean and that 'I intimated, that if the coal supply was not put right, I would respectfully ask leave to haul down my flag, and I would publish my letter to the Commander-in-Chief in every paper in England.' In one sentence he had admitted to both blackmailing his superior officer *and* planning to release confidential information to the press. Next, in commenting on some recent manoeuvres, he said that Vice Admiral Gerald Noel of the Home Fleet 'had no idea how to handle' his fleet and had 'made every possible mistake for a man to make'. Then, having upset one admiral by vilifying him, he upset another – Fisher – by praising him. Fisher was, he said 'the best man … we have got in the British Navy, or have had for many years'. The Admiralty should 'make him the War Lord'. Since Fisher was desperate to be made Second Naval Lord, this suggestion was most unwelcome.

And so, there it was. The long-awaited speech was, by the standards of Beresford's glory-days, a sad thing. There was no detail, no delving into statistics, no evidence to support his assertions. At fifty-six years of age Beresford was losing his edge. His speech was a mixture of well-worn assertions, cheap jibes and generalities. He had ignored the points pressed on him by Fisher and we can safely presume that he never consulted Thursfield.

After the fun came the reckoning. First off the mark was the *Evening Standard*, which criticised Beresford for revealing that he had 'remonstrated with his commander-in-chief' about coal stocks and had threatened to publish his correspondence with the Admiralty. Next, Noel wrote to the Admiralty to protest at the 'personal attack made on me in my official capacity by Rear Admiral Lord Charles Beresford in his speech'. He added 'I cannot allow that this officer – my junior – is at all in a position to judge on the question of Naval Tactics, as he has but small experience in the matter.' He accused Beresford of having attacked him 'to further his own ends'. Worse still, Noel was a serving officer so could make no public reply.

The controversy that Beresford had stirred up led the London Chamber of Commerce to write to *The Times* to distance itself from some of his pronouncements. Sir Albert Rollit, MP for Islington South, wrote on the Chamber's behalf to say that they were not able to accept all Beresford's proposals. Beresford did score one success though when the committee passed a resolution in support of his call for an officer 'for the particular duty of preparation for war'. This officer was to 'sign annually a statement that all requirements for war could be attained'.

Hammering on the Parliamentary anvil 1902-03

* * *

Seven weeks after Beresford had told the London Chamber of Commerce that Parliament was 'moribund' the sitting MP for Woolwich (Colonel Hughes) resigned. Within hours the local party had offered the nomination to Beresford. His election address followed so swiftly as to suggest that he already knew of Hughes' intention. He would, Beresford said, support Lord Salisbury's Government, oppose Home Rule for Ireland, support old-age pensions and promote the introduction of compulsory military training in schools.

Attempts were made by the United Irish League, the Liberal Party and the Labour Party to select a candidate to oppose him but the sixty delegates could not agree on what to do. By default Beresford was elected unopposed on 25 April. His triumph was diminished by an Admiralty letter of the same day reprimanding him for his having divulged information about coal stocks in the Mediterranean. This, he was told, had been 'imparted to you in virtue of your position as Second in Command H.M. Naval Forces in the Mediterranean'. Their Lordships reminded him that he was not 'at liberty to communicate information acquired in an official capacity'. Beresford declined to accept the reprimand and insolently replied that 'it is possible for anyone to get the tonnage of coal at Malta'. (This clearly was not true since in July Beresford asked in the Commons what those coal stocks were.)

* * *

Beresford's first public act as an MP was to make a confession. It appeared in a letter to *The Times* of 29 April. He declared that *he* had been the person responsible for the letter which had appeared in the *Daily Mail* on 21 June 1901 (see previous chapter). It had been 'a very grave mistake' for which he took all the blame. With the ink on the reprimand letter of 25 April barely dry, a second one followed on 1 May. This time the language was more severe. He was informed of Their Lordships' 'grave displeasure' at his breach of Article 682 of the King's Regulations'. They were surprised that 'an officer in whom such confidence had been shown as to appoint him to an important position in one of H.M.'s principal Fleets should have set an example so subversive to discipline'.

The next day *The Times*, which for nearly a year had vilified Arnold White as the guilty party, published an unreserved apology. In doing so the paper admonished Beresford for his cowardly use of White to protect him from public opprobrium. The end of the *Daily Mail* letter saga took place in the Commons on 5 May when Beresford had to apologise for having allowed the House to be misled. He admitted that he wrote the letter but, since 'The constituted authorities never wrote to me to ask me if I had written that letter' he had not felt it necessary to own up. Disingenuously he added 'When I came home the other day ... I immediately took steps to show that I alone was responsible for the letter.' He could have corrected the accusation against White at any time in the last ten months but chose not to do so because he feared an Admiralty reprimand. Only when he had safely returned to Parliament and had the cover of Parliamentary privilege did he confess.

LORD CHARLES BERESFORD AND THE MEDITERRANEAN SQUADRON.

TO THE EDITOR OF THE TIMES.

Sir,—In *The Times* of the 25th reference is made in a leading article to a letter over my signature which appeared in the public Press last summer. The publication of that letter was a very grave mistake, but all blame (which I own is thoroughly deserved) for that mistake should be laid on my shoulders as the person solely responsible.

I am, Sir, &c.,
CHARLES BERESFORD.
Park Gate-house, Ham-common, April 28.

Beresford's confession

***

Never willing to miss an opportunity to enlarge the services, Beresford proposed in June that 'physical and military instruction' should be taught in schools. The Secretary to the Local Government Board told the Commons that 'physical instruction given in a public elementary school is left to the discretion of the managers' and that it was 'obvious that military training would be unsuitable in schools for little boys, girls, and infants'. Beresford refused to accept this rebuff and for the rest of the year he pursued this topic with vigour. He wrote to the Duke of Devonshire, who was responsible for an *Education Bill* in the House of Lords. Through his secretary the Duke replied that Beresford needed to approach the President of the Board of Education, Lord Londonderry, with a request to include such training in the Education Code (the National Curriculum of those days). Beresford claimed that when he approached Londonderry he was informed that 'marching and rifle shooting could only be dealt with by the war office'. Leaving aside the military aspect of his proposal, Beresford had made a very good case. He referred to the fact that 'during the late South African war a large number of recruits could not pass the reduced military standard' and that 'nine-tenths of the people get no physical training whatever'. These arguments failed; only a much more deadly war finally persuaded governments that the nation was in a poor state of health.

"CHARLEY."

A character sketch of Beresford speaking in the Commons

Beresford next went into action during the debate on the estimates for 1902-03 on 20 June. The particular vote under discussion was the expenses of the Admiralty Office. To show his disapproval of the Admiralty as a whole, Beresford had tabled a motion to reduce these expenses by a nominal £100. He had done this he said 'in order to call attention to the state of the administration of the Admiralty, or rather the want of system, to which he attributed all their lack of preparation, as well as a great deal of the extravagance and the mismanagement'. His speech was splattered with vacuous generalities such as 'want of organisation' and 'the system was rotten', and he laid claim to just about every improvement in the service in recent years. There was coal in the Mediterranean (not enough until he made shortages public); the fleet was inefficient and 'an absolute waste of money'; the level of reserves in men was 'a crying danger to the State'. And so it went on until the patience of the chairman was exhausted. Calling Beresford to order he observed that 'The noble Lord seems to be travelling over the whole field of the Navy Estimates. I fail to see how he can make that relevant to this Vote.' Beresford, he said, had to show 'some inherent deficiency in the Board of Admiralty which is responsible for the circumstances to which he refers'. After a protest by Beresford, the chairman allowed him to continue, which he did. All these deficiencies, he declared, 'were the results of there being no one directly responsible for the efficiency of the Navy'.

H O Arnold-Forster, MP, Financial Secretary to the Admiralty 1900-1903

After listening to Beresford's diatribes against the Admiralty, the Financial Secretary to the Admiralty, Arnold-Forster, challenged members to 'deny that the impression he gave was an extremely vague one'. All Beresford was asking for was 'an efficient Navy; but the Navy is efficient now'. Turning to the detail of Beresford's claims, Arnold-Forster demonstrated to the House that an increase in the Malta coal stocks had been authorised before Beresford had even arrived in the

Mediterranean. As to the additional battleships recently sent out, these had been laid down three years before Beresford had asked for them to be sent to the Mediterranean. He could also have added, had they not been confidential, quotes from Fisher's letters to the Admiralty on the deficiencies of his fleet. The plain fact was that there was no evidence that Beresford's agitations in the Mediterranean had achieved anything.

What the Commons made of this is hard to tell. There is a clue, though, in a letter of 16 July written by Arnold White to Captain Percy Scott on HMS *Terrible*. Scott seems to have contemplated enlisting Beresford's help over the reform of gunnery training. White doubted that Beresford would be of much use since 'on the occasion of his last speech in the House of Commons there were exactly eleven Members present including the Treasury Bench. No Cabinet Minister thought it worthwhile to stay to hear him.'

* * *

In August 1902 George King-Hall found Beresford 'in low state of mind' after being told that the Admiralty would not employ him again. In consequence he went off to America in the following month. It is hard to know what to make of this. King-Hall is a dependable informant, so it is safe to assume that he accurately recorded what Beresford had told him. Perhaps Beresford had asked for employment and received an evasive or vague reply. Whatever the case, in early October rumours began to circulate that the Woolwich seat would soon be vacant because Beresford was shortly to take up the command of the Channel Fleet. His secretary, though, declared that this was 'pure and simple conjecture'. The denial was undermined by Beresford being promoted to vice admiral the next day, although this does not appear to have been made public until 17 October when it was announced in *The Times*.

* * *

On 10 June Fisher, now returned from the Mediterranean, became Second Naval Lord – one step away from the highest post in the Navy. He had been chosen by Lord Selborne as the only man capable of devising a root-and-branch reform of the Navy's education system.

Fisher's education reforms appeared in December and are known as the *Selborne Scheme*. His scheme addressed the discontent amongst engineer officers with their low status and poor chances of promotion. To overcome these problems Fisher proposed a single system of entry and training for all naval officers – executive, engineers and marines.

They were to enter the service aged 12 or 13 and train together 'until they shall have passed for the rank of Sub-Lieutenant between the ages of 19 and 20.' Few of Fisher's reforms were more ferociously condemned than this attack on the class system in the Navy. The idea that executive officers should train and share a mess with men commonly called 'greasers' was anathema. Yet one officer came out with a forceful defence of the scheme: Beresford.

Beresford's support was not entirely unexpected since in June he had tabled a Parliamentary question which referred to the engineers as not being 'satisfied with their status'. He asked what the Admiralty was doing about the matter and was told that it 'is engaging the attention of the Admiralty very closely'. At that time he gave no sign of his own views, but after the scheme's announcement he gave an interview to the *Western Morning News* in which he described it as 'a brilliant and statesmanlike effort'. At last 'the Board have recognized that the present status of naval engineer officers could not continue, in fairness either to themselves or to the Service'. He welcomed the fact that the engineer would receive 'that recognition to which the importance of his duties and responsibilities justly entitles him'. Beresford even welcomed the part that referred to the marines; their new status would be 'received with the greatest satisfaction'. He concluded that 'the plan is one that has been thoroughly matured and well thought out'.

* * *

Nothing more had been heard about the Channel appointment since October. In January 1903 a fresh rumour declared that Beresford was to be appointed to the command of the Mediterranean Fleet. Once more his secretary issued a denial. Then in February Beresford himself announced his appointment to the Channel Fleet two days before it was officially made public. He did this at a meeting of the Executive Committee of the Woolwich Conservative and Unionist party. Two hundred supporters heard him announce his resignation after only 10 months and 2 days as their MP (the resignation took effect on 26 February).

According to the *Manchester Guardian* the Admiralty had told Beresford that if he did not take the appointment he would be forcibly retired. Such a move would have been a disaster since his sights were still set on being First Naval Lord. He absolutely had to remain on the active list, even if to do so meant abandoning his agitations. This explanation goes a long way to explain the lack of enthusiasm that Beresford showed in his three appointments as commander-in-chief.

Chapter 17
The Channel Fleet 1903-05

On 17 April 1903 Beresford took up command of the Channel Squadron. (Confusingly its name was changed to Channel Fleet three weeks later and to the Atlantic Fleet at the end of 1904. I shall refer to it as the Channel Fleet throughout this chapter.)

Accompanied by his staff, Beresford raised his flag on HMS *Hero* before boarding the *Majestic*, on which the outgoing commander, Vice Admiral Sir A K Wilson, VC was preparing his handover. On deck Beresford stood side by side with Wilson as the crew marched past, each man's name being called as he saluted his new commander. Wilson departed the next day. He had expressly forbidden any ceremony; neither the fleet nor Portsmouth was to permit any ship to acknowledge his going. In civilian clothes he slipped ashore and disappeared into the crowds – the antithesis of his replacement's ostentatious leave-takings.

Portsmouth naval yard in 1903

Before leaving to join the rest of the fleet Beresford held a reception for his senior officers and a host of shore-based naval and garrison personnel. Then on 27 April he set sail for Berehaven to join his fleet of six battleships, two armoured cruisers and three smaller cruisers. The *Majestic* was a large ship of 14,900 tons. She carried four 12-inch and twelve 6-inch guns and had a crew of 772 men. Her top speed was 17.5

knots. On-board was his flag staff, which included Captain Hugh Evan-Thomas as flag captain, Michael Culme-Seymour as flag-commander and Charles Roper as flag-lieutenant. *Majestic's* commander was Henry Pelly, while Beresford's rear admiral was the Hon A G Curzon-Howe, who was later replaced by the Hon Hedworth Lambton (later called Meux).

Admirals came and admirals went as the mighty fleets of the British Empire ploughed the seas. Most appointments went unnoticed beyond their appearance in the *Gazette* and *The Times*. Beresford's appointment was another case. Just two weeks after he had boarded *Majestic* his new portrait by Charles Furse RA was unveiled at the Royal Academy. *The Times* commented that 'Lord Charles Beresford is so well known to all the world that everybody can judge whether his portrait is a true one ... As a picture, too, it is excellent; the uniform, the rail, the rigging, give a sufficient suggestion of the ship ... the painting is full of vigour.'

Beresford's fame now preceded him when his fleet made the customary summer tour of British ports. As his ships lay at anchor in port after port, an eager press and public would jostle for a sight of the famous admiral. Captain Henry Oliver, who had served on the *Majestic* under Wilson, recalled that Beresford was so besieged by visits from journalists and MPs that 'it was difficult to get access to him about Service matters, and anything arranged was forgotten as soon as you left him'. This was the new Beresford. The Beresford who almost felt it was beneath his dignity to command a fleet, preferring to converse with journalists and correspond with agitators, rather than pay attention to his command.

Beresford's showy parades also caused problems for Pelly as he cleared up the mess left by the crowds that poured onto the decks of the fleet. Visitors would arrive in tugs and boats to spend long hours on-board. By the time they prepared to leave, the local boats had long since stopped work, leaving Pelly to arrange alternative transport. These chores, though, did not stop him from describing Beresford as 'a marvellous man ... to serve under ... ever thoughtful for all his juniors'.

The full extent of Beresford's inflated view of his command is revealed in a story that Commander Richmond (later Admiral Sir Herbert Richmond) overheard. 'A lady asked him "Tell me, Lord Charles, who in war would be what I may call the 'Generalissimo of the British Fleet'". Charlie replied, without any hesitation "Oh, I should" "But, says she, would Lord Selborne appoint [you] to this position over the senior men" "Perhaps yes, perhaps no; but the Nation would call for me".'

The foredeck of HMS Majestic showing two of her four 12-inch guns

Despite the pomp and glory, Beresford's health was beginning to trouble him. Oliver recounted the lengths to which his chief went to disguise his condition. On one occasion he had planned a tactical exercise of vice admiral versus rear admiral. Sick with gout, he remained in his cabin while Oliver took command. To cover this deceit Beresford appeared on the bridge as the *Majestic* sailed into Berehaven at the end of the day. Only later did Curzon-Howe discover the trickery; he was furious and felt he had been 'scurvily treated'.

* * *

The first of Beresford's big visits was to Belfast in May 1903. Things started badly when the fleet was leaving Lamlash on the Isle of Arran. The flag staff knew that Beresford could not be trusted to remember details, so they arranged that Oliver would explain the course to him; later, Evan-Thomas would go over it again. To cover themselves they also left a copy with the flag-lieutenant on the bridge. The fleet was hardly at sea before Beresford gave a wrong signal, which caused the rear admiral to enquire what course they were following. Beresford exploded as the fleet sailed on at 90 degrees to the planned course. He had not only forgotten all that he had been told, but he had also lost the piece of paper. And so it was that when the fleet sailed into

Belfast Lough, the Mayor and Corporation had been standing on the quay for half an hour awaiting the delayed ships.

From Belfast the fleet sailed on to Dublin. On its first full day in the city, Beresford and his officers lunched with the Duke (Victoria's third son) and Duchess of Connaught and later met the Lord Lieutenant. On the following day the Lord Mayor set national animosities aside and gave a dance for Beresford and his party – the first time this had been done for a naval visit since 1879. The *Observer* newspaper noted that the entertainment of more than 100 naval officers 'had caused no stir', which it put down to Beresford being 'one of the most popular of Irishmen'.

* * *

Beresford next turned his attention to the combined exercises of the Home Fleet (under Wilson) and the Mediterranean Fleet (under Admiral Compton Domvile). Wilson commanded Fleet B1 at Berehaven and Beresford commanded Fleet B2 at Madeira. Domvile's fleet, at Lagos (off the Portuguese coast), represented the enemy as Fleet X. Wilson and Beresford had to attempt to join forces in order to fend off an attack by Domvile. The *Manchester Guardian* described the exercises as 'unprecedented in magnitude' both in terms of the number of ships and the area of ocean involved. In his memoirs Beresford eulogised the '72 battleships and cruisers, with nearly 40,000 men, all under the command of one admiral'. It had been 'probably the strongest Fleet ever brought together in the history of the world'.

* * *

While the manoeuvres were proceeding Lord Salisbury died on 22 August. As soon as he could find time, Beresford sent his condolences to Balfour, who had been Prime Minister since 11 July 1902: 'I have always regarded you with such genuine affection and respect that you will know how honestly I sympathise with you, in the great loss you have sustained in the death of your Uncle.' Once more he tried to entice Balfour to join him at sea, but the wily Prime Minister knew how to keep his distance.

* * *

With the manoeuvres over, Beresford's fleet returned to home waters and more visits. His ships made their way through thunderous seas to Scarborough, arriving on 11 September. So rough was the weather that the Mayor and his party were unable to board *Majestic* and had to satisfy themselves by welcoming the fleet from the deck of a local paddle-steamer. Beresford announced that four of his ships were to be open to the public since 'The officers recognized that the taxpayers had every right to see the ships they had to pay for.' Later in the day 355 of his men enjoyed a dinner at the Grand Hotel Restaurant as guests of the town, followed by a trip to the circus. There was also a dinner for warrant officers, free access for the men to local entertainments and trips round the bay to view the six battleships. On Sunday the fleet's bands entertained the local people in the town.

The visits to the ships went less well. By Sunday the heavy sea had virtually cut off the fleet from the shore. The men waiting to go on shore were told to remain on-board; others were stranded in the town. Some townspeople were compelled to spend the night on the *Majestic.* Beresford expressed his 'bitter disappointment' at his men being prevented from 'coming to the splendid entertainment' that the town had provided for Sunday evening.

* * *

In the autumn, when Beresford's fleet was steaming off the coast of Spain he came very near to losing a warship. A midshipman on the *Prince George* later described how he was reading in his hammock at 10.00 pm when he was flung to the deck by a violent shock. He and the rest of the crew rushed to their stations. Standing by his boat he felt the ship list to port and then settle by the stern. Then came the order 'Away all boats'. It seemed that the ship was about to sink.

Within minutes boats from other ships had arrived. For an hour water poured into *Prince George* faster than it could be pumped out. Bulkheads gave way under the pressure and the steering engine room flooded. The men frantically stuffed the gaping hole until finally the flow was checked. Beresford then ordered the fire engines and hoses from other ships to help with the pumping. Soon it was clear that the ship would survive and Beresford took personal command as she limped into port.

The collision of the *Prince George* and the *Hannibal* had occurred when the fleet was manoeuvring with lights out. Daylight showed that the damage to *Prince George* had been massive, with a hole 24 ft. 8 in. by 6 ft. 6 in. in her side, which had been driven inwards 1 ft. 8 in. The captain of *Prince George* appeared before a court-martial but was 'honourably acquitted' after two days. Beresford got off less lightly. He was reprimanded 'for the near-loss of a battleship by holding night manoeuvres with lights out'. In Beresford's defence the *Manchester Guardian* said 'it will be an evil day if naval officers are debarred from this necessary practice'. His fault, the paper declared, was not proceeding without lights but entrusting such a manoeuvre to the two captains involved who had '[not] been long enough in the fleet to get accustomed to their Admiral'. It was a story that exemplified the two sides of Beresford's character: that the ships collided was due to his risk-prone behaviour; that the *Prince George* was saved was due to his masterly handling of emergencies.

* * *

Despite the collision Beresford received a Knight Commandership in the King's birthday honours list in November. However, the new year of 1904 opened disastrously for him when he suffered serious injury after being thrown from his horse while hunting. The date of the accident is not known, but it would appear that he was too badly injured to return to London immediately after the accident. All we know about the injuries is that Lady Charles told the press that 'he sustained concussion to the brain and also injured his back, so that for some days he lost the use of his legs'. He was still too ill to leave the house on 22 January and so missed the memorial service for his beloved Admiral Keppel. Nor could he attend the inaugural dinner of the Ireland Club (which he had helped to found) on 25 January. He then missed the hoisting of his flag in his new flagship, HMS *Caesar* on 2 February, finally reappearing in public on 6 February for an audience with the King. He may even have struggled to keep that appointment since he did not leave Claridges Hotel, where he stayed during his illness, until 9 February.

This was possibly the worst accident that Beresford had sustained. More importantly, it is arguable that it had permanent consequences. We have already noted that Beresford's speeches had deteriorated in recent years but from 1904 onwards there seems to have been an acceleration in his mental decline. The conjecture that his concussion did some lasting damage does not seem far-fetched.

One of Beresford's first tasks once he had recovered was to welcome the German Kaiser on his visit to Gibraltar in March. He laid on a suitable display to greet his adored Emperor: as the imperial ship approached *Caesar* her passage was lined by the fleet's boats. Beresford recalled that 'Every boat burned a blue light, all oars were tossed, blades fore and aft, in perfect silence, the midshipmen conveying their orders by signs.' At dinner Beresford continued the drama. When he pronounced the toast 'Emperor of Germany' a rocket from *Caesar* was followed by a salute from all the guns of the fleet. And, as the Emperor left, the Union flag fluttered on the Rock while the fleet's searchlights played over it. This pomp and glory were, though, somewhat dampened when yet two more reprimands arrived from the Admiralty. On this occasion some remarks that Beresford had made on prize-firing and gun turret sights had been deemed 'neither called for nor necessary and not borne out by the facts'. This rebuke was followed ten days later by another concerning remarks Beresford had made alleging that the Admiralty had been slow in fitting 'improved turret sights' to guns. Their Lordships regretted that he had permitted himself 'to comment on their action with so little consideration or knowledge of the facts of the case'.

One of HMS Caesar's 12-inch guns

Brighter times should have followed with a visit to Majorca in April to exchange civilities with King Alfonso of Spain, but the event was marred by muddles. On the first day, when Beresford and his officers landed to attend a reception given by the King, he found there was no seat for him within the royal suite. He returned to the *Caesar* 'evidently much annoyed', noted *The Times,* and had to content himself with an apology from the Prime Minister. On the following day Beresford sat on the King's right-hand side at a banquet on the Spanish royal yacht in honour of the British fleet. Two days later his non-appearance in a procession led to rumours of diplomatic frictions. In fact Beresford's barge had become stuck in some mud so leaving him unable to land. He apologised to the local governor 'who perfectly appreciated the situation'. Any perturbation in relations was smoothed over by a dinner given by Beresford for the Spanish authorities on 28 April. Beresford later received the thanks of Edward VII, who found his speech 'judicious and appropriate'.

* * *

During his Channel command Beresford was surprisingly positive about Admiralty policy. He described Selborne as 'a genius' who was the only First Lord he had known 'who appears to me to have grasped thoroughly what the work is'. Of Selborne's reforms he said they were 'most satisfactory' but he seemed unaware that the reforms were all Fisher's work. So confused was he that he told Balfour 'you can always get on with a gentleman [Selborne]' but not with 'the half caste [Fisher]'. Fisher had become First Sea Lord on 20 October 1904 and had been feeding Selborne policy papers for since mid-1902. (In accepting the appointment he had revived the old term 'Sea Lord' to replace that of 'Naval Lord', which had been in use since 1828.). So this particular letter is of great importance given what was to come. It is clear evidence that, at the start of Fisher's reign as First Sea Lord, Beresford approved of his reforms. His later venomous opposition was based on personal factors, not on principle.

* * *

Beresford's next reprimand was not long in coming. Its origins lay in the North Sea. On the night of 21-22 October a group of Hull trawlers was fishing at Dogger Bank in the North Sea when, out of the darkness, came several Russian warships. After raking the trawlers with their searchlights, the warships sped on – they were heading for the Far East to do battle with the Japanese fleet. About half-an-hour later a second group of Russian ships appeared. This time they opened fire on the defenceless trawlers. When the warships departed shortly afterwards they left behind one trawler sunk, two men dead, six wounded and five damaged boats. It was an international incident of the first order. Fisher, ill in bed with flu at the Charing Cross Hotel, recalled ships and men from far flung seas in anticipation of a full-scale attack from Russia. But when he heard that the Cabinet was contemplating war Fisher leapt from his sick bed, donned his admiral's uniform and dashed to Downing

Street, where the Cabinet was in session. He browbeat the Cabinet into staying its hand.

Hull trawlers under attack from the Russians 21-22 October 1904

Meanwhile Beresford happened to be near Gibraltar – right in the path of the southbound Russian fleet. His ships were cleared for action and the men slept by their guns. But as the fleet lay silent and alert in the dark, Beresford nearly triggered an incident of a different kind. He had sent off a group of destroyers for exercises and had then forgotten about them; as the destroyers returned in the dark they narrowly missed being fired on by their own fleet.

The Dogger Bank incident blew over at the beginning of November, but not for Beresford. A few weeks later, in a letter to the Admiralty, he declared that 'being quite satisfied with the excellence of the gunnery of the Channel Fleet' he would only have used four battleships to stop the advancing Russians. This, he said 'would only be chivalrous under the circumstances'. There was outrage in the Admiralty. The Director of Naval Intelligence declared that 'If this statement became public property, the taxpayers would probably enquire why they were paying for the other half [of the Fleet].' It was not long before yet another reprimand was on its way to Beresford. He was told that 'sentiment' had no place in war and, had he encountered the Russians, 'their Lordships would expect you to make use of the whole of the force at your disposal.'

***

Beresford was coming near to the end of his command when the Dogger Bank incident took place so he may have feared for his future.

All was well, though. On 19 November his appointment as commander-in-chief of the Mediterranean Fleet was announced, with the acting rank of admiral. But then a snag arose.

Fisher had not forgiven Beresford for his chivalrous attitude towards the Russians so he decided to terminate Beresford's Channel command a month early to show the Board's disapproval. With a month of Beresford's time at his disposal, Fisher asked him to take the presidency of a signal committee. Beresford stormed into the Admiralty and told Fisher that 'he did not intend to be superseded, nor would be go on a Committee'. Fisher replied 'Well, then, you will not go to the Mediterranean.' Beresford continued, said King-Hall:

> 'You dare to threaten me, Jacky Fisher. Who are you? I only
> take orders from the Board. If I have to haul my flag down on
> 7th February, I will resign the Service, go down to Birmingham,
> get into the House and turn out both you and Selborne.'

Beresford himself confirmed having made this threat in a letter ten months later to Carlyon Bellairs in which he concluded 'It made him pipe down. He will never threaten me again.' Fisher had his way over Beresford's early departure, but Beresford never served on the committee.

This meeting marked the watershed in the Beresford-Fisher relationship. Whatever tiffs and disagreements there might have been prior to February 1905, there is not a shred of evidence of any bad relations between the two men. But from early 1905 Beresford had become Fisher's sworn enemy.

* * *

On 17 May Beresford arrived in Queenstown to go on to Liverpool. His mother died in London two days later and her memorial service took place on 23 May. The death of her husband had left Lady Waterford deranged. Unable to recall visits from her sons she had berated them for neglecting her. Lord Marcus threatened to cut notches in her table each time he came to prove that he had visited her. It is not surprising, then, that neither Lord Marcus nor Beresford attended the funeral, although their wives did. When he came to write his memoirs, Beresford made only one trivial reference to his mother.

Although Beresford was adored by his men, even his admirers, such as Pelly, found his command of the Channel Fleet slack. As we have seen, there were lost signals, muddles over prestigious visits, and an atmosphere in which pomp took precedence over practice. Pelly was disparaging about Beresford's exercises, which seemed to contribute little to preparation for war. There were 'all sorts of competitions and drills'; attacking and defending Portland Bill; and endless 'away all boats' orders. In the latter case Beresford would even order the boats out in rough weather, often resulting in their being unable to find their ships again.

Carlyon Bellairs MP, a co-conspirator with Beresford in his attacks on Fisher

If we add to this picture Beresford's squabbles with the Admiralty, his laid-back attitude to attacking the Russians, and his recklessness with *Prince George* and *Hannibal*, there is a sense of a man with his mind only half on the job. His forgetting the destroyers off Lagos could have resulted in a disastrous incident. Time and again Beresford was rescued by his staff from his carelessness and inattention. In his memoirs he found almost nothing to say about his high commands. While he wrote forty pages on the few days of the bombardment of Alexandria and 123 pages on the Sudan, he could manage only twelve for the Channel Fleet.

Despite this apparent lack of interest in fleet command Beresford accepted the Mediterranean appointment. His motivation was no doubt prestige, as his friend Captain Sir William Pakenham, then naval attaché in Japan, told a correspondent: 'He will be glad to get to the Med^t. It has always been considered the highest honour in our Navy to command there.' Also he would be 'a full admiral too. That means nearly £400 a year more.' And so, on 27 May, he went to the Palace for the customary royal blessing before returning to sea.

YEARS OF ANTAGONISM 1905-1910

Chapter 18
The Mediterranean command 1905-07

Beresford's new command ran from 1 May 1905. As was often the case with him, there was no yearning to join his fleet. It was not until 3 June that he took a train from Victoria station to travel to Genoa. At the station, Lady Charles with one daughter, four admirals (including Fisher) and various other dignitaries provided a grand send-off. Finally on 6 June Beresford raised his flag in HMS *Bulwark*.

HMS Bulwark, Beresford's Mediterranean flagship 1905-1907

On the very day that Beresford arrived in the Mediterranean, a letter of his appeared in *The Standard* in which he advocated joint manoeuvres between the American and British fleets. In the United States the letter was favourably received, with President Roosevelt indicating his approval. At home the reception was more problematic, particularly since the letter's publication breached regulations, The letter was an early indication of his growing disdain for his masters.

Beresford took command of the Mediterranean Fleet in a mood of smouldering revolt against Fisher and the Board. Officers were now either friend or foe, the latter being those in Fisher's favour. The Beresford camp included Rear Admiral Hedworth Lambton (later Meux) in command of the Cruiser Division. Another Beresford ally was his Chief of Staff, Captain Doveton Sturdee. Others such as Rear Admiral Bridgeman (Beresford's second-in-command) and Captain Reginald Bacon on *Dreadnought* were neutral at this stage. In due course both would suffer the full force of Beresford's odium. Others, like Beresford's flag captain, Osmond Brock, seemed to have avoided the fray.

The Mediterranean command was the plum sea posting. When Fisher held it he took the opportunity to test the fleet and his methods almost to destruction. Beresford was too old, too tired and too grand for that. His command was to be in the majestic style.

Beresford's first fleet visit was to Algiers on 20 June. There was the usual round of dinners given and dinners received, mixed with fetes and illuminations. The local Lloyd's agent, who had lived in Algiers for 23 years, could not recall a fleet that had received a 'more cordial, spontaneous, and enthusiastic' welcome in the port. The conduct of the thousands of men had been 'exemplary' with 'not a single case of drunkenness or disorder'. This, said the Algerians, was in marked contrast to 'the conduct of liberty men from other foreign fleets'. 'No doubt', he added, 'the agreeable personality of Lord Charles Beresford contributed very largely to the good impression left upon the population'. It was Beresford at his best and heralded well for his two year posting.

In July Beresford was the chief mourner at the Gibraltar funeral of six men killed by a burst steam-pipe on HMS *Implacable*. He led 1200 sailors through the town of Gibraltar with its closed shops and businesses. From there he took his fleet for combined exercises off Lagos, where he was joined by the Atlantic and Mediterranean fleets. There was a gentle start with two days of light-hearted sailing competitions in a fresh wind. Seven boats capsized on one afternoon, while the galley of *King Edward VII* sailed to victory. Beresford, on *Bulwark*, hosted an evening of entertainment for the officers of both fleets. On the Sunday there was a visit from the King of Portugal and a salute of 21 guns. As to the more serious purpose of preparing for war, there were steam tactics in which ships moved in unison; towing practice; night torpedo exercises in which, despite the clear sky, the torpedo boats failed to find their targets. These small-scale tasks were followed by battle exercises between squadrons with Beresford as umpire.

* * *

We have seen that Fisher's recall of Beresford one month early from his Channel command, combined with his determination to put Beresford on a committee, had driven Beresford to declare open war on his superior. These two events clearly date the beginning of Beresford's vendetta against Fisher to around February 1905. But if those clashes were the tinder, the spark came from Fisher's promotion to Admiral of the Fleet in December. The significance of this promotion lay in retirement ages. As an admiral, Fisher would have retired in January 1906; as admiral of the fleet he would be in post until January 1911. By then Beresford would be 64 years old – too old to be offered the post of First Sea Lord. In one stroke his greatest ambition had been thwarted. Now his only hope of commanding the Navy was to oust Fisher. Captain Thomas Crease, one of Fisher's assistants, attributed much of what happened next to 'Lady Charles' disappointment and spite over not becoming the wife of a First Sea Lord, so cutting a big figure in London society'.

Just a week after Fisher's promotion Beresford vented his anger in a letter to Bellairs. Admiralty policy was now 'one of T H R E A T' and 'a great number of good men have been put on the beach'. Fisher, he said, ran a system of favouritism with appointments going to 'the few who agree with any decision or proposal made by authority'. Those who disagreed 'are sent to bad Stations, personally threatened with annihilation, or refused appointments altogether'. As to Fisher's capacities, 'the Service knows, he never was a Seaman, could not handle a Fleet' and was 'also known not to have any original ideas in his head'. He continued, 'Nearly all the reforms he has ... instituted he had in my handwriting, with the exception of the Education Scheme.' The situation was so bad that Beresford was contemplating giving up his command in order to 'let my Countrymen know the facts of the case. There is no question that I would have the whole Service at my back.' This particular letter is the most important document we have on the origin of the vendetta. Beresford had been writing to Bellairs since at least 1892. He trusted him totally and held nothing back – yet no letter before 12 December 1905 is at all critical of Fisher. That this letter followed only days after Fisher's promotion decisively shows that Beresford's antagonism towards Fisher lay in jealousy and in nothing else.

* * *

It was in 1906 that Beresford began to develop an irrational and distasteful hatred for Prince Louis of Battenberg. Battenberg had been born into a German family in 1854 but moved to Britain as a young boy. He was naturalised as a British citizen and entered the Royal Navy as a cadet in 1868. Contemporary accounts show him as a consummate officer of unswerving loyalty to his King and country. By 1900 he was

Assistant Director of Naval Intelligence with the rank of captain. He became Director of Naval Intelligence in 1902 and was promoted rear admiral in 1904. Battenberg first raised his flag in 1905 in command of the Second Cruiser Squadron. Known to be a strong supporter of Fisher, he was now to become the target of Beresford's vicious rumour-mongering. Beresford's aim was nothing less than to destroy Battenberg's career.

Prince Louis of Battenberg

Beresford's chosen weapon was the parliamentary question; his henchman was Bellairs. In a letter to Bellairs, Beresford explained that '[Battenberg] may be a Naturalised Englishman now, but he is a German, was born in Germany, all his property is in Germany, and he always uses German servants.' It was 'absolutely wrong' that he should go there [the Admiralty]' since it would then 'appear that there is no British Officer of his own Rank who is good enough to take up the position'. Beresford then provided Bellairs with three draft parliamentary questions. The first asked whether the government was 'aware that there is a very strong opinion throughout the Navy as to the desirability of placing a German Prince in the position of Second Sea Lord'. The second asked 'whether the said German Prince is, or is not, a Naturalised British Subject'. With the third question Beresford lost all restraint, asking 'Whether it is a fact that during the time this German

Prince was Director of Naval Intelligence, he employed German servants, who had charge of Dispatch Boxes, and took them from the Admiralty to the Prince's house, and from the Admiralty to the Prince's estate in Germany?' Bellairs never asked these questions. For once, someone was able to restrain the increasingly unhinged admiral.

The curious reference to Battenberg becoming Second Sea Lord (a post he did not hold until 1911) is explained by a letter that Captain Rosslyn Wemyss of HMS *Suffolk* wrote to his wife later that year. The rumour went that Battenberg had been offered the post but 'refused the billet because he thought the feeling in the Navy would be against it'.

At the same time that Beresford was attacking Battenberg, he began to plot the downfall of Fisher. He had been feeding lines of attack to Bellairs for some time. Now he sought other supporters. One of his chosen tools was Lady Jessica Sykes. Conveniently, Sykes was also the sister-in-law of Captain William Pakenham, then a naval attaché in Japan. Beresford briefed Sykes on how Pakenham could assist in his intrigues. In February he asked her to use 'any means of ventilating the views of the Navy on the questions I have brought to notice' that she could.

* * *

In early 1906 Captain Reginald Bacon had taken command of Fisher's new battleship, *Dreadnought*. Knowing that he was going to the Mediterranean, Fisher asked Bacon to write home to tell him how the fleet was receiving his reforms. This Bacon did in six or seven letters, of which four have survived. In his memoirs Bacon said he thought his reports would help 'Sir John see any weak points in the Admiralty proposals which were being discovered by the brains of those at sea'.

His first surviving letter was written on 31 March. He described how, after three months in the Mediterranean, 'I am more than ever impressed with the soundness and absolute necessity for the proposed changes [Fisher's reforms]'. He made specific comments on how much better the midshipmen were now that 'they know that whether they pass or not depends on their working at sea – not merely attending school'. He also praised the engineers' reforms and forecast that the 'the present agitation will die out'.

In his next letter Bacon reported on a conversation that he had had with the Prince of Wales, who was concerned about opposition to Fisher's reforms. In his letter of 15 April Bacon listed the main gripes of the officers in the Mediterranean, including 'not being consulted more by the Admiralty' and a 'want of information'. He also remarked that 'The King and the Prince of Wales ... [were] very much disturbed at the Service agitation headed by Lord Charles Beresford and Admiral Lambton.' His final letter of 24 April dealt once more with fleet reactions to the Selborne scheme.

Reginald Bacon, as admiral in 1915

No one in Beresford's fleet knew of these letters until one of them surfaced in 1909. Had Beresford been aware of their existence they would have further fuelled his determination to drive out Fisher – and Bacon, too.

* * *

While Bacon was writing home about the mood of the fleet, Beresford made a visit to Greece in April where, once more, his lack of attention to detail had unpleasant consequences. King George of Greece had informed Beresford of his intention to visit *Bulwark*. On boarding the ship he was astonished to see that Beresford had not troubled to don full-dress uniform. Aggrieved, the Greek King complained to Edward VII, who instructed his private secretary, Sir Charles Hardinge, to inform the Admiralty of 'Beresford's insulting and slovenly conduct'.

* * *

In early June the Admiralty announced plans for combined manoeuvres. In large part these were to test how well a powerful maritime nation (Britain) could defend its commerce against a weaker power (Germany). This was to be simulated by an enemy force (Blue) putting to sea under Admiral May. Later a British force (Red) under Beresford and Wilson would put to sea from various ports, so simulating a dispersed British fleet searching for enemy raiders. Beresford and Wilson had to find each other and combine forces in order to overcome the enemy. *The Times* comfortingly observed that 'no sooner was that point reached than the whole of the Blue Fleet was overwhelmed, dispersed, and put to flight'. The paper drew further comfort from the fact that Beresford had won even though the Blue Fleet was much larger than could be realistically expected in war. While acknowledging that such exercises 'are not and can never be the real thing', the paper's conclusions were gratifying for both Beresford and the Admiralty. Beresford's own comment on the manoeuvres came in a letter to Fisher's youngest daughter, Pamela: 'Just finished the manoeuvres when all comrades have been fighting like devils for conciliation and murdering each other for the love of God.'

* * *

At the end of 1905 Balfour had resigned as Prime Minister, to be replaced by the Liberal Party leader, Sir Henry Campbell-Bannerman. This brought a new First Lord: Lord Tweedmouth. His arrival had little impact on Beresford until the subject of Beresford's next appointment came up in July 1906, when Tweedmouth offered him the post of Commander-in-Chief of the Channel Fleet. The correspondence has not survived but we have Beresford's summary in a letter that he wrote to Tweedmouth in the following year. According to this summary Beresford accepted the command on the condition that he was given 'a properly fitted despatch vessel'. (This may seem trivial, but Beresford seems to have used this vessel in order to spend as little time as possible with his fleet.) He accepted the command on 7 August, expecting to take charge of 66 vessels, including sixteen battleships, six armoured and three unarmoured cruisers.

Whatever were the reservations on each side, the appointment seemed settled on 7 August. Then Beresford learnt on 2 September that his future fleet was to lose two battleships. He protested to the Admiralty that 'the policy [was] unsound, more particularly with regard to the training of officers and men for war'. At this stage there was no suggestion that he might rescind his decision to take up the post.

* * *

Meanwhile, fleet life continued with late summer visits to Venice and Fiume in August. At Venice Beresford used his despatch yacht to provide a lunch and serenade for the city's officials. Then his flagship led the fleet out to sea, each ship playing the Italian national anthem as it left its anchorage. At Fiume (then part of Austria-Hungary) the fleet was welcomed by the local governor, Count Nako. The festivities included a banquet for 800 people at which the Count toasted the friendship of King Edward VII and the Emperor of Austria-Hungary. Beresford replied by toasting the Emperor who eight years later would unleash the war that Beresford so eagerly anticipated.

* * *

When the French submarine *Lutin* sank without trace after leaving harbour at Bizerta on the morning of 16 October Beresford sprang to assist. He immediately despatched a battleship, a cruiser and a destroyer to the scene. He also offered tugs, but the French admiral telegraphed to say he had sufficient. The presence of the British ships proved vital since they carried underwater lamps, which neither the French nor the Danish salvage vessels possessed. The rescue party located the submarine and put a cable round her at a depth of 150 metres. Despite the prompt assistance of Beresford's fleet and the Danish vessel, none of the crew was saved. The submarine was raised, though, and repaired, only to sink again in 1907. On the second occasion there were no fatalities – and no need for Beresford's help.

* * *

One major part of Fisher's reforms was his redistribution of the fleets. For the whole of the previous century Britain had maintained independent fleets scattered around the globe. This had two consequences. First, it was costly; second, no attempt was made to concentrate forces where war was most likely. Fisher was under pressure from Parliament to cut the estimates *and* to better protect Britain from a possible attack in home waters. This he did by scrapping all those ships that were too small to fight or too slow to run away. This released men and money for better-armed and faster ships in home waters. Despite these changes he still came under press criticism over the total number of battleships in full commission in home waters. Whether as a result of this criticism or not, in October he proposed the creation of 'a new Home Fleet and a Reserve Fleet, both under one Admiral'. The core of this would be seven battleships and four armoured cruisers, which he had brought back from other stations. It was not obvious at the outset how this move would impact on the Channel Fleet. Certainly Beresford expressed no immediate concern.

The new Home Fleet was to be built around the three reserve divisions at the Nore, Devonport and Portsmouth. Fisher argued that these divisions had demonstrated the viability of his nucleus crew system and that they could be put under a single admiral who would take them to sea for regular exercises and training. The Nore division would be fully manned so that the new Home Fleet could respond instantly to a surprise attack. He planned to augment the three existing divisions with seven battleships and four armoured cruisers withdrawn from foreign stations.

A few days later various command changes were announced by the Admiralty. Beresford, as expected, was to go to the Channel Fleet. Vice Admiral Sir Francis Bridgeman would take the new Home Fleet. One other appointment would have caught Beresford's eye: Prince Louis was to be second-in-command of the Mediterranean Fleet. His rumoured elevation to Second Sea Lord had not transpired.

Two weeks later Beresford was promoted to admiral. His career was still prospering, notwithstanding his recent clashes with the Admiralty. This is clear proof that, despite all that has been said about Fisher's supposed animus for Beresford, he did nothing to impede the latter's career. It would be Beresford himself who would use his new command to bring about his own downfall. His capacity to self-destruct needed no help from others.

Shortly before Beresford's promotion he received an Admiralty letter of 23 October announcing the transfer of the torpedo craft of the Channel Fleet to the Home Fleet. The loss of 36 vessels reduced Beresford's next command to 26 vessels. Fisher's own explanation for this was hinted at in his paper on the Home Fleet, published in December. Whereas two years earlier 'France and Russia were our most probable opponents', now 'our only potential foe ... [is] Germany'. In his view, the fleet facing Germany (the Home Fleet) needed a plethora of torpedo craft to defend its battleships from a German attack. Conspiracy theorists are apt to see Fisher's motive as a desire to harm Beresford, but strategic logic was on Fisher's side. Germany *was* the potential enemy and the Navy *was* weak on the south-east coast.

The Mediterranean command 1905-07

* * *

Beresford never seemed to have enough disputes on his plate to satisfy him. In December, with only weeks remaining of his Mediterranean command, he picked a needless quarrel with the Admiralty. It arose over a pamphlet, *The Truth About the Navy*, which had been reprinted by *The Spectator*. The Admiralty had sent copies of this as part of their regular distribution of material to ships' libraries. Only one officer in the Navy took offence: Beresford. In a lengthy (and expensive) telegram to the Admiralty he claimed that 'The pamphlet is also political in character ... I consider it most insidious for authorities to issue under official sanction one set of views under such circumstances and not to issue as well under official sanction the views of contrary opinions.'

In a minute to the Board Fisher explained that it was he who had recommended circulation of the pamphlet as 'an outside point of view'. But it was not the pamphlet that bothered Fisher: it was Beresford's attitude. Beresford, he told the Board, 'has consistently and persistently thwarted Admiralty Policy at every opportunity and hardly ever does he receive an order without some private or public representation on his part of an improper character'. Then he turned to the heart of the issue, rightly commenting 'yet never has an Admiral received such consideration and been permitted such licence'. 'Why?' asked Fisher. Because 'it has been rightly decided in the past that to take the proper steps would have been to make him a martyr'. And there lay the Admiralty's dilemma. In post Beresford endlessly criticised, challenged and flouted the Board. But if he were sacked he would do the same with the added freedom of being a martyr on half-pay.

* * *

On the penultimate day of the year Beresford was astounded to receive yet another letter from the Admiralty outlining further fleet changes. Additional transfers of vessels to the Home Fleet would reduce his Channel command to 21 vessels. Against the Home Fleet's 244 vessels, Beresford would have fourteen battleships, four armoured cruisers and three unarmoured cruisers – a total of 21 vessels. It will be recalled that back in July he had been offered 66 vessels. So far Beresford had accepted the fleet reductions with little comment. Now the Admiralty had gone too far.

Much of the wrangling over Beresford's appointment had been exacerbated by his being in the Mediterranean. (Letters were reaching

153

him up to two weeks after despatch.) In January 1907 Beresford was able to confront the First Lord when he visited the Mediterranean to inspect the new naval works at Malta. There he told Tweedmouth that he could not accept the appointment. Beresford set out his reasoning in a lengthy letter to the First Lord dated 22 January, concluding: 'I could not undertake to accept the command of the Channel Fleet under the total alteration of its component parts and its defined duties.'

Fisher rather doubted that Beresford was seriously interested in the Channel Fleet: 'My conviction is he wants to get into Parliament and hates the Channel' he told the King's Private Secretary, Lord Knollys. Nevertheless, on 28 January Tweedmouth, Fisher and Beresford put their signatures to a minute recording an agreement which set out three *modus operandi* for the Channel and Home fleets. First, Beresford could detach the destroyers from the Home Fleet for 'exercise and manoeuvres' whenever he wished. Second, he could similarly detach the Fifth Cruiser Squadron. And finally, 'in time of war' Beresford was to have overall command. In consequence the two fleets 'will be exercised together at such periods as will be decided by the Admiralty on the representations of the Commander-in-Chief of the Channel Fleet'.

* * *

The time had arrived for Beresford to leave the Mediterranean Fleet. It was an emotional parting – he broke down when replying to a toast at a club dinner in his honour. Whatever his relationship with the Admiralty was, his officers adored him so it is understandable that leaving the cosy world of the Mediterranean Fleet for the more hostile territory of a home command (where the Admiralty was near enough to assert its authority) gave him some qualms.

The send-off was royal as Beresford in *Bulwark* followed by Lady Charles in *Surprise* sailed between the ships of the fleet in two lines. The decks were lined with saluting men and the bands played. Guns fired in salute, with the rear admiral's flagship despatching the final farewell to their beloved commander-in-chief.

As if presaging times to come, *Bulwark* arrived home at Portsmouth after an exceedingly rough passage, during which a stoker was killed. After being greeted by the port officers, the crew mustered on the quarter deck as Beresford, in civilian clothes, took his final leave. A loud 'Three cheers for The Chief' rang out. Then again, and then again. Did Beresford realise, as he walked down the gangplank, that life would now be down-hill to a bitter end?

While Beresford's own account of his two years in the Mediterranean records the bold and successful innovations of a great commander, the reality was more mixed. Something was lacking that made his command lacklustre. Health does not seem to have been the problem. Possibly the Mediterranean climate had helped rid him of his aches and pains. At 60 years of age he told Sykes that 'I am very fit, thin and energetic as ever [and] really feel stronger & fitter than when 30.' Wemyss, surely with some exaggeration, had never seen 'anybody look so well and so young as he does' while Midshipman Oswald Frewen, observing Beresford jumping down into a boat in a choppy sea, thought he did so 'in the most sprightly manner considering his age'. 'Admirals,' he added, 'are not in the habit of doing this.' Nor was it any lack of success in creating a happy atmosphere. Wemyss spoke for many when he told his wife that 'the Admiral is extremely civil' and was no doubt only one of many who could record that '[he] is perpetually asking me to dine + lunch'. 'Everything and anything amuses him, and he gets more pleasure out of life than almost anybody I ever came across.' No one had a bad word to say about the comradely side of Beresford's fleet.

HMS Surprise – Beresford's despatch vessel

Nor was it a matter of technical failures. There were even moments to please the Admiralty. For example, the fleet gunnery was a success, as Beresford told Pakenham in 1905: 'the nine Battleships have averaged 23 hits out of an average of 90 rounds'. He thought this was a record. This achievement was recognized by the Admiralty when Their

Lordships signalled their appreciation of Beresford's 'development of gunnery efficiency of Med^n Fleet'. There is additionally a partially legible note in November 1906 on Beresford's Admiralty record which shows approval of the recent battle results. Beresford also managed to set a new record for coaling by loading *Bulwark* at a rate of 251.1 tons per hour.

That leaves us with two explanations as to what was wrong. First, and most obviously, Beresford conducted his command in an atmosphere of more or less open warfare with the admiralty. His disloyalty to his masters was astonishing. Not only did he freely discuss their failings (as he saw them) with fellow officers but he was also liberal with his opinions when entertaining his guests. Then there was the pointlessness of so many of his attacks. There was his unnecessary letter in *The Standard*; his needless attack on Prince Louis of Battenberg; his lining up friends and colleagues to attack Fisher; his pointless dispute over *The Truth About the Navy*; and, towards the end of his command, he began to circulate stories of the Home Fleet being a fraud. At some time during this command Beresford was also in trouble for addressing the commander-in-chief of the Atlantic Fleet as 'Vice Admiral Commanding' instead of as 'Commander-in-Chief'. Admiral Lord John Hay commented 'Certainly he holds the record ... of contempt and insubordination.'

This leads us to the final and principal cause of the problem: attitude. True, Beresford adored being a famous and popular admiral who could parade himself around the courts and ports of the Mediterranean. But be could neither stomach the detailed work nor accept his inferior position. He was a disgruntled and reluctant subordinate to Fisher. In accepting the Channel command, nothing would change except the depths of his bitterness at not being First Sea Lord.

* * *

Before Beresford could take up his next command, he received a piece of distressing news, although with a silver lining. On Christmas Eve 1906 two trains collided at Enderlin in North Dakota. Ten passengers died at the scene, of whom one was Lord Delaval Beresford, the youngest of Beresford's brothers. He had been on his way from Canada (where he possessed ranches of 76,000 acres) to Mexico (where he had two ranches totalling 120,000 acres). Just how rich Delaval was is not clear. One rumour put his wealth at $2,000,000. Another put the value at $1,000,000. There was no doubt that Beresford was about to inherit a very substantial sum. How much he was likely to get depended in part on the claims of two women. In Mexico a certain Flora Wolf, who called herself Lady Flo, and who had lived with Delaval for many years as his housekeeper, claimed that she was married to him. Then there was also a woman in Ontario in Canada who declared that Delaval had married her many years previously in Ottawa but had disappeared two weeks later.

Beresford took charge of the situation, leaving Southampton on 30 January 1907 to travel to New York. He had one month's leave but, being Beresford, did not return until 10 April. (This is despite the fact that the Boston Evening Transcript reported Beresford as having been granted probate on 26 February.) When he arrived in America he declared that he would be there for about three weeks. In fact his business took more like eight weeks, and he seems to have visited San Francisco and Chicago in the States, as well as Mexico and Canada. True to his capacity for getting into trouble, he refused to deal with Flora Wolff. In consequence a writ was issued in Texas requiring him to appear in court. Rather than face his claimant, he put it around that he was off to Santa Fé and then took a train to San Francisco, so evading the police. He hid in Mexico until he was safely able to make his way to New York. (Despite these tactics, several American newspapers carried reports of his giving $10,000 to Flora Wolff, plus the right to remain in Delaval's house.)

On his return to England Beresford was a very rich man since he and Lord Marcus were the only substantial beneficiaries of the estate. They do not appear to have sold the estates at the time since Beresford told Lord Londonderry in 1909 that he hoped to sell the Mexican ranches. Also, he described in his memoirs their continued management after that date. One ranch failed in 1909 when a drought killed all the livestock. He sold the Ojitos ranch for $190,000 in 1910 according the *Victoria* Advocate. Another ranch was sold in 1912 and the third was still in their hands in 1913.

Chapter 19
The Channel Fleet 1907-08

Four months after leaving the Mediterranean Beresford arrived at Portsmouth to take command of the Channel Fleet.

Beresford's officers, some willingly, some reluctantly, were to be drawn into the coming two years of his violent attacks on the Admiralty. They included: his chief of staff, Captain Frederick Sturdee; his intelligence officer at the Admiralty, Captain Arthur Hulbert; his signal officer, Lieutenant Charles Roper; and his flag captain, Captain Henry Pelly. At the time only Sturdee was known as a potential Beresford ally.

One further officer, though, needs special mention given the role he was to play in Beresford's vendetta against Fisher. Beresford's second-in-command. Vice Admiral Sir Reginald Custance has been described as possessing 'narrow, dogmatic, and inflexible opinions [which] were delivered with an uncommon degree of venom ... He lacked the mental flexibility to benefit from debate.' Added to his intellectual stiffness, 'he lacked ... personal warmth' and was of a 'suspicious nature'. In a damning finale, this observer concludes that 'his arrogant and unbending approach deprived his work of lasting value, and his life of close society'. He was also a bitter opponent of Fisher. As second-in-command, Custance had charge of HMS *Majestic* with Captain Ernle Chatfield (a future First Sea Lord) as his flag-captain. Chatfield later recalled that Custance showed the flagship no mercy. '[He] insisted on manual housing of the anchor, even tho' there was machinery to do it', while Chatfield's endeavours to run the ship were impeded by 'the daily wearing routine Admiral Custance had imposed'.

* * *

The diminished fleet that Beresford took over in mid-April consisted of fourteen battleships, four armoured cruisers, two second-class cruisers and one third-class. Beresford took up command of the fleet in mid-April. His flagship, HMS *King Edward VII*, was a pre-dreadnought battleship of 16,350 tons displacement. With her 18,000 hp engines she could make 18.5 knots, burning coal from her 2000-ton capacity bunkers. Manned by 777 men she carried eight 12-inch guns, as well as smaller calibre armament. She was a magnificent ship and a worthy floating stage for Beresford's pompous style of command.

There was very little significant activity in the fleet at the start of Beresford's command, other than a ball given for Beresford and his officers on 10 May at Weymouth – a town that held him in great affection.

The ship's company on HMS King Edward VII c 1908

If the story of Beresford's Channel command were limited to the activities of the fleet, there would be little to tell. As it was, his two years of command were littered with disputes with the Admiralty, making these years some of the most vivid of his life.

The first major dispute between Beresford and the Board began in late April. Beresford had been bombarding the Admiralty with letters, which led Fisher to accuse him of using his staff to prepare 'ammunition for you to fire off at the Admiralty'. He urged that they 'should avoid friction and undesirable correspondence' and suggested that they meet. Beresford denied that there was any friction between him and the Board. If any friction were to arise, 'I am off'. Then followed twenty-three words against which we have every right to judge what was to come: 'If a Senior and a Junior have a row the Junior is wrong under any conceivable conditions or discipline could not go on.'

One of the main areas of dispute during Beresford's Channel command was war plans. On appointment, a commander-in-chief received a brief war orders document from the Board. This set out the likely role of his fleet in war. In response to this the commander was required to produce his own war plans. Beresford turned this routine task into a *cause célèbre*.

It all began when Beresford intimated to Fisher that he wanted to see Wilson's war plans. In response Fisher asked Beresford not to request these plans since they were out of date. Instead Fisher enclosed a document with 'eight different ideas', which he hoped would be useful.

Beresford's response was immediate. He was 'loath to appear discourteous' but could not see why he should not have access to Wilson's plans which 'must be of infinite utility to me'. In reply Fisher enclosed a paper which, he said, 'embodies all that is useful'. He added that 'I don't want to get into a correspondence and will wait till we meet.' Having failed to get satisfaction from Fisher, Beresford wrote to Tweedmouth, who also declined to supply Wilson's plans.

A short while later, Beresford handed-in what he called his 'sketch plan', which was a first attempt to fulfil the Admiralty's request for war plans. In the Admiralty's reply, Beresford was informed that Wilson had been requested 'to rearrange the War Plans on which he would have acted, so as to make them applicable to present conditions'. Nevertheless, Fisher was not pleased with Beresford's plan which, he said, 'employed more battleships, cruisers, &c., &c., than the British Navy possesses'. What most annoyed Fisher, though, was Beresford's attitude. Wilson, in his six years of the Channel command, had not submitted one single document 'calling into question the wisdom of Admiralty Policy' whereas 'within a month of Lord Charles Beresford assuming the command we have received a mass of insubordinate letters'.

To resolve the war plans dispute the Admiralty issued new war orders to the commanders-in-chief of the home ports and of the Atlantic and Home Fleets. Beresford was reminded that 'The Fleet which will be placed under your command on the outbreak of war will be such as appears to their Lordships most adequate to meet the situation'. This was a firm reminder that he was to stop telling the Admiralty how to distribute its ships. He was promised a monthly order of battle 'with the ships likely to come under your orders' and was asked to submit his 'detailed plans … under the several contingencies of an outbreak of war'.

In fact nothing came from Beresford other than disputatious letters. There was no option now but to call him in. But first we need to backtrack and catch up with Beresford's fleet command from April to June.

* * *

Shortly after the Weymouth visit Beresford was once more reprimanded by the Admiralty for a further incorrect use of modes of address. He had asked the commanders-in-chief at Chatham and Devonport to address him as 'Admiral in Command of the Fleet'. The commanders got into trouble too since they had agreed to this arrangement when they should have known better.

In May Beresford announced that his fleet would shortly begin its summer cruise around the British coast, taking in Yarmouth, the Humber, Queensferry, Aberdeen, Inverness, Invergordon, Cromarty, the Isle of Man, Aberystwyth, Liverpool and Lamlash. The tour began at Grimsby and Cleethorpes at the end of June, where the fleet received the usual enthusiastic welcome when nearly 40,000 people visited its ships. On shore, the streets of Grimsby were decorated in honour of the fleet and free passes were handed out to the 4000 men. There was the usual lunch and reception, which Beresford flatteringly described as 'the most gigantic he ever remembered'. For the men there were sports and other entertainments throughout the visit. There were similar events at Yarmouth on the same day when Custance arrived with the Second Division. One thousand bluejackets were entertained in the town, while Custance held a reception on his flagship. In the evening the fleet's searchlights gave a display to the town. Beresford meanwhile took three destroyers to Hull, where he lunched with the Wardens and Brethren of Trinity House (the lighthouse authority) and had tea with the mayor.

Channel Fleet visit to Grimsby 1907

On 3 July the Channel Fleet arrived unannounced in the Firth of Forth. Perhaps Beresford had forgotten to advise the Lord Provost of his visit because his mind was on other things: he had received a peremptory order to appear in the First Lord's office on 5 July. Leaving his fleet, the troublesome admiral departed for London.

* * *

Tweedmouth's decision to call Beresford to account was a turning point. True, no firm action followed, but it was the first time that the Admiralty had attempted to rein in their most vociferous critic. This is then a good moment to take a look at Beresford's style of command at what was (theoretically at least) the peak of his career.

Lord Tweedmouth, First Lord of the Admiralty 1905-1908

By 1907 Beresford was a public figure of the first order. His self-importance knew no bounds; his speech and manners became more pompous by the day; his popularity with the public had no equal in the fleet. Not that fleet life interested Beresford any longer. Sub-lieutenant Lionel Dawson on *King Edward VII* recalled that Beresford was hardly ever to be seen around the fleet. When he appeared it was invariably on the quarter-deck, where he came up the hatchway, looked around and remarked: 'Carry on, please, Mr Officer of the Watch.' He addressed the men in a sonorous voice as if they were at a public meeting or on the Commons benches, while his language reflected the past. He would say 'catchers' rather than 'destroyers' and use out-of-date terms such as 'lee-line' and 'weather-line'.

Beresford lived well and entertained in style. He had his own Irish stewards, including those for his personal barge. Wherever he went one or more bulldogs would accompany him, while a seaman trailed behind with dustpan and brush. In his quarters he had his own bathroom with a large tin bath in which he bathed every morning. His cabin was 'cosy rather than luxurious' according to a journalist's account and was littered with personal belongings and photographs of royal and public figures.

Nothing got in the way of Beresford's pleasures. On deck there was his large motor car, which had to be landed by derrick at every port of call. Naturally he had his own driver. His passion for fishing remained undiminished although he had adapted his style to suit his station. A typical trip needed three men to clear a path and help with locating a suitable stretch of bank. Behind them would be minions with lunch-baskets and endless equipment.

Yet beyond the pomp and the pleasure, there was not much else. However much Beresford had desired the Channel appointment, it had come too late. No longer did he have ambitions at sea. He saw himself as the only man who could save the nation from its effete defence policies. His dreams were of politics and power in high places. The post had come too late in another sense as well: the state of his brain. When Frederick Ponsonby, King Edward's Assistant Private Secretary, quizzed Beresford on how safe Britain was from invasion he enjoyed 'a breezy talk' but, he told Fisher, it was 'very difficult to pin him down to any serious criticism of existing methods'. As soon as Ponsonby tried to pursue one point Beresford gave 'an outburst of oratory on another'.

Allied to the state of Beresford's brain there was the question of his general health. In the cold damp Channel he was again suffering from gout and phlebitis, often being confined to his cabin or ashore. While his absences are hard to establish precisely and mentions of his health are infrequent, it is nevertheless clear that he was far from a full-time commander. He had taken up his command on 15 April and he seems to have left the fleet for three months from mid-November onwards. (We will examine those three months in more detail shortly.) Even between those dates he was not always present. Basically, Beresford was too old, too sick and too bored to fulfil the terms of his command.

There was also the question of what role Beresford thought he was playing. He was supposed to be a full-time commander-in-chief, yet he was totally dependent on his staff on almost all matters. He claimed that war could come in an instant, while he ran his fleet in a very relaxed manner, including giving his men three-night long weekend leaves once a month. He also continued leaking secret information to politicians and journalists. Just the day before the momentous 5 July meeting he sent Bellairs a list of battleships absent from his fleet on various dates. Such information should have been treated as most secret, but Beresford spread it like confetti.

So, on 5 July Beresford found himself in Tweedmouth's office to answer to the First Lord and the First Sea Lord. On entering Tweedmouth's office Beresford noted a fourth person: departing from custom, a stenographer was present to ensure that Beresford could not dispute what he said and agreed to. As a result we have a verbatim record of the meeting.

Tweedmouth opened by drawing attention to Beresford's recent letters. The Admiralty had asked for war plans; all they had received were acerbic letters. The First Lord took particular exception to a Beresford letter of 27 June, at the heart of which was his refusal to produce war plans 'unless I know what ships are available to carry these plans out, and where such ships are to be found'. Later in the letter he had written 'I have not the remotest idea as to the number of Torpedo Craft and Submarines in Home Waters'. (Against this remark Fisher had scribbled 'Is this really seriously stated!') Tweedmouth then pointed out that on 14 June, when he gave Beresford his new war orders, he had said that they were 'agreeable' to him. How, he asked, could Beresford accept war orders one day and thoroughly reject them thirteen days later?

Having established the origins of his concern, Tweedmouth presented Beresford with four questions: (1) what vessels did he consider he needed? (2) what further information did he need on the order of battle? (3) 'Why do you not try to cultivate good and cordial relations with the Admiralty?' and (4) would he explain why he called the Home Fleet 'a fraud and a danger to the Empire'? As a precaution against Beresford's leaky memory, Tweedmouth handed him the list of questions before the discussion began.

On the first question, after various digressions, Beresford declared 'If you will let me work this one out, I will send you an answer.' When it came to the second question, Beresford had clearly not studied the documents that he had already received from the Admiralty and was unable to specify his needs. The third question on cordial relations gave him the opportunity to patronise his superiors: 'You will allow me to smile for at least ten minutes over Question No. 3. There is no question of cordial relations. I do not care about having rows with anybody. I never did.'

When it came to the last question, Beresford put up a vigorous if disingenuous defence. He did not deny that he had called the Home Fleet a fraud, but his remark was of no consequence since his letter to Tweedmouth had been 'a private letter'. When Tweedmouth pointed out that the letter had not been marked private, Beresford retorted 'We have all written much stronger things than that on important questions of that sort.'

Towards the end of the meeting Fisher and Tweedmouth tried to rescue something from the farcical discussion. They offered to make Beresford's cruisers up to six (the same number that Wilson had had) and to give him two divisions of destroyers, with their attendant vessels. To this offer Beresford replied 'I cannot see that thing straight off. I will write to you.' Fisher retorted 'You must have thought about it. You have been writing about it for months.' Beresford, perhaps realising that his displays of ineptitude put him in a poor light, added 'it is a fair offer'.

* * *

Following the meeting Beresford had to make amends for having neglected to inform the Lord Provost of Edinburgh that his fleet was to visit the Firth of Forth. He wrote a grovelling apology in which he claimed that he thought that such visits were not notified in advance. He chose to forget that on his visit in 1903 he had given the usual notice.

The First Lord's formal offer of additional ships was despatched by the Admiralty secretary on the same day as the meeting. Beresford was asked whether he wished to 'allow the present arrangements to continue' or to accept the ships as offered. The following day Fisher wrote a private letter to Beresford in which he emphasised his desire for cordial relations. Both of them, he said, needed to guard against 'liars trying to make mischief' by spreading rumours about the two of them.

Later Beresford wrote an official letter to the Admiralty in which he set out his considered response to the four questions posed by Tweedmouth. Without a word of apology or a hint of shame he declared that his relationship with the Admiralty could not be more cordial; also his charge against the Home Fleet was justified by an Admiralty memorandum of December 1906. Within a mere eleven days of being called to account, Beresford had shrugged off every charge against him. To emphasise his lack of contrition he now requested two more battleships and three more unarmoured cruisers.

The Admiralty's response came at the end of the month in a letter in which the Board confirmed the offer made at the 5 July meeting. Beresford was given his additional cruisers, twenty-four torpedo boats and their auxiliary vessels. At the same time he was reminded that the Board could not enter into discussions with officers over the 'disposition of the fighting fleet', which was a matter 'solely for the decision of the Board of Admiralty'.

* * *

The fleet visits continued when Custance took the Second Division to Aberystwyth at the beginning of August, while Beresford took the First Division to the Isle of Man. Next, the Fleet was at Liverpool where, for a fee of 1s, the citizens could take a steamer from the Prince's Landing Stage to visit the warships out in the Mersey. As the three-mile long fleet steamed up the river, *The Times* reported that sightseers trained telescopes on the bridge of the flagship. As their hero came into view there were cries of 'There's Charlie Beresford.'

In what the *Manchester Guardian* described as 'a breezy speech to journalists' Beresford referred to the Navy as 'a rate of insurance for the commerce of the Empire'. He went on 'I sympathise with the people of the Peace Society. They want us to reduce our armaments. If we reduce our armaments it is absolutely certain we shall have to go to war.' These off-the-cuff remarks were roundly criticised by the *Manchester Guardian*, which declared that 'he perhaps failed to realise ... that the fleet is not the only possible form of insurance'. The paper went on to refer to the work of a peace conference at the Hague and called Beresford 'thoughtless' for not seeing the role this could play in preventing war. Meanwhile *The Daily Express* had published Beresford's offending words, which came to the attention of the Admiralty. In a Board telegram he was ordered to 'take immediate steps' to contradict 'the facts of the interview'. Beresford appealed to the *Daily Express* journalist Ralph Blumenfeld to help quash the story, even going so far as to tell him that the interview had never taken place.

There was then an indifferent fleet visit to Blackpool on 9 August. The beach traders cursed as the arrival of the fleet led to a mass desertion of their pitches. Nor did the weather help. On the Saturday the crowds were unable to board Beresford's ships in the choppy sea. Later, as the mayor and his guests sat down to the onshore lunch given in Beresford's honour, he and his flag staff remained marooned on the flagship.

The Channel Fleet 1907-08

* * *

In September Beresford and Frederick Ponsonby were both guests at Wynyard, one of the homes of the Lord and Lady Londonderry, both of whom were stalwart Tories. Beresford grabbed the opportunity to bombard Ponsonby with his complaints. He criticised the recent gunnery scores, which he said had been conducted under 'unfair conditions'; the Home Fleet was 'a fraud and a deception'; and Fisher's nucleus crew system (an economical method of manning ships in reserve) was 'unworkable'. What Ponsonby most noticed, though, was not so much Beresford's technical criticisms, but that 'his conversation was impregnated with a hatred of Fisher'. Little did Beresford understand the adverse impression he had left on Ponsonby. When thanking Lady Londonderry for her hospitality ('I never enjoyed myself more') he mistakenly noted his 'good fortune' in meeting Ponsonby. As the King's Assistant Private Secretary, Ponsonby would ensure that the Sovereign was informed about Beresford's increasingly deranged behaviour.

* * *

As the autumn approached Beresford's interest in the war plans dispute was distracted by the arrival of Rear Admiral Sir Percy Scott to take charge of the First Cruiser Squadron in the Channel Fleet. This comprised the *Good Hope, Argyll, Hampshire, Duke of Edinburgh, Black Prince,* and *Roxburgh.* In just over a year, Scott was to prove to be Beresford's nemesis, although at some cost to Scott too.

Scott was a difficult and pushy man of great ability, with a distinguished record as an innovator in naval technology. Above all, he was known throughout the Navy for his exceptional gunnery skills, with his ships achieving hit-rates of 80 per cent or more. When he first joined the Channel Fleet Beresford tried to lure him into his anti-Fisher camp. Scott's refusal sealed his fate. Only his ejection from the fleet would satisfy Beresford.

In mid-October Beresford took charge of the combined forces of the Channel Fleet, the Atlantic fleet, The Nore Division of the Home Fleet and the Fifth Cruiser Squadron for exercises. These began by blocking the passage of the Channel at Dover, night torpedo attacks and raids on the East Coast. Beresford's first chance to humiliate his unwanted subordinate came at Cromarty. He had ordered Scott to watch the entrance to Cromarty Firth and prevent the enemy from leaving. Scott was not told whether enemy vessels were in the bay but he had been instructed not to move until he was certain that the bay was empty. Not having received any further signals, Scott remained on station with his cruisers strung across the mouth of the bay. After the exercise Scott was mortified to find that he had been severely criticised in a fleet memorandum for having 'remained in a dangerous position'. Beresford accused him of having failed to move despite a signal from the *Sapphire* to the effect that the enemy had left Cromarty. Scott always maintained that he never received the *Sapphire* signal and that Beresford had never asked him to explain his actions. He had been condemned without any right of reply. Furious and aggrieved, he sat down to write a letter of complaint to the Admiralty, but events overtook its completion

Rear Admiral Sir Percy Scott

The manoeuvres over, the Channel Fleet sailed south for Portland. Because the weather was foggy, Beresford left the ships to make their own way. By the time the *Good Hope* had moored, the *Roxburgh* was already outside the Portland breakwater carrying out rifle practice. She asked Scott's permission to remain there. In reply Scott signalled 'Paint work appears to be more in demand than Gunnery so you had better come in in time to look pretty by the 8th instant.' This was a reference to the fact that the Channel Fleet was shortly to take part in a visit of Kaiser Wilhelm to Britain. Beresford had issued a memorandum requiring ships to be spruced up for the visit, which specified that 'The ships are to be in all respects ready for sailing and painted externally by the 8th November.' In other words, there was no requirement to paint on any particular day.

Beresford knew nothing of Scott's signal and would never have done so but for Sub Lieutenant Dawson, who happened to visit the *Good Hope* on 7 November. In the mess he overheard an officer say 'That was a very typical signal of Percy's.' On enquiry he was told the full story, which he related to the Flag Lieutenant and the Signal Officer on his return to the flagship. Beresford immediately sent for the *Good Hope's* signal log.

Scott was commanded to present himself 'in frock coat and sword' on the flagship on the following day, 8 November. As he reached the quarter-deck he found himself facing Beresford with his rear admirals and flag staff. What happened next is best told by the *New York Times* as it reported the story four days later:

> 'The staffs were ordered to fall back out of earshot. The three Admirals alone walked slowly aft to the ensign staff and stood there. Before them stood Sir Percy Scott at attention. A dead hush fell upon the spectators.

> 'Lord Charles Beresford produced a paper. His voice could just faintly be heard above the lap of the waves against the ship's side reading a general signal to the fleet in which he described Sir Percy's reply to his signal to paint ship in preparation for the arrival of the German Emperor as "contemptuous in tone and insubordinate in character."'

Having said his piece, Beresford dismissed Scott who was, said Dawson, 'a changed Sir Percy'. Stunned, he crossed the quarterdeck 'silent and white-faced ... his gait was slow and dragging'. As in the Cromarty incident Beresford gave Scott no chance to explain his behaviour. He was judged and sentenced in public and without redress.

Beresford wrote that same day to the Admiralty to demand Scott's removal from his fleet 'after such a public insult to my authority'. At the same time, Beresford copied Scott's offending signal to the whole fleet while ordering the *Good Hope* and the *Roxburgh* to expunge it from their signal books. While the Admiralty found Scott's signal 'inexcusable' they declined to punish him further. Beresford now banned Scott from all dinners and social functions, other than those where Scott had to be present as part of his duties.

The German Emperor had been due to appear in the Channel on 11 November, where he was to be greeted by twelve battleships, nine cruisers, two scouts and 22 destroyers all commanded by Beresford. But when dawn broke that day dense fog obscured the German yacht and Beresford's newly painted fleet was unable to escort the royal party into harbour. At least, though, Beresford could bask in the glory of attending the royal banquet given in honour of the Emperor. Scott was not invited (he was too junior) but his presence when the Emperor paid his formal visit to Portsmouth on the following day must have irked Beresford.

* * *

The enormity of the paintwork incident obscured another occasion when Beresford publicly criticised his fellow officers without giving them a chance to comment. On this occasion his remarks concerned the actions of officers in the Home Fleet and appeared in a fleet memorandum. It has not survived, but Bridgeman's account makes it clear that the document both criticised his officers and attacked the Admiralty's shipbuilding policy.

Bridgeman complained to the Admiralty about two of Beresford's remarks. First, his statement that the destroyers under Commodore Bayly (later Admiral Sir Lewis Bayly) had not been properly trained and second, his charge that the unarmoured cruisers were fundamentally unsound. These remarks reflected 'on the competence of the Commander-in-Chief of the Home Fleet' and 'on the policy of past and present Boards of Admiralty'. Beresford was ordered to re-issue the memorandum with the offending paragraphs removed.

* * *

On 11 November Beresford had been at Spithead for the German Emperor's visit. The next time that he was with the fleet was on 17 February 1908 – an absence of 3 months and 4 days. This can only be described as curious behaviour for a man who insisted that war could come at an hour's notice and whose official leave was 30 days beginning on 12 December. Why he was absent for such a long time is not clear. During that period he attended a state banquet, received the freedom of the Salters' Company, visited the Whitehead torpedo works, attended firing experiments at Kentish Knock, observed HMS *Hero* firing experiments, attended a Savage Club dinner, attended boxing and wrestling championships at Weymouth and spent Christmas with the Londonderrys. Then he fell ill and took up residence at Claridges Hotel. He recovered enough to leave London on 13 January, after which he went to Brighton to recuperate. How ill Beresford really was is unclear. Viscount Esher, a courtier whose ear was ever close to the ground, told

Fisher that Beresford was 'shamming illness in order to draw Ministers to his bed side'. There is no evidence that any minister obliged.

Whether Beresford ever intended to return is not known, but in the end he was forced back by an ironic circumstance. Custance, who was in command in Beresford's absence, came ashore when his flagship went into dock for repairs. This left Scott as the only admiral with the fleet and, by default, acting commander-in-chief of the Channel Fleet. Beresford's return was instant.

* * *

While away from his fleet Beresford brooded on the Admiralty's disposition of his officers. He convinced himself that he was being persecuted by the removal of key members of his staff. In a lengthy letter to the Admiralty he declared that 'it has come to my notice that a feeling has arisen in the Service that it is prejudicial to an officer's career to be personally connected with me on Service matters'. Beresford gained this impression through the confluence of three events. First, Sturdee was to leave the fleet and have his own command in order to qualify for flag rank. Then there was Custance who was being moved to another command; and finally, Rear Admiral Montgomerie, who was in command of the destroyers, and who was coming to the end of his one year appointment. 'The removal of three such important officers from my command' would, said Beresford, 'add enormously to my already exceptionally hard work.' These changes had 'the appearance of a wish to handicap and hamper me in carrying out the responsibilities'.

In their reply the Admiralty described Beresford's allegations as of 'a very serious character' and they asked for evidence to support them. Beresford was reminded that Sturdee had chosen to take a command and was to be captain of the *New Zealand*. As to Custance, there was no truth that he was about to be moved. That left Montgomerie. The Admiralty pointed out that when Montgomerie had been transferred to Beresford, he (Beresford) had been told that it was a one year appointment. It seems likely that Montgomerie gave up his post because of ill health since he died in the following year. This was not the last that was to be heard of the alleged victimisation of Beresford's officers. In 1909 he added more names to the list and was still complaining about it years later. He never, though, produced an iota of evidence to show that any officer's career suffered from working with him.

All in all Beresford's first year with the Channel Fleet had been a dismal experience. He was sixty-two years old as his second year commenced and not one step nearer his ambition to be First Sea Lord. Retirement at sixty-five loomed. It was time to step up the pace and finally force Fisher out.

Doveton Sturdee as vice admiral

Chapter 20
The Channel Fleet 1908-09

As Beresford's second year with the Channel Fleet began, gloom overcame him. He was, he told White, 'sick of the attacks on me' and forecast that he would soon be found 'enjoying myself on the ranch in Mexico'. The public would forget about him. Three days later Bellairs received a rant about Fisher – 'the author of a naval evil'. Referring to Fisher's 'favouritism, espionage, [and] spoiling officers' careers who will not bend the knee' he declared that 'Things cannot go on much longer as they are'. Not content with letting off steam to his friends, Beresford also fed regular diatribes to leading members of the opposition. To Balfour he complained that 'the Navy has been ruled by Fleet Street for the last 3 years' and had put out 'false impressions' of the fleet. These stories needed to be 'deflated' and the truth about the 'terribly neglected' fleet made public.

In addition to his rumbling discontent about naval matters in general, Beresford was still furious with the Admiralty for their lack of public support over the paintwork incident. In February 1908 he had received permission to distribute the Admiralty's letter of 13 November of the previous year, which had called Scott's signal 'inexcusable'. When circulating the letter, he told his officers that 'It is their Lordships' desire that the Officers of the Channel Fleet should know that the Commander-in-Chief had the full support of the Admiralty in his severe condemnation of the signal referred to.' This was a gross exaggeration given the exasperation felt by the Board at Beresford's precipitate action.

When the promised parliamentary statement of support came it simply told the House that the Board had already expressed their 'grave disapprobation' of Scott's signal. It had taken Beresford four months to extract this 'support' for his action, but it was the best he was to get. In any case, a much more significant event was about to overtake him.

* * *

The Prime Minister, Henry Campbell-Bannerman, near to death, resigned on 4 April and was replaced by Herbert Henry Asquith, who immediately sacked the First Lord. In place of Tweedmouth he brought in Reginald McKenna from the Board of Education. Asquith had chosen McKenna because he thought him more likely to curtail the Admiralty's insatiable capacity for spending money. In this Asquith was to be disappointed, but McKenna did achieve something that Tweedmouth could never do: the dismissal of Beresford.

Prime Minister Herbert Henry Asquith MP in the Commons

What Beresford thought of the change we do not know. He was perhaps indifferent since he submitted a request for additional ships during the week that the government was being reconstructed. A more astute admiral would surely have waited to know who was to be the new First Lord before submitting such a controversial claim. He requested that 'a mining vessel and a division of submarines may be attached to the Channel Fleet' so that he could carry out mining and submarine exercises. The Board declined the request five days later, saying that 'at present the training of these branches ... [is] sufficiently provided for by the periodical combined exercises'. Slade noted in his diary that '[Beresford] will not sit down under the rebuff'.

It was not long before McKenna was made aware of the simmering Beresford problem. In an early briefing for his new master Fisher told McKenna that 'It is unprecedented the lengths to which Lord Charles Beresford has been permitted (I think wrongly) to flout the Admiralty.' He did not, though, recommend immediate action but rather 'to wait now till the autumn, when probably matters will arrange themselves'.

Reginald McKenna MP, First Lord of the Admiralty 1908-1911

The year, though, was to be dominated by public scandals rather than private recriminations. Beresford's precipitous descent began five days later on 1 May when he and Fisher were both guests at the prestigious annual Royal Academy dinner. Beresford cast caution aside when, in front of the Prince of Wales, the Prime Minister, senior government officials and leading members of society, he sought to avoid shaking Fisher's hand. Fisher refused to accept the rebuff and chased his subordinate round the dining room until he was compelled to surrender.

Beresford, now beyond reason, followed this effrontery with a similar incident at the royal levée ten days later. Fisher was talking to Winston Churchill (President of the Board of Trade) and Lloyd George (Chancellor of the Exchequer), when Beresford passed the group. He bowed, shook hands with the two politicians, but when Fisher offered his hand, Beresford turned his back and walked off. But no action was taken, causing the King to curse his government as 'a pack of cowards'.

It may have been these two incidents that prompted Fisher to plan the curtailment of Beresford's command. The Home and Channel Fleets

The Channel Fleet 1908-09

were to become one fleet, he decided. Given Beresford's past 'marked antagonism' to the Admiralty, he could not see how the Board could expect to receive 'cordial co-operation' in this change. So Fisher set about choosing a date when Beresford should go. There was no question of dropping him before the manoeuvres finished on 25 June. Also, it would be awkward to make the change over before Custance had been promoted in July. In the end, Fisher and McKenna agreed on 4 March 1909, when Beresford would have served for two years.

Beresford knew nothing of these plans. Instead he was basking in the glory of a visit by the French President to Britain. On 25 May there was a banquet on *King Edward VII,* at which he made a short speech praising the French Navy and 'the gallantry of its officers'. Things did not go so well a few days later when it was the turn of the French Consul to host a banquet at Dover. Once more Beresford spoke, this time about 'the wide community of interests' of the two countries. However the evening was marred by press reports that he had refused to sit next to Scott.

On the same day as the Dover banquet the Cabinet had a brief discussion of the Beresford situation. McKenna suggested that the imminent strategic exercises would be better carried out by 'officers who will be in a position to make use of that experience subsequently'. This led him to suggest that Beresford should be dismissed before 15 June, when his fleet was due to sail to Scandinavia. The Cabinet demurred and asked McKenna to request Beresford to produce more detail of his complaints.

* * *

On 1 June, after nearly a year of failing to submit war plans, Beresford returned to the task. The first document that he wrote that day was an updated version of his sketch plan of 13 May 1907. The new plan went far beyond the role of the Channel Fleet in war, disposing as it did of 286 vessels. It was clear that Beresford assumed that he was to be commander-in-chief of all vessels in home waters in war.

The Admiralty response came ten days later. As to the plan, the Admiralty had no intention of agreeing to anything so detailed in advance of war. However, since they could hardly tell Beresford that he was being increasingly side-lined in their plans for the amalgamation of the Home and Channel Fleets, no attempt was made to give him any feedback on his plan. Of the sketch plan, for which Beresford had been waiting for approval for a year, he was merely told that the Admiralty were glad to receive it, but they wanted to 'study alternative plans of action for the British Fleet in war'.

Beresford's world was steadily falling apart. The next blow was the departure of Custance on being promoted to admiral. He had been Beresford's most loyal supporter and conspirator through all his recent battles with the Admiralty, so his leaving came at a delicate time. His departure, Beresford told Captain de Robeck of HMS *Dominion*, 'is a terrible loss to me personally'. Custance was 'the best Admiral all round in the Service' and 'a great personal friend to me as well as the most loyal Second in Command'. But the loss of Custance would soon seem a trivial matter when compared to the flood of disasters that were now to engulf Beresford.

* * *

With the Cabinet reluctant to dismiss Beresford, his fleet set sail for Norway where, before the manoeuvres began, there was to be a formal visit to the King and Queen of Norway at Christiania (now Oslo). With him went his new second-in-command, Vice Admiral Sir Berkeley Milne. Where Custance had encouraged Beresford's excesses, it is likely that Milne urged caution. But he had arrived too late to forestall the denouement that was to unfold over the next three weeks.

The fleet arrived at Christiania on 19 June. During the following day Beresford's flagship welcomed in turn a Norwegian vice admiral, a senior general and the Ministers of Marine and Foreign Affairs. There were 15-gun salutes for the military men and 17-gun salutes for the politicians. In the evening the royal couple gave a dinner at which Beresford was seated on the Queen's right-hand side. After proposing a toast to the King and Queen, he received the Grand Cross of the Order of St Olav. Much to Beresford's chagrin, Scott was made a Knight Commander at the same time. It was during this dinner that an innocent request triggered the next phase of Beresford's persecution of Scott. Scott recalled that, while sitting at table, someone approached him and asked if he could 'provide some little surprise for the morrow' when the fleet would be inspected by the royals. He recalled that 'the request rather upset my appetite' as he wracked his brain for an idea.

The next day the royal party, in the dispatch vessel *Surprise*, were taken round the fleet. As they approached *Good Hope*, to the astonishment of all, the side of the ship bore the phrase 'LEVE KONGEN' (Long live the King) in gigantic white letters. When the *Surprise* drew closer, the letters turned out to be made of men – twenty for each letter – standing on a wooden frame. There were loud cheers at the sight and the Queen photographed this ingenious tribute. But Beresford was not amused since Scott's device meant that he had disregarded his order that the men were to be in blue ceremonial dress. He was so angry, despite the spontaneous delight of the royals, that he wrote a formal complaint to the Admiralty. Scott, he said, had put him in 'a very false position'. What the Admiralty made of this pathetic complaint is not known.

HMS Good Hope with LEVE KONGEN faintly visible on her beam

The next day Beresford found yet more reason to berate his rear admiral. It was 9.30 in the morning and the *Good Hope* was using a kedge anchor to turn the ship 8-points to starboard. When the manoeuvre had been completed Scott found the anchor to be fast in the mud, so he sent out a cutter to retrieve the anchor but without success. During this operation Scott was ordered to repair instantly to the flagship where, he recalled, 'in a loud and angry voice' Beresford lambasted him for using a cutter to retrieve a kedge anchor. Scott's account continues: 'He then asked me why I was not on deck during the evolution, and on my informing him that I was, he angrily exclaimed that he had two eyes in his head and that he did not see me.'

That evening there was yet a further brush between the two men at another public dinner. Scott was supposed to sit five places away from Beresford but when he arrived he found that the only vacant seat was the one on Beresford's right. The Mayor guided Scott to the seat but Milne noticed Beresford's horrified look and 'he shoved the Minister of War and himself along and so saved the situation'.

After the diplomatic engagements of Christiania, the Channel Fleet sailed to its rendezvous with the Home Fleet for manoeuvres. Even before the manoeuvres had started Beresford had upset the Admiralty over the presence of journalists. It was usual practice for numerous reporters to sail with a fleet on manoeuvres. On this occasion Beresford had requested that they be excluded. The Admiralty agreed, only to find that Beresford was filling up his ships with his friends. Crease told White that this was 'not to report the manoeuvres personally, but to assist in the agitation afterwards!' The Admiralty ordered Beresford to disembark his guests before the manoeuvres commenced.

* * *

It was on 1 July that an incident occurred that was to overwhelm Beresford and lead directly to his dismissal at the end of the year. It all began innocently enough when Beresford's fleet was in two columns and was to turn through 180 degrees. The *Good Hope* log book described what happened:

> '7.4 Ordered by Flag to turn 16 pts towards Argyll who was 6 cables on port side. Considered this dangerous – therefore turned to starboard.'

The flagship queried whether the *Good Hope* had turned to starboard to avoid a collision. *Good Hope* confirmed this was so. And there the incident would have ended had it not been for the press.

It was *The Times* that set things off when it reported, under the title 'A Strange Occurrence in the Channel Fleet', that, 'Had the signal been obeyed the *Good Hope* and *Argyle* would have collided, as did the *Victoria* and *Camperdown*.' This was a factual statement, confirmed by the unruffled exchange of signals on the day. Yet Beresford chose to read the article as declaring that he had given a dangerous signal. And no better example of a dangerous signal could be cited than Tryon's, which sank the *Victoria* in 1893 (see Chapter 10).

Matters were made worse by a letter from the MP Arthur Lee (the man who later gave Chequers to the nation) in *The Times* of 6 July in which he said it was common knowledge that 'the Commander-in-Chief of the Channel Fleet ... is not on speaking terms with the Admiral commanding his cruiser squadron on the one hand, or with the First Sea Lord of the Admiralty on the other'. He called on the Admiralty to put an end to this 'grave scandal'. This was followed by an attack on Beresford in the *Manchester Guardian*, but it was *The Times* that delivered the *coup-de-grâce* on 8 July:

> 'We say frankly that if, as is alleged, Lord Charles Beresford is at loggerheads with the Board of Admiralty, or with any individual member of it, he is, in our judgement, *ipso facto* in the wrong.'

> 'If, as is also alleged, he is not on speaking terms with one of his flag officers, he is equally in the wrong, since it is his duty before all things to do nothing to impair the discipline, good order, and good feeling of the fleet under his command.'

His behaviour was 'a deplorable example of indiscipline and insubordination to the Fleet'. He faced, said the paper, 'the historic alternative *se soumettre ou se démettre'* (submit or resign).

Beresford's behaviour was now everyone's concern. The Cabinet asked for a report on his relations with Scott and the King was more determined than ever that he should go. There were further questions in the Commons on 9 July, focused on the licence that the Admiralty had given to Beresford. 'Were,' asked H C Lea, MP for St Pancras East, 'the rules and regulations of the Navy ... only to apply to the humbler ranks, stokers, for example, while Lord Charles Beresford is to be allowed to break them with impunity?' There was no answer from the government benches.

Beresford now put up Bellairs to asking a parliamentary question as to whether naval officers could sue for libel. McKenna answered that they could if on half-pay or retired. Bellairs next asked whether, in that case, the Admiralty would 'recognise their special obligation to defend an officer whose reputation is assailed by falsehoods circulated in a paper of repute?' McKenna knew of no such case.

McKenna was determined to put an end to the dispute. In the Commons he pronounced that the Board 'are satisfied that the manoeuvre was not dangerous'. That, he hoped, would draw Beresford's fire. Then he called Scott into his office and told him that he was to be withdrawn from the Channel Fleet. He was to take charge of a squadron of first-class cruisers, which would pay a visit to South Africa to coincide with a convention on the federation of the South African colonies. It appeared to be a clear victory for Beresford, but Beresford had only received a short stay of execution.

* * *

In the Admiralty's bad odour and with much of the press against him, Beresford seized upon a royal inspection of the Channel Fleet as a chance to rebuild his relationship with the King. Anticipating this visit, he told Captain John de Robeck that he would take the opportunity to 'address myself to a high personage in the manner you suggest' in the hope that the King would support him in his hour of desperate need. The visit took place on 7 August, the party comprising the King, the Queen, the Prince of Wales, Princess Victoria and Fisher. They were greeted by four scouts and thirty-six destroyers and escorted to Portsmouth where they visited Beresford on *King Edward VII* and Admiral Sir Berkeley Milne on *Hibernia*. After lunch they returned to the royal yacht. As soon as the royal party had gone, Beresford seized his pen and wrote an obsequious letter to the King, saying he would 'never forget the day' since 'Your Majesty's kindness and charm reminded me so clearly of those happy days gone by which can never be erased from my memory.' The King's reply offered little consolation. After expressing his 'great pleasure and satisfaction' at the visit and offering his congratulations on 'such a splendid Fleet', he closed with a warning: 'Trusting nothing will occur to prevent you continuing to hold the high and important position which you now occupy.' Later, in her own letter, the Queen wrote: 'let me repeat what I said before … always try and sacrifice personal grievances'. He should remember 'England expects every man to do his duty.'

The visit was overshadowed by an announcement in *The Times* that Beresford was to 'vacate the command of the Channel Fleet in March'. He had heard nothing of this and wrote to McKenna for an explanation. Was the report true, he wanted to know. If so, why was his command limited to two years when Wilson had held the post for four years? In his reply McKenna enigmatically declared that the article 'contains much information which … is unknown to me'. In any case, he told Beresford, his command was 'held at His Majesty's pleasure' although it was also the case that 'the commands of the important fleets have usually been held for three years'. It was an oddly vague letter, but it was all McKenna was going to offer.

* * *

When autumn arrived Beresford was able to indulge in his visits to British ports, where the public's admiration for their favourite admiral remained undiminished. He took a division of his fleet to Scarborough on 25 September and was warmly greeted by the Mayor who promised that the town 'would do its utmost to make the visit enjoyable'. That night Beresford joined his officers in a ball. On the next day special trains brought visitors from as far away as Hull and Bradford while 400 men marched through the town, where they each received presents of tobacco, a pipe and a tea ticket. When the fleet team played football against locals the result was a suitably diplomatic draw. Afterwards Beresford held an at-home on-board ship for over 700 guests, while on land there was a concert in Marine Drive. At the end of the four day visit the fleet departed in bright sunshine, parading along the coast in a long line for the delight of the Scarborough citizens.

The fleet visits still left time for Beresford to send critical letters to the Admiralty. In October he complained that 'no tactical training of one large Fleet against another has taken place since October 1907' and said it was 'my duty to inform Their Lordships that it is of the first importance to pursue the practical investigation of the tactics of one large Fleet against another'. This request was turned down on 24 October. On the next day he finally replied to an Admiralty's letter of 1 July. Around this time Beresford also sent Bellairs a long list of points to use in attacks on the Admiralty. These included a lack of stores, the cost of defects, 'false economies', the weakness of the British fleet compared to that of Germany, and Channel Fleet battleship shortages at various dates.

***

On 2 December Beresford put to sea again 'to shake up my people well before Xmas'. He was, he told Lady Londonderry, planning 'a tremendous attack on the Western Front on the top of Portland Hill'. The next day, apparently unaware of the cataclysm that was only days away, he breezily wrote to the Board and optimistically assured them that he would do this utmost to 'fulfil my duty in furtherance of their instructions'. This outburst of loyalty only lasted two days, to be broken by a letter to Walter Long, a leading Tory MP. Having told him that Fisher 'would not remain in Office 48 hours if it was not for the King', he added that 'I have only to make two speeches to put things right'.

Beresford's arrangements for generous Christmas leave for his men were abruptly halted when a secret message came from the Admiralty. They 'have heard something', was all Beresford could tell Lady Londonderry. Now he had to keep half his fleet fully-manned over the Christmas period, although it would be Milne who would sit out the festive period at Portsmouth.

Despite Beresford being in bed with gout, his planned attack on Verne Citadel on Portland Island went ahead on 8 December. Over 10,000 bluejackets and marines took part. In reporting this action in one of his regular fleet letters to the Admiralty, he departed from his usual style of simply listing what the fleet had done. This time, perhaps in view of the oddity of this exercise, he justified his action, saying 'These

Landing Parties are good for the health of the men; they take men out of the ships who otherwise do not go ashore and they are good exercise for all.' More fulsomely, he told the Queen of Norway that 'Altogether it was splendid.'

Beresford and his BBBB bulldogs 1909

Unable to ingratiate himself with the British royals, Beresford had written to the Queen of Norway, offering her a bulldog pup as a Christmas present. This was no ordinary dog. It was a 'B.B.B.B. – the Beresford Battleship Bulldog Breed'. He claimed the father (not owned by Beresford) was worth £1000 and 'I would not take £500 for the mother'. Despite these persuasions, the Queen declined the gift. Having failed to find a royal home for one pup, Beresford disposed of four in January by giving them to four of the battleships. On this occasion, he revealed that the mother was called 'Some Time' probably a reference to the German Navy's toast of 'The Day'. The sire was now said to be Beresford's, he having refused an offer of £2000 for the dog. (Sir Henry Lucy recalled that the sire was 'a trifle stout and short of breath' and used 'to groan direfully at the unwonted exercise' of following his master around the ship.)

The Channel Fleet 1908-09

***

And then it came – the letter from McKenna – on 19 December. Beresford's command was to be terminated on 24 March 1909. It was dismissal, although Fisher and McKenna had dressed it up as an unavoidable administrative change. The Board had decided that home commands should be for two years, so that both the Channel and Home Fleet appointments would fall vacant at the same time. Archly, McKenna thought 'this decision will probably not be unwelcome' to Beresford 'after a continuous and distinguished tenure of chief commands lasting six years'.

There was not the least possibility that Beresford would view his truncated command as anything other than a brutal attack on his reputation, which he would exploit to the full. It happened that Walter Long MP was on-board the *King Edward VII* when the letter reached Beresford. Fisher had got word of what they were plotting: 'Walter Long hopes to be First Lord of the Admiralty and ... Beresford is his prophet and his First Sea Lord!' With surprising moderation, Beresford replied (with Long's help) to McKenna in calm tones. The termination of his command was 'not either convenient or pleasant to me', he wrote. It was particularly inconvenient since only in August he had asked McKenna 'to give me early intimation of your decision in order that I might make my arrangements'. He was also aggrieved that he was to go on to half-pay while Bridgeman was to receive another appointment. Beresford's supporters were outraged at his dismissal and at least one public meeting was held in protest.

Part of the reason for Beresford's moderation in his reply to McKenna was his determination to replace Fisher as First Sea Lord. He was unsure how best to engineer this outcome. Should he 'sit still and do nothing' or should he 'make a statement', he mused in a letter to Long. He chose political intrigue. First he talked to Asquith who, he told Admiral Noel, commander-in-chief at The Nore, 'knew that the state of morale of the service was very grave'. Beresford's contacts with Asquith continued and they dined together on 10 February. There was 'a long talk about naval affairs', which left Beresford with the impression that Asquith 'knows a great deal of what is going on and is very uneasy about it'. Beresford was pleased with Asquith's response but, in reality, Asquith had no time for the rebellious admiral. He told his wife that he was tempted to 'cashier' Beresford.

Beresford decided to go out in style and wrote to the Admiralty for permission for one last cruise. 'In the ordinary course it would be rather silly to approve this in view of the re-arrangement of the ships on March

24', Fisher told McKenna, but 'let him have his fireworks'. And so, with a stiff wind blowing, Beresford's ships left the Portland roads and headed for the north coast of Ireland. As the last ship reached the open sea, only the *Surprise* was left in the roads. On-board was Lady Charles, symbolising the couple's increasing isolation. Before returning home, Lady Charles called at the Royal Sailors' Home at Weymouth to hand over a signed portrait of Beresford – his 'parting gift on relinquishing the command of the Channel Fleet'.

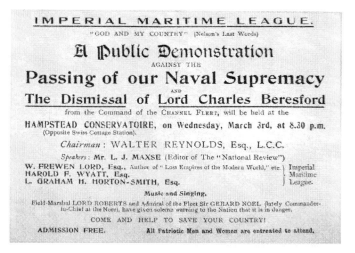

A ticket advertising a meeting to protest at Beresford's dismissal

There were two farewell dinners, the first given by Beresford's captains at the Royal Hotel in Weymouth. Twenty-eight captains attended, including Captain R F Scott who was to die three years later on his fatal journey to the South Pole. Two days later Beresford gave a dinner on-board his flagship at Portland. Hundreds of officers heard him wish 'good-bye, good luck and God-speed' as he thanked them for their 'loyalty, energy, and enthusiastic manner'. He added: 'I haul down my flag with very great regret.' He also wrote to Lady Londonderry, sending her a 'boatswain's ball and chain' and one of his admiral's flags 'as owing to being dismissed before time for doing my duty I shall probably never use it again unless there is war'.

The scenes on 24 March, when Beresford took leave of his ship and set foot on the Portsmouth dockside, were such as had not been witnessed in living memory. Outside the dockyard gates there was a large crowd of cheering supporters, whose cries did not diminish until Beresford's train to the town centre had moved off. In the town the streets were packed with cheering crowds, the trams filled to capacity and the roads lined on both sides by cars flying Union Jacks. At Waterloo Station in London later in the day the same frenzied sight greeted the dismissed admiral. Despite the attempts of the police to keep the platforms clear, Beresford could barely descend from his train. A seething mass sang 'For he's a jolly good fellow' as he made his way to the exit. There was only one jarring note. For all the enthusiasm of the populace there was no one of any note to greet Beresford on his return. After a career of just under 50 years, his reception committee was limited to Harold Wyatt and Lionel Horton-Smith, two members of the cranky Imperial Maritime League. Two days later Beresford paid the customary visit to the Palace. His career was over.

Beresford (with raised hat) on HMS King Edward VII taking leave of his fleet 24 March 1909

Chapter 21
Career's end 1909-10

Before Beresford had left his fleet he had consulted Balfour as to what he should do next. Since it was clear that he was determined to agitate, Balfour advised him to first talk to Asquith. After a meeting with the Prime Minister on 30 March, Beresford returned home and wrote him two letters. The first, formal and lengthy, set out his critique of naval policy. At the heart of his grievances was his allegation that 'During the whole of my tenure of the command of the Channel Fleet … that force … has never, even for a day, been equal to the force which it might encounter in Home Waters.' He also objected to there being two fleets in the Channel instead of 'one large homogeneous Fleet, complete in all units'. Then there were the reductions in his fleet before he took it over, the lack of combined fleet exercises and the weakness of the Home Fleet. He concluded: 'I should be wanting in my duty' if he did not report such matters 'at this critical moment in the destinies of the Empire'.

The second letter, a handwritten scribble, was blackmail. Beresford told Asquith that 'I do not intend to make any public statement until after the 14th. April by which time you will no doubt have had leisure to verify the remarks contained in enclosure No. I [his main letter].'

Asquith suggested to McKenna that there should be an enquiry. Fisher, Esher and Knollys objected strongly but McKenna favoured the idea as the 'surest way to bring immediate peace'. And so, just inside Beresford's blackmail deadline, Asquith informed his bothersome admiral of the decision.

It has been said by some authors that Asquith accepted an enquiry because it gave him an opportunity to conduct a fishing expedition into the Admiralty's archives. During his years as Chancellor and Prime Minister he had fended off one demand after another for money for the Navy. To him the Admiralty was extravagant and out of control. This explanation is absolutely incompatible with what happened over the next few months. In the two weeks of setting up the Enquiry, Asquith dithered about the membership, initially including Viscount Esher and Admiral A K Wilson. He removed them after a protest from Beresford. At the same time, Asquith made no attempt to draw up a list of witnesses. This he left to Beresford, who produced seventeen names, all carefully chosen to bolster *his* case. As to the terms of reference, Asquith left those to Charles Ottley at the Committee for Imperial

Defence. In short, the Prime Minister showed not the least interest in the purpose or the procedures of the Enquiry.

The eight terms of reference dealt with the adequacy of the Channel Fleet during Beresford's appointment; the degree of readiness of the Home Fleet; the alleged deficiency of small craft; the suitability of British torpedo craft for the work they had to do; the distribution of the fleets in Home Waters; the lack of war preparation at the Admiralty; and whether or not the Admiralty should provide war plans to commanders-in-chief at sea.

The Enquiry met for the first time on 27 April, its members being Asquith, Lord Crewe (Lord President of the Council), Lord Morley (Secretary of State for India), Sir Edward Grey (Foreign Secretary) and Richard Haldane (Secretary of State for War). McKenna attended for the Admiralty, with Fisher as his technical adviser. Rear Admiral Sir Charles Ottley, who was secretary of the Committee for Imperial Defence, was the secretary. They met on fifteen occasions and produced 334 pages of proceedings with 250 pages of appendices.

The proceedings themselves further illustrated Asquith's insouciant approach to the Enquiry. With no agenda, he opened the Enquiry by simply asking Beresford to begin. He presumably intended that the committee would work its way through the eight headings drawn up by Ottley, but, from the moment Beresford began, the committee never once regained control of the agenda.

The hilarious exchanges between the rude and often incoherent Beresford and the inept committee have been explored in detail elsewhere (Freeman 2009). In brief, Beresford so failed to keep to the point that both he and the committee often lost track of the discussion. Time after time when asked a factual question about his fleet, Beresford could not recall the answer. He made wild allegations that he could not substantiate, swore that certain documents existed that did not, and denied the existence of others that were then produced at the meetings. The authoritative naval historian of this period, Arthur Marder, was of the view that the Enquiry demonstrated 'the absolute incompetence of the man and his inability even to comprehend, much less to substantiate his charges'.

An anonymous early draft of the report boldly stated that 'It is plain upon the evidence that Lord Charles has failed to prove his case.' This version was far too candid for public consumption so a new draft was prepared, which drew three conclusions. First, that there had never been any danger to the country from the Admiralty's arrangements during the period under review. Second, that although the 'arrangements [were] quite defensible in themselves' they were 'not ideally perfect'.

The Board had not 'taken Lord Charles sufficiently into their confidence' while he in turn had failed to 'carry out the spirit of the instructions of the Board'. Third, they recommended 'the development of a Naval War Staff'.

The report had Asquith's indecision stamped all over it. If he had thought that, by an even-handed allocation of fault, he could end the dispute, he was grievously mistaken. As Esher noted, there were 'no words of appreciation' for all that Fisher had done to build a Navy with the power to repel any invader. Fisher berated the *'cowardly document!'* Beresford, on the other hand, was 'in ecstasies', Balfour told Esher. Indeed, Beresford's public reaction was one of jubilation.

Reactions aside, the damage was done. The committee had sought to vindicate the Admiralty without enraging the accuser. The results were disastrous for Asquith. Fisher was driven into retirement (with the fig-leaf of a peerage), for want of any display of public support. As to Beresford, newly emboldened, he dropped plans to stand for his old East Marylebone constituency and promptly signed up for Portsmouth. The juggernaut that Asquith had sought to halt in its tracks was now unstoppable.

The first sign of serious trouble was when Beresford wrote to Asquith on 23 October 1909, accusing the Admiralty of having victimised various officers who had been associated with the Enquiry. Then, before Asquith had had a chance to reply, Beresford sent copies of their recent correspondence to the press. Meanwhile McKenna prepared a lengthy rebuttal of Beresford's accusations, which appeared in *The Times* on 24 November. In enormous detail McKenna showed that every one of Beresford's accusations was without foundation. Beresford's central point was that serving with him had harmed officers' careers. To rebuff this McKenna looked at the fifteen officers who had joined Beresford in 1907. Two of the four captains had been promoted to flag rank. The other two had received more responsible appointments. Four out of five commanders had been promoted. Three out of six lieutenants had been promoted. Most importantly of all, the two men who Beresford claimed had been seriously persecuted (Hulbert and Sturdee) had been promoted to captain and rear admiral respectively. Despite McKenna's total demolition of the accusations Beresford was to repeat them in his 1912 book *Betrayal.*

* * *

If Asquith had any doubt as to his error, the scene in Portsmouth on 18 December when Beresford arrived to fight a by-election would have erased it. Even before his train had arrived, the Town Hall was besieged by thousands of people. As he left the station, Beresford's carriage was drawn by bluejackets. The public had spoken: Beresford was the victor.

So assured was Beresford of winning the election that he refused to speak at outdoor meetings nor would he 'canvass the electors individually' since he had 'too much respect for their intelligence'. Later he claimed that it was his doctors who had forbidden him 'to address open-air meetings'. Accident prone as ever, Beresford's electioneering came to an abrupt halt on 1 December when a General Election was announced. This was, he fumed, '[a] disenfranchisement of the constituency' which was 'an unprecedented violation of constitutional usage'.

Beresford took an active part in the General Election, speaking on behalf of many other candidates, his enthusiasm being boosted by a rumoured promise from the Conservatives to give him the post of First Lord, should they win.

Beresford's own election at Portsmouth was a triumph. He and the Liberal Unionist Bertram Falle, topped the poll with 16,777 and 15,592 votes respectively. Both Liberal candidates trailed well behind and, despite the industrial nature of the constituency, the Labour candidate received a mere 3529 votes. Naturally Beresford attributed the Conservative success at Portsmouth to their fighting on 'the question of adequate naval defence of the Empire'.

BITTER HARVEST 1910-1919

Chapter 22
Return to the back benches 1910

Beresford's first chance to attack the government's naval policy came on 2 March 1910, when McKenna presented a supplementary estimate. The circumstances were such as to allow both sides to claim victory. The estimate was for costs in the current year attributable to laying down four 'contingent' dreadnoughts. (Four dreadnoughts had already been approved for 1909-10 but the government had agreed to lay down four more should they be needed to keep pace with German shipbuilding.) McKenna presented the additional ships as evidence of the government's serious commitment to naval defence. Beresford, on the other hand, claimed that he and his friends had not been 'scaremongers' after all. He asked McKenna to 'give us credit for saying what we think in the interest of the defence of the country'.

It was a good start for the new MP but at sixty-four years old Beresford increasingly lived in the past as when he reprinted his memorandum of 1886 calling for a Naval Intelligence Department. What the relevance of a twenty-four year old document was to the issues of 1910 is unclear. At the same time he published a second pamphlet setting out a proposed shipbuilding programme. This called for 16 battleships to be built by 31 March 1914. His total programme for 1910-14 would cost £70m, which he suggested should be financed by a loan.

The Commons enjoyed a rare spectacle in the estimates debate on 14 March, when Beresford and McKenna clashed time after time. The rows began with the dreadnoughts. Beresford accused McKenna of talking 'about nothing but "Dreadnoughts"'. 'If I took him down to Aldershot and showed him heavy artillery, and no cavalry and no infantry, he would probably think it strange', said Beresford, but the fleet 'would no more be effective without cruisers, stores, etc., than artillery could be utilised without cavalry and infantry'. Next they clashed over what the true figure for new construction was. Then came torpedo boats, which Beresford maintained 'are not suitable for the North Sea'. And he should know, he said, since 'there is nobody in the whole Service who has worked these torpedo-boat destroyers like I have'. In fact the Admiralty had designed these torpedo boats for work near the British coast, so Beresford's point was irrelevant.

After that Beresford moved on to repairs, claiming that he once had to wait six months for a destroyer to be repaired. Not so, said McKenna: 'I investigated the facts, and I discovered that it was not six months but six weeks.' After further clashes on the lack of marines, the slowness of new shipbuilding, the risks of a bolt from the blue attack, and the size of the fleet, Beresford returned to German tramp steamers. The Admiralty had proof that these armed tramps existed, he claimed. McKenna denied this. Beresford then referred to the letters produced at the Enquiry. McKenna retorted: 'The statements of the Noble Lord are absolutely without the slightest foundation.' Beresford then shifted his ground and attacked McKenna for not having exercised the fleets enough in recent years. Such bickering was all the great admiral had to offer the House.

* * *

On 6 May King Edward VII died, un-reconciled to his once bosom friend. Beresford rushed off telegrams of sympathy to various members of the royal family, but only perfunctory thanks were returned. While Fisher had been summoned by Queen Alexandra to sit with her dead husband Beresford had to content himself with being invited to St George's Chapel to pay his last respects. When writing to the new King George V he referred to 'the kindness, generosity and affection' that Edward Prince of Wales had shown him 'in those happy years gone by'. He knew George V too well to suggest that the rift had ever been healed.

* * *

When the American President Roosevelt was in Britain in May 1910 Beresford arranged a dinner in his honour. The guest list testified to Beresford's standing and his breadth of contacts. In addition to MPs and admirals, there were Lord Curzon, Sir George Armstrong (proprietor of the *Globe* newspaper) and the composer Edward Elgar. Only a few days later, he organized a similar grand occasion for Field Marshal Herbert Kitchener, recently returned from his post as commander-in-chief in India. This time the guests included a bevy of ambassadors and a glittering array of dukes, duchesses, viscounts, countesses and other peers.

* * *

The Navy estimates were back in the Commons in June and July, offering Beresford many opportunities for intervening in the debate. On 8 June he talked about the food during his years in the Navy: it 'was always excellent'. Although food had improved recently with the introduction of refrigeration and on-board bakeries, for most of the nineteenth century it had been abominable. Why Beresford chose to deny this is a mystery. On the same day he had opinions to offer on the medical side of the Navy: there was a deficiency of 60-70 surgeons and a need for two hospital ships. Under the pensions vote Beresford made a typically sympathetic plea for the needs of the ordinary seamen. He argued that the widows and children of men 'who get killed or maimed or diseased in the Service' were not recognized. Pensions in these circumstances should be more generous.

King George V

In the debate on shipbuilding on 14 July, Beresford was highly critical of the way the government juggled expenditure between financial years. This gave him the chance to mock the consequences, saying 'the Government are going to lay down five ships for this year and call this year's ships next year's ships, because the five ships last year, we were told, were this year's ships, and they were no more this year's than the four contingent ships are last year's ships'. It was good debating fun and contained a truth: there were so many revisions of building programmes, and so many ways of counting building (voted, laid down, being built, launched, fitted out) that the figures were baffling. The same could have been said of German shipbuilding, but Beresford preferred to overlook this.

Both Beresford and the Secretary of State for War, Richard Haldane, found themselves guests of the Cutlers' Company in Sheffield in October and it was Beresford who replied to the toast 'The Defensive Forces'. He declared that 'he wished to see the Navy put in an unassailable position by the unanimous vote of the people'. Despite being the Navy's number one critique, he added 'Criticism should cease, he said, and 'those in control of our Navy' should be left to run it. In a strange twist of logic Beresford declared that the 'competition in armaments' was caused by Britain reducing its expenditure. Haldane began his speech by praising the work of the Committee for Imperial Defence and then went on to support Beresford's view that 'our Navy should be our first line of defence'. He did not, though, offer any strong support for Beresford's assertion that the Navy was critically short of either men or ships, limiting himself to saying 'Our Navy might possibly have to be made stronger.'

At the end of the same month Beresford made a populist speech on the Navy to his constituents. Ignoring all that he had done to alarm the masses as to the state of Britain's defences, he said that any apprehension was entirely 'created by the speeches of Ministers themselves'. After declaring that the naval scares had been justified, he then claimed that he 'avoided scares'. Having painted himself as a disinterested party he went on to suggest that the Navy required £60m of additional expenditure, more ships and more men. Incoherent as the speech was, it was loudly cheered.

Beresford's first year back in politics had been marked by his aimless and unfocused agenda. At the heart of his difficulties was his inability to form alliances. Not only did he ignore the front bench of his own party, but he never saw the value of working with other backbenchers. He took topics up almost at random and quickly dropped them. Rarely did he follow an issue through to any conclusion.

Return to the back benches 1910

* * *

Edward VII had died in the midst of the first phase of the great constitutional crisis of the Commons versus the Lords. This had been brought about by the House of Lords rejecting Lloyd George's Budget in December 1909. Asquith had reached an agreement with King Edward VII whereby he would, if necessary, create 500 Liberal peers to push the Budget through the Lords. Edward's death left this scheme in ruins since the inexperienced King George V could hardly be expected to support such a bold and constitutionally risky innovation. That left only one option: a General Election. So, in December Beresford found himself at the hustings for the second time that year.

The government saw this as a good moment to get Beresford off their backs. Asquith persuaded Edward Hemmerde, then MP for Denbighshire East, to stand against Beresford in Portsmouth. *The Times* saw Hemmerde as 'a keen controversialist' who would give Beresford 'the sort of hard-hitting sporting fight that he liked'. When the Labour Party decided not to field a candidate the election became a head-to-head contest. The *Manchester Guardian* thought that Beresford was 'disquieted' at the prospect and forecast that the election would not be such 'plain sailing' as on the previous occasion. Since Beresford's triumphal election, Parliament had laid bare 'his futility as a general politician' and 'the Beresford myth has been sadly damaged'. Now he faced the 'formidable opposition of one of the ablest and keenest of the younger Liberals'. When the result came, both Beresford and his fellow Unionist had held their seats, although Hemmerde had cut Beresford's majority from 3195 to 1710.

One triumph gained was followed by one lost. In December the King asked Asquith to make Beresford an admiral of the fleet on his retirement in February 1911. Writing to McKenna, Asquith said that he had 'no personal objections' provided that Beresford was taken off the active list. However, he feared that it would be said 'that we were trying to buy his silence'. That, though, was 'not worth 5 minutes' purchase'. Beresford suspected that he would not be promoted so he asked Walter Long to launch a campaign in his favour. He wanted his case 'to be heard' and provided Long with sixteen pages on his career to use as ammunition. But before Long could act, McKenna stamped on the proposal. He explained to Asquith that there were two types of promotion to admiral of the fleet: ordinary and extraordinary. Only three ordinary admirals of the fleet were permitted and there was no vacancy at that time. As to the extraordinary category, it was only used to *retain* an active office whose services were 'indispensable'. This could hardly be said of Beresford. Asquith sent McKenna's letter to the King and no more was heard of the matter.

Chapter 23
Member for the Navy 1911

At the same time that Beresford's promotion efforts were faltering, he inherited a collection of Nelson relics from Lady Meux, the wife of a London brewer. These included Nelson's sword which, in 2002, was sold for £336,650. These gifts might have been some comfort to Beresford as he struggled to throw off an attack of bronchitis, which had struck him down at the end of 1910.

When the new Parliament assembled in February Beresford made a sad sight as he leaned on his stick to be sworn in. He was not too ill, though, to engage in an odd exchange in the Commons the next day, when Arthur Lee asked a question about a booklet of notes on the risk of invasion. Lee wanted it to be published 'officially', although it was openly on sale. Beresford leapt in to ask whether it was usual for 'an official Admiralty document to be signed by one member of the Board?' McKenna said it was frequently so, to which Beresford riposted 'They are not published like that, Sir?' Like so many of Beresford's Parliamentary interventions, its purpose, other than to annoy McKenna, was obscure.

On the following day, Mr Rowland Hunt, the MP for Ludlow, asked about the arrangements for discussing the *Declaration of London*. (This was a new multinational treaty, which dealt with blockades and contraband. Although it was ratified by quite a few countries it never came into effect.) Possibly no subject excited Beresford more in 1911. He pressed to know whether it would be discussed separately from the *Naval Prize Bill*. Asquith replied that 'Parliament will have full opportunity of discussing the provisions of the *Declaration* before His Majesty is advised to ratify it.'

Beresford's intervention over the *Declaration* was his last political comment as an active naval officer. On the following day, his sixty-fifth birthday, there was no news of his long-desired promotion. With a bitter heart he noted that *The Times* approved the withheld promotion, since 'No one knows better than Lord Charles Beresford that Admirals in active service should nowadays be men of almost superhuman endurance.' Beresford, the paper suggested, would not 'cavil' at this rule. 'Exceptional promotion ... needs to be rare and should always be such as to command universal assent.' Beresford, the paper continued, suffered from 'the dangerous endowment of an interesting personality'.

Member for the Navy 1911

* * *

In keeping with his often remarkably progressive views, Beresford voted in favour of the second reading of the *Women's Enfranchisement Bill* on 5 May. If enacted, this bill would have given the vote to women householders. It is beyond the limits of this book to follow the tortuous story of how a bill that was supported by 255 votes to 88 never became law.

When the naval estimates came back to the House in May, Beresford asked for enhanced pensions for widows of men killed in action. Bringing the reality of service life to the chamber, he said 'I maintain that a man who is blown up in the boiler-room, who dies from sunstroke or dysentery through hard work is losing his life just as much in the service of the country as the man who is killed by shot and shell.' And, for those who did not understand the consequences of this, he added that the widow of a man killed in action received 5s a week plus 1s 6d per child. That same widow, if her husband were accidentally killed, received only a gratuity.

In late May Beresford, in another display of his progressive side, gave his strong support to the government's *National Insurance Bill*. He described it as 'one of the greatest Bills we have ever seen'. He continued, 'It is a Bill not only to relieve the poor, but to relieve the sick poor', the neglect of whom 'has been a shameful case ... for a great many years'. He went on to praise the doctors who cared for the poor under schemes run by the Friendly Societies: 'no class in the community have acted more loyally or more sympathetically or in a more kindly, chivalrous spirit to the poorer classes'. When it came to women, and wives in particular, he once more displayed his intuitive understanding of the plight of the poor. Referring to their proposed contribution, he said 'I do not believe the women can pay 3d. per week. The pennies are everything to the women ... You take threepence from a poor woman who has got a sick baby, and it may make just the difference of a little more milk to save the child.' As to the proposed maternity payments, 'The maternity money ought not to go to the men. The 30s ought to go to the women and to nobody else.' It was an astounding intervention in support of Liberal policy.

* * *

By the middle of the year *The Declaration of London* was back in Beresford's sights. He forecast that it would encourage 'a secretly organized attack upon our trade routes, because it will be open to an enemy to convert merchant ships into men-of-war'. Next he organized a meeting of retired admirals at the Westminster Palace Hotel. The 102 admirals expressed 'grave concern' at the 'menace' that the *Declaration* possessed. They foresaw enemy powers arming merchant ships in war, which would then be used to sink neutral vessels bringing food to Britain. The meeting called for 'a Select Committee or a Royal Commission' to study the treaty before it was ratified. A few days later Beresford, replying to a telegram from the Imperial Merchant Service Guild, said that, if ratified, the treaty would draw 'the teeth and claws of the British lion'. He spoke again about the treaty on 28 June at a huge rally in the City. The *Declaration*, he said, posed 'a grave emergency' and had only been possible because Asquith and Lord Loreburn (Lord Chancellor) 'had been led away by some of those wild, hysterical ideas that were not inseparable from democracy'. The bill was back in the Commons on 29 June when Sir John Butcher, MP for York, moved an amendment to stop its ratification. Beresford spoke at great length on the protection of merchant ships before concluding that 'if the *Declaration of London* becomes ratified' then Britain would 'be worse off than we were under the old scheme of working under the *Declaration of Paris* when privateering was abolished'.

* * *

Things brightened a little for Beresford in June when he was appointed to the Order of the Bath (Knight Grand Cross) in the Coronation Honours list of 20 June. Then, within a week, he received an Honorary DCL from the University of Oxford. That, in praising Beresford, the University orator recalled the boiler incident of 1885 was almost to suggest that he had achieved nothing as laudable in the following twenty-six years.

* * *

Shortly after the university ceremony a German gunboat arrived outside the Moroccan port of Agadir on 1 July. It had been sent, following a recent uprising in the country, in the hope of weakening the ties between France and Britain. International tension increased sharply with fears of imminent war. But the British and French governments stood firm and Germany backed down. Beresford had no faith in Asquith's capacity to handle the situation and pleaded in a letter to him that 'no communication will be made to Germany which would give her an opportunity of declaring war immediately'. The British fleet was too dispersed and it would take until Sunday to have '20 Battleships and 11 armoured Cruisers' available. Since Beresford was writing on Thursday, this meant he would have been happy to see all-out war three days later! Asquith no doubt smiled mockingly as he disposed of this presumptuous advice.

Winston Churchill MP as First Lord of the Admiralty c 1911

On 24 October Winston Churchill, at the Home Office, swapped offices with Reginald McKenna at the Admiralty. This followed a disastrous meeting of the Committee for Imperial Defence on 23 August at which the Admiralty had declared that, in the event of war, it would not be able to supply ships to transport troops to the continent – at least not until the German Navy had been defeated. Asquith hoped that the more energetic Churchill would better understand the need for the Army and Navy to act in unison. One of Churchill's first actions at the Admiralty was to ask Beresford for his assistance. They met, but nothing came from their discussions. Churchill also asked Fisher to visit. They instantly took to each other and were to meet and correspond regularly – in effect Fisher became Churchill's mentor. As for Beresford Churchill's arrival at the Admiralty only provoked him to more excesses. From now on he would both continue his vendetta against McKenna for past slights and start a new one against Churchill for his handling of the Admiralty and – worse still – for his accommodation with Fisher.

A few weeks later there were further changes at the Admiralty as Churchill got to grips with his new ministry. In came Admiral Sir Francis Bridgeman to replace A K Wilson as First Sea Lord, with Prince Louis of Battenberg coming as Second Sea Lord and Captain Sir William Pakenham as Third Sea Lord. Beresford called the appointments 'admirable'. This was purely for public consumption since, as we know, he had no language harsh enough to describe his view of Battenberg. He wondered whether the outgoing sea lords had resigned or been pushed out, but for now held his tongue.

***

On the evening of Friday 1 December, the Marquess of Waterford failed to return home from inspecting his estate. A search found his body in the River Clodagh. The inquest concluded that he had slipped and fallen into the water, where he drowned. In one of Ireland's largest funerals of recent years, Beresford's nephew was buried on 6 December in the family tomb at Clonagarn. Beresford and his two surviving brothers William and Marcus were amongst the chief mourners.

Chapter 24
Home Rule 1912

For some time Beresford had been preparing a book to avenge his sacking, the Enquiry, and his failure to be promoted to Admiral of the Fleet. His publishers had announced its appearance for 5 December 1911 but the day had come and no book had appeared. Rumours quickly spread. Some said that the book had been withdrawn, some that it required 'corrections of detail' and others that the cause was the change of First Lord. They were all wrong. Libel was the issue. Beresford had included something like twenty pages attacking Captain Reginald Bacon, who had declared them libellous and repaired to his lawyers. Beresford's own explanation was that the delay was 'in part due to a desire to correct and revise it after an absence in Canada' but also because of Churchill's appointment. He felt the 'publication of a severe stricture on our naval administration' straight after the appointment was not 'fair play'. *The Betrayal* finally appeared 28 January 1912.

The book was a relentless and polemical attack on the naval administration of the last ten years, but it was also no more than a rehash of old gripes. Beresford's targets included the Selborne Scheme (this had 'deceived' the parents and the cadets); the 'espionage' which required officers to 'report secretly upon brother officers'; the ship-scrapping policy; fleet distribution; the lack of docks and the failure to develop Rosyth; the Home Fleet ('a fraud upon the public'); the commands of the Channel, Atlantic and Home fleets; and Fisher and McKenna for creating a manpower shortage. Beresford's own summary captured the tone of the book well enough: 'the naval policy of the years 1902 to 1909 was mistaken in every important particular'. As for the officers who had disagreed with those policies, Beresford claimed that 'several ... have been placed on half-pay and kept without employment, or their Service careers have been summarily terminated'. 'These officers were right; the Navy was right; and the authorities were wrong.'

The *Observer* newspaper noted that the book had 'much reduced dimensions and character from the expectations we were led at first to expect'. This comment suggests that Beresford had either cut more than the libellous passages, or that he had oversold the book prior to publication. *The Times*, too, was not impressed, nor was it convinced by Beresford's arguments. For a start, having read the book, they found little evidence that it had been amended in the light of the new Churchill regime as Beresford had claimed. Whilst the paper admired 'all that emphasis of expression, conviction, and full-bodied denunciation of which the gallant Admiral is a master', it found little satisfaction in the content, which was '[a] long tissue of criticisms and accusations' which Beresford had already repeated many times. The paper took particular issue with Beresford's assertion that 'throughout the eventful years from 1902 to the autumn of 1911 Lord Charles Beresford alone has been right, while successive Boards of Admiralty, and the successive Governments, Unionist and Liberal, that they have served have been wilfully, culpably, and almost criminally wrong'. The editorial concluded by expressing the paper's 'regret that Lord Charles Beresford has seen fit to publish his book and to call it *The Betrayal*'.

Publication day for the modern author is likely to involve a rush of signings and public appearances. Back in 1912 no one raised an eyebrow at Beresford being in Russia when the book came out. On his way home he stopped in Berlin, where he lunched with the Emperor. The *New York Times* imagined this to be 'particularly piquant' since 'the Admiral is regarded in Germany as one of the Fatherland's most incorrigible English foes'. That Beresford was in Berlin only a few weeks after a similar visit by Lord Haldane did not go unnoticed in Paris, where commentators puzzled over the meaning of the Emperor's attentions to British politicians. Was this, the papers wondered, a *rapprochement* between the two powers?

* * *

After speaking in the Commons on the mixed bag of rifles, army pay and church vestments, Beresford turned his attention to a more serious matter: the naval estimates. He attacked Churchill for saying that 'the foundation of naval policy was finance'. 'Surely,' he said, 'the foundation of naval policy is not finance, but requirement.' No doubt Churchill would have wished to agree with him, but a minister has to respect the limits of the Exchequer; a backbencher is free to demand the Earth. To emphasise the gulf between the two men, Beresford bemoaned the eight cruisers that Churchill proposed to build. 'He knows we want thirty-six.' He then went on to criticise Churchill for taking account of the threat posed by Germany's growing Navy. Churchill should concentrate on 'Imperial defence and leave Germany alone'.

Beresford was in a more constructive mood two days later, when Churchill proposed the appointment of an additional civil lord to the Admiralty. Some members opposed this, but Beresford declared that it would 'prevent a good deal of unnecessary expense'. On the same day

Beresford expressed his dissatisfaction with the numbers of men being recruited to the Navy. Saying that the Navy had been 20,000 men short in 1909, he was not impressed with the recruitment of 3000 men in each of the last two years. Uncharacteristically, he phrased his short speech as an observation and made no effort to urge his points.

The following day Beresford continued his argument in the columns of *The Times* when he told his readers that the government's two keels to one policy (laying down two warships for each one laid down by Germany) was 'interfering in a high-handed manner with Germany's naval affairs'. Britain should forget Germany and 'make out plans for the defence of the Empire'. He wanted all those naval bases in far-flung places that had been cut back to be restored. For a man who, as Commander-in-Chief in the Channel, had so persistently drawn attention to the threat to British ships in home waters, his new insouciance about home defence was amazing.

* * *

On the night of the 14 April the RMS *Titanic* sank on her maiden voyage, with a loss of over 1500 lives. A week later Beresford wrote to *The Times* to praise 'the dauntless heroism of those employed in the engine and boiler room departments, and artisan departments (such as the carpenter and his crew)'. These people, he said, had been 'passed over without comment' in all the press reporting. '[They] remained at their posts', he continued 'when they must have known that a death – the most terrible and painful it is possible to conceive – awaited them at any minute.' After 'the muffled sound of the ice tearing through the ship's side ... they knew that the pumps would not check the rising water, yet for over two hours they remained at their posts'. He declared that 'All honour and respect to those men whose names will be recorded on the role of fame for gallantry in a sudden and unlooked-for disaster.' No other admiral could have written a letter like that. What a great popular novelist Beresford would have made! A week later he wrote to *The Times* again, this time calling for a fund 'on the lines of the General Hospital Fund for the relief of the relatives of those in the merchant service who lose their lives at sea'.

Five weeks after the loss of the *Titanic*, Major Archer-Shee MP moved to reduce the salary of the President of the Board of Trade by £100. This was in protest against the Board's failure to provide 'efficient regulations for accommodation in boats on passenger ships'. With the recent *Titanic* disaster in mind Archer-Shee attacked the Board's failure to update regulations to take account of the huge size of modern ships. Beresford at first supported him. He began with a long discourse on water-tight doors (to which he had strong objections) and then turned to analysing the cause of the sinking, while admitting he knew nothing about it. But he cut across Archer-Shee's argument when he warned the Commons 'do not overdo the question of boats' and went on to explain why ships should *not* carry enough boats for all their passengers. Anticipating the debate that rages today with the modern obsession of eliminating all risk from life, he warned the House 'we must remember that we should never be able to build anything that will float, and that will not meet with disaster'.

RMS Titanic sinking on 14 April 1912

A short while later Beresford resurrected his interest in the need for more and better physical education. He was acutely aware of the poor physical condition of young men – something the country as a whole only realised when the First World War arrived. In pursuit of this interest he introduced a bill to promote physical education in schools. It was given its first reading and ordered to be printed. It does not seem to have got any further.

On the same day that he was opening up the physical education issue Beresford was also busy pursuing the subject of the Mediterranean. In a press statement he asserted that the Government had 'determined virtually to abandon the naval defence of the Mediterranean'. He warned that 'the nation must decide, and that quickly ... whether or not they will permit the weakening to breaking-point of what is the main link in the defence of the Empire.' This weakness, he added, was 'the natural development of the policy of reducing the Navy which was initiated in 1904'. (What Beresford did not know, and Parliament was not to learn until Sir Edward Grey's statement to the Commons on 3 August 1914, was that this was a considered policy. Unable to afford enough ships and men to fully defend both home waters and the Mediterranean, the government had entered into a secret understanding with the French, whereby, in war, France would protect the Mediterranean and Britain would protect the Channel.)

Beresford's next letter to the press quickly followed on 22 July when he declared that there was a grave situation which required 'instant action'. 'The Mediterranean has been abandoned, and that abandonment was intended to be permanent.' He demanded immediate action on five fronts: the food supply was 'to be secured against panic'; selected merchant vessels were to have 'guns and trained gunners'; the garrisons at Malta, Gibraltar and Egypt were to be strengthened; more naval vessels should be fully-manned; and naval recruitment should increase by 5000 men per year.

Churchill was in Beresford's sights in a supply debate in July when Beresford attacked his lack of preparation for imminent war, focusing on an alleged insufficiency of manpower. When Churchill challenged him over his remarks, Beresford retorted 'Who is more likely to know all about the men than I am?' Then he plunged into a personal attack on Churchill, saying 'I do not doubt the ability and courage of the right hon. Gentleman. He has got plenty of ability and courage, but a statesman wants more than that. Without being the least bit offensive, perhaps I may point out that you often find plenty of ability and courage in the gaols of our country ... I have no faith in him and the statements he makes.' Beresford had moved into the final phase of his political career: he had become a purveyor of abuse.

Beresford returned to attacking Churchill at a Primrose League meeting at Evesham in early August. Churchill, he declared, was the 'most eccentric individual placed over the Navy'. Referring to when Churchill had crossed the floor of the House in 1904, Beresford said 'He ratted from their side and was the father of the "Little Navy" Party in the House of Commons.' As to his performance as First Lord, 'He had had his chance. He had been at the Admiralty for eight months, and he had miserably failed.' He concluded 'things were worse than in the infamous administration of Mr McKenna'.

Home Rule 1912

* * *

The 28 September 1912 was one of the most momentous days in Ulster's history. Sir Edward Carson, MP and leader of the Ulster Unionists, had become the driving force in rallying the Ulster Protestants behind his notorious plans for rebellion against the United Kingdom government. Their first public act was the signing of the Covenant, which committed its signatories to 'using all means which may be found necessary' to defend 'for ourselves and our children, our cherished position of equal citizenship in the United Kingdom'. Carson signed first. The rest of the first page was completed with the signatures of six church representatives, Lord Castlereagh and the local MP James Chambers. Beresford, who played a prominent part that day, presumably signed on the next page. He had taken his first step towards open rebellion against the Crown.

Sir Edward Carson signing the Covenant on 28 September 1911. Beresford was present but is not identifiable in this picture

By October the Commons had resumed its business and Beresford was there on the seventh of the month when the official report on the sinking of the *Titanic* was debated. The Enquiry had concluded that, in part, the accident was due to the ship's 'excessive speed', so the House was no doubt grateful to Beresford for telling them that 'the ship was going too fast'. He warned members not to attempt to 'secure the safety of life' through 'sentimental theories'. What was needed was 'practical utility'. Once more he questioned the value of having lifeboats for all on-board: 'you add enormously to the weight on the ship, and you may affect her stability'. (Previously he had decried sufficient lifeboats on the grounds of the difficulty of launching them.)

* * *

It was Bridgeman's retirement, though, that most riled Beresford in December. He had heard rumours that it had been less than voluntary and seized the opportunity to vilify Churchill. On 11 December he asked Churchill in the Commons for 'the full circumstances' surrounding Bridgeman's resignation as First Sea Lord on 6 December. There followed a bout of what the *Manchester Guardian* called 'a singularly determined piece of heckling' by Beresford as he quizzed Churchill. Was there 'no other cause,' asked Beresford. No, said Churchill. Who proposed the resignation, asked Beresford. Churchill hesitated and asked whether Beresford was speaking for Bridgeman. On Beresford's assurance that he had had no contact with Bridgeman, Churchill conceded that he had initiated the resignation.

During a later debate on Bridgeman's resignation, Arthur Beck, MP for Saffron Walden, accused Beresford of having told everyone that 'that there is a scandal, and that my right hon. Friend the First Lord of the Admiralty is such a tyrannical person that no one can work with him unless absolutely prepared to be subservient to him' and then had refused to substantiate this accusation. Beck then launched into a diatribe on Beresford's methods:

> 'ever since he came back from sea he has been raising these questions in connection with the Navy. Every little bit of scandal, everything that could drive a wedge between different officers holding His Majesty's commission, has been seized by the Noble Lord'

People, Beck continued, recalled Beresford's 'courage on the occasion of the taking of the *Condor* into action' but:

> 'It is to us [the younger MPs] little less than a tragedy that he who has played such an honourable part in the Navy, who has held almost the highest post it is possible for a naval officer to hold, should in this House for what appear to us after the most careful investigation to be merely party purposes, make charge after charge which he is unable to substantiate.'

Throughout this tirade Beresford remained seated, laughing at each new charge. 'It is not a laughing matter,' declared Beck, as he called for Beresford to rise to his feet and 'substantiate the charges he has made'.

When Beresford did stand up, it was not to clarify, but to confuse. He launched into an attack on Churchill saying that 'Since the First Lord has been in office there have been five – this is the fifth – Sea Lords that have left the Admiralty.' (All the previous changes of personnel had been reported to Parliament without a question being asked.) When challenged by Churchill as to what difference of opinion he was supposed to have had with Bridgeman, Beresford refused to reply. Churchill could take no more and furiously turned on Beresford. It was his habit, said Churchill:

> 'to make a number of insinuations – insinuations of a very gross character, some of which transgress the limits of Parliamentary decorum; to cover the Order Paper with leading and fishing questions, designed to give substance and form to any gossip or tittle-tattle he may have been able to scrape together, and then to come down to the House, not to attempt to make good in fact or in detail, or to advance any evidence or any authority for the statements he has made, but to skulk in the background, waiting for an opportunity, after the Minister has spoken and when no further reply is possible, to utter another long string of disconnected statements and assertions which he hopes will confuse the issue and awaken disquietude in the mind of the public.'

There was much more to the debate (it ran to 14,000 words). At the end it was clear that Churchill could have handled Bridgeman's resignation more adroitly, but at least he had had the satisfaction of saying what so many must have felt for so long. Meanwhile the *Manchester Guardian* hoped that if the subject came back to the Commons, 'it will be from someone more capable than Lord Charles Beresford of handling a case without ruining it'.

It was a disastrous year end for Beresford. The Commons was losing patience with a member who showed no respect for its conventions and no self-restraint in his abusing its members.

Chapter 25
Slowing down 1913

In the naval estimates debate on 27 March 1913 Beresford made his usual demand that the government spend more money. His justifications went back as far as 1888, as if what happened twenty-five years ago had much relevance in the new age of oil, aeroplanes and dreadnoughts. He accused Churchill of being 20,000 men short 'if you go to war now' – a charge which Churchill dismissed as 'a travesty of the position'. If need be, every ship in the Navy could be mobilised in twenty-four hours, Churchill insisted. Ever a man of coal, Beresford next attacked the Navy's increasing dependence on oil: 'Oil in tanks in reserve is very easily destroyed; you cannot destroy coal.'

On 31 March Beresford again attacked Churchill's manning provision. He said he could prove 'our being 20,000 men short' but gave no detail when challenged by Churchill. Perhaps thinking that his case had been weak, he later added 'If, by some wave of a fairy wand, the First Lord could have six "Dreadnoughts" to-morrow, he could not man them unless he paid off ships now in commission.' Churchill riposted: 'How many "Dreadnoughts" more than the Admiralty now possess or have in prospect are they expected to provide crews for?'

On that same day Beresford was a pall-bearer at the funeral of his adored Field Marshal Lord Wolseley, who had died on 25 March. With other high ranking dignitaries, dressed in his blue frock coat with gold epaulettes, Beresford bore the coffin into St Paul's Cathedral. Memories of the Sudan must have come flooding back. That moment of unsullied triumph had been the high point of his career. Ever since he had found himself fighting his superiors and his political masters. No one else had placed so much faith in him as had the dead field marshal.

After speaking in Portsmouth in support of Field Marshal Lord Robert's campaign for national service Beresford returned to Ireland for a house party given by the brewer Viscount Iveagh, a ball given by Lady Paget, racing at Punchestown, a ball given by Viscountess Iveagh and further races at Leopardstown. He then returned to England for his new passion of yacht racing. At Crouch his six-metre yacht, the *Bunty*, came second.

This short break was followed by attending a Mansion House meeting arranged by the Aerial Defence Committee of the Navy League on 5 May. The Duke of Argyll expressed the mood of the meeting when he declared, anticipating the summer of 1940, that they should aim to achieve '[the mastery] of the blue air overhead as well as the blue waters round our shores'. Beresford did not speak, but concurred with Admiral Sir Edward Seymour in his view that the Navy's support for stronger aerial defence was evidence of their being 'not entirely satisfied with the Navy'. The following day Beresford and other colleagues formed a Unionist Aerial Defence Committee.

Edelweiss II – the same class as Beresford's Bunty

One of Beresford's more bizarre Commons interventions took place on 6 June during a debate on naval pensions. He brought the discussion round to one of his favourite topics: Greenwich Hospital pensions. He declared that the seamen who had paid 6d a month had been 'robbed'. Nobody knew how much money had gone into the fund: 'was [it] £2,000,000 or £8,000,000', he asked. Was the House on tenterhooks as they heard of the poor seamen who had been deprived of their pensions? Macnamara brought the House to its senses by reminding Beresford that the six-penny reductions had ceased in 1834 – seventy-nine years earlier. 'That does not make any difference', replied Beresford.

Beresford was on better form in the victualing debate on the same day, when Colonel Arthur Lee spoke on the Navy's rum ration, saying he objected to 'subsidising personal habits'. Beresford then gave the House a learned discourse on rum in the Navy. It was not the rum ration that caused drunkenness, he argued, but the rum that teetotallers did not take up. The nine-sixteenths of a penny that the Admiralty offered for forgoing the ration was too small to be worth taking. In practice, Beresford said, 'It goes into the mess, and other men get the advantage of it.' He continued: 'If you gave the men who do not want the rum a fair price, it would go a long way to encourage temperance.' It was a fine example of Beresford's skilled use of his knowledge of the arcane details of naval practice.

After another week of yachting, Beresford was in the House for the *Government of Ireland Bill* on 10 June. He once more declared his willingness to commit treasonable acts should Home Rule be forced on Ulster:

> 'I am an Ulster man, born and bred. My boyhood was spent in Ulster, and I have spent my life in the British service. The breath of my life has been discipline – to obey orders or to give orders. I will say this, however, that if the Government send troops over to Ireland I shall offer my services to my countrymen, even at my age, and poor though my services may be.'

On 4 July Beresford visited the Imperial Scout Exhibition in Birmingham and spoke to the assembled boys. He praised them for their 'zeal and enthusiasm' and said that the way to get rid of hooliganism was 'to teach lads to do something useful'. Then he presented, as a prize, his old sextant, which he had had since 1859. Ten days later, and fifty-four years since Beresford had left school, his former teacher, Montague Foster died. At Foster's Naval Academy he had taught both Beresford and Scott of the Antarctic.

Around the time of Foster's death, Lord Midleton (the ennobled St John Brodrick, a leading Conservative) received a request from Beresford to join the Unionist Party front bench. When Midleton passed on the request to Bonar Law, he remarked that 'I cannot understand the suggestion from one who acts as a free lance.' This is the only occasion when Beresford is known to have openly sought office, as opposed to having conspired to gain it.

If Beresford's hopes of the front bench were fanciful, his harassment of Churchill was real. When the shipbuilding vote came up for debate, Beresford made a long and detailed attack on the First Lord over the Navy's increasing use of oil in ships: 'we have up to now depended upon coal which we could produce, but now we are going to depend on oil, which we cannot produce'. Nor did the Admiralty have adequate storage facilities. Churchill, he said, 'has not put up his store tanks in sufficient numbers'. Even if there had been the storage capacity

Slowing down 1913

Beresford was still concerned about relying on oil from Romania and Mexico. He trusted the government of neither country.

Not content with this onslaught, Beresford wrote to the press on 20 July with a brutal attack on Churchill and his Admiralty administration. He declared that 'The authority of the Board has been usurped by one man.' There was no evidence in the rest of the letter that Churchill had usurped his powers or ignored his Board. All he seems to have done is to have taken decisions that Beresford disagreed with.

* * *

Beresford lost interest in the Commons during the rest of the year. In September the results for the year's yacht racing were announced. Beresford and a Mr Baird had raced *Bunty* 51 times, coming first on seven occasions, second on twelve occasions and third on eight occasions. Then it was on to Balmoral where for ten days or so Beresford was a guest of the King. He attended the Braemar Gathering (at which he was 'a prominent figure'), took part in a Balmoral ball and watched a royal command performance of *The Headmaster*.

Shortly after his intimacies with the Monarch, Beresford went off to join his anti-Home Rule colleagues in Ulster to make plans for a provisional government. This would seize power and declare independence, should the British government ever impose Home Rule on Ulster. Beresford willingly joined this proposed insurrection and became a member of the Volunteer Committee. One wonders what the King made of all this.

In October the Weymouth Town Council discussed the fact that Beresford had still not taken up their 1909 offer of the freedom of the borough. They had invited him to a public banquet in 1910 'but the date was inconvenient and Lord Charles promised to communicate later'. They were still awaiting his call. Beresford was abashed when he read of this in *The Times* and promptly wrote to express his 'great regret'. He could not recall any offer of another date. His letter, though, was so ambiguous, that the Council could not work out whether Beresford still wished to take up the honour.

On home territory in late October Beresford told his constituents that 'Ulster was terribly in earnest' against Home Rule. She would 'arm one hundred thousand men to prevent it'. 'Did Mr Asquith,' he asked, 'seriously think that our soldiers and sailors would advance light-heartedly against a people whose flag was the Union Jack?' He again spoke on Home Rule at Reading on 1 November. Confident that the Unionists, who had rejected Home Rule in 1886 and 1893, would do so again, he said that 'the English would not desert them [Ulster] in their hour of trial'.

From mid-November 1913 to mid-February 1914 Beresford disappeared from public life. In part this was the result of Lady Charles' health. As he told Lady Londonderry, 'I am told to take her away.' They left for Turin and the Riviera on 21 November. A month later Beresford had returned to shoot at Hall Barn, the home of Lord Burnham. He had perhaps taken the trouble to come back because the King was shooting there as well. He returned to Cannes before the year end and remained (with one short trip home) until 6 February. Lady Charles followed in March. This leisurely existence was all part of Beresford slowing down, although war was to bring great changes to his life.

Chapter 26
Last days of peace 1914

Early in 1914, Bonar Law received a letter from Almeric Paget (rear-commodore of the Royal Thames Yacht Club) about the state of Beresford's morale. Beresford was, he told Law, 'disturbed in his mind' at the way 'he is ignored by the powers that be ... in all matters referring to Naval Policy'. Only the Ulster question prevented him from resigning. Another sign of Beresford's depressed state comes in a letter that he wrote to a Mr Vesey later that month. He had been shocked to find that Arthur Lee had announced that the Unionist Party intended to support Churchill at the Admiralty. After delivering a long diatribe against Churchill's reign and forecasting that 'there will be panic bye and bye' Beresford declared 'In these circumstances you can quite see that my loyalty to the Party will prevent me speaking anywhere, as, if I did, I would bring out the whole facts.'

When Beresford finally returned to political life it was to attend an Ulster Association banquet on 11 February. He was asked how military men in Ireland should act if civil war broke out and replied 'As long as you are under the pennant and under the colours obey your orders – and Ulster will understand.' This was the opposite of what he had said only a few months ago, which was perhaps a sign of just how difficult the Ulster question was to be.

Beresford was then put out of action by an attack of flu and had to cancel his attendance at a Primrose League demonstration in Portsmouth. On 18 February he was well enough to attend the Commons. His illness then recurred, causing a United Empire Club dinner in his honour to be postponed. He also had, yet again, to put off his receipt of the Freedom of Weymouth. Indeed, he told Law on 2 March that he and his wife were still 'seriously ill with influenza'.

* * *

On 20 March fifty-seven army officers based at the Curragh Camp in Ireland resigned their commissions to avoid being ordered to take up arms to enforce Home Rule on Ulster. We shall not go into the muddles and confusions that led up to this incident, which has been so fully explored elsewhere. Suffice it to say that Asquith declared the affair to be a misunderstanding and the men were quickly reinstated, while the Secretary of State for War, Colonel Seely, lost his office.

Beresford saw a chance for mischief. Towards the end of March he told the press that he knew 'for a fact' that 'many naval officers' would 'resign their commissions' if they were called upon 'to take part in coercing Ulster'. Indeed, he added, they would resign 'even if the army is alone used for this purpose'. It was a typical Beresford statement, purporting to speak for others yet not providing any evidence to support his claim. But it was Churchill's actions that most drew his attention.

Curragh Camp – seat of the 'mutiny' in 1914

During the alarm over the loyalty of the British troops in Ireland, the Cabinet had taken various precautions, including moving some naval ships into the Irish Sea. Beresford wanted to know the details. He asked Churchill in the Commons :

> 'Whether a battle squadron was ordered to proceed home with dispatch from Spanish waters; whether the order was cancelled by wireless one night during the passage home of this squadron; whether a flotilla of destroyers was ordered to proceed with dispatch to Lamlash or the North of Ireland; whether the order was cancelled by wireless during the passage of these vessels to their destination; whether His Majesty's ship *King Edward VII* and her sister ships were ordered to embark field guns; whether these orders were subsequently cancelled; whether he will state to the House what was the emergency which necessitated these orders being given; whether he will state to the House why the orders were countermanded; and whether the orders were given originally by the Board of Admiralty as a Board or by his own authority?'

Churchill confirmed that the Cabinet had ordered the squadron under Vice Admiral Lewis Bayly to go to Lamlash so that it 'would be in proximity to the coasts of Ireland in case of serious disorders

Last days of peace 1914

occurring'. The order (which Churchill read out) had been sent on 19 March. Two days later, said Churchill, 'when it was clear that the precautionary movements of troops to the various depots had been carried out without opposition' the order was rescinded. As for the field guns, these had been requested by Bayly 'for exercising his men on shore at Lamlash if the weather was bad'. Bayly's memoirs make clear that he had asked for the guns on his own initiative at a time when he had no knowledge of the feared insurrection.

Beresford had called the offer of special arrangements for the Curragh Army officers 'outrageous'. Despite this, the next day he asked whether, since 'an assurance has been given to certain officers and regiments in the Regular Army that they would not be employed against Ulster, a similar assurance will be given that the Fleet or ships of the Fleet shall not be so employed?' Churchill replied with words that could as well have come from Beresford: 'Sir, the officers and men of His Majesty's Navy are expected to obey without question orders which reach them through the proper channels from lawfully constituted authority.'

Nothing would silence Beresford on the subject and he spoke twice in April. On the first occasion he bizarrely accused Churchill of planning to use battleships to defend land-based munitions dumps. On the second he attempted to prove that the ministers concerned had acted improperly over the Curragh affair.

It was only a small step for Beresford to move from his indignation over the Curragh incident to his own proposed participation in Ulster's insurrection. In the Commons towards the end of April he admitted that 'we have broken the law' by running guns into Ulster but this had been justified because 'there was a plot to surround us with the most enormous number of military men and to cow us into submission to the Home Rule Bill'. Had he spoken these words outside the Commons he would no doubt have been arrested.

* * *

During the weeks that were dominated by the Curragh incident, Beresford also attended two anti-Home Rule demonstrations. On 4 April there was a huge 'no coercion' demonstration in Hyde Park, at which, according to the *Manchester Guardian*, he was 'cheered so much that he could hardly get a word in edgeways' but he did manage to declare that the *Home Rule Bill* was 'the most cowardly plot and intrigue that had ever been concocted'. It had all been 'organized by Mr Winston Churchill, the Lilliput Napoleon'. He was 'a danger to the

State'. Ten days later Beresford was at a 'No Surrender' demonstration in Belfast. In the same week he went to Antrim Castle for the presentation of colours to two battalions and attended a review of the North Belfast Regiment. This unusual interest in the Army was perhaps his way of emphasising his loyalty while at the same time plotting a rebellion against the Crown.

After attending the Royal Academy Banquet and a dance given by Lord Curzon on 4 May, Beresford was present at a lunch for the retired Admiral Bosanquet on 7 May. He then went to Manchester to speak once more on Home Rule. Beresford introduced himself as 'an Irishman, a loyal Irishman, and an Ulsterman'. Asquith, he said, was faced 'with civil war in Ulster if Home Rule is passed, and civil war in the rest of Ireland if it is not'. This was 'the gravest indictment of the Government'. He then let rip at Churchill and the government. The former was the man who organized the 'wicked and cowardly plot'. This he had done 'out of frenzy and vindictiveness because Ulster would not listen to him'.

In this hectic round of anti-Home Rule activities, Beresford found time to attend a Covent Garden gala performance for the King and Queen of Norway. He then set off for Weymouth where, five years one month and eighteen days after the town had offered him the freedom of its borough, he finally received the honour.

The long hot summer of 1914 continued for Beresford as he proceeded from one anti-Home Rule event to another. Mid-June found him on Woodhouse Moor in Leeds, where 30,000 people gathered to hear him, the Duke of Norfolk and Lord Milner (the ex-High Commissioner for South Africa) speak. When Sir Mark Sykes (MP for Hull Central) attempted to address the crowd, the platform was besieged by Irish Nationalists singing, shouting and throwing stones. The platform party had to be hurried off to safety as they were overwhelmed from the rear. Women fainted and injured men were carried off in ambulances. Beresford, who was the biggest draw at the event, was able to speak without interruption. The day was so chaotic, though, that the reporter failed to record what he said or the wording of the resolution passed by the throng.

* * *

And then the world changed. On 28 June the Austrian Archduke Ferdinand and his Duchess were assassinated in Sarajevo. *The Times* remarked that 'The political effects of the tragedy of Sarajevo can only be broadly surmised.' It is not therefore surprising that Beresford's

Last days of peace 1914

letter drawing attention to the 'appalling catastrophe towards which we have been drifting for over two years' made no reference to Balkan politics. He, like the Cabinet would for the next month see Ulster as the looming catastrophe, and not the ambitions of the Triple Alliance. In a letter that was weak on logic, he said 'There must be a General Election or civil war ... The issue must be Home Rule and separation or the maintenance of the Union.' Neither choice was an option. Indeed, each of the three possible government moves (Home Rule, Home Rule excluding Ulster, and the status quo) had enough do or die opponents to render it unthinkable.

When the government proposed the purchase of a controlling interest in the Anglo-Persian Oil Company (now BP) in July Beresford raged against what he termed a 'gambling transaction ... [for] which we have no security whatever' since 'the First Lord of the Admiralty himself acknowledged that the Mediterranean route might ... be blocked and we should have to send the oil ... round by the Cape'. He thought the cost was too high and he wanted to hear more about Churchill's proposals for the defence of the supply route. Despite his arguments, a mere 48 MPs voted against the purchase, which went ahead with a majority of 180. It turned out to be one of the best investments ever made by a British government.

***

On 10 July, with war now three weeks away, Beresford, along with most of the Navy, still saw only a minor role for submarines. They were important, he told the North East Coast Institution of Engineers and Shipbuilders, but were useful for 'defence rather than attack'. A submarine was limited because '[it] could only operate by day and in clear weather, and it was practically useless in misty weather'. Then there was the health aspect. He declared that a week in a submarine 'got to the bottom of the health of the officers and men'. How would they fare in war, he asked. Further, 'there was great anxiety as to whether they were going to sink a friend'.

***

And so, as Europe hurtled towards war, Beresford, along with his 40 million compatriots innocently carried on their daily lives. On 13 July he went over to Ireland to attend an Orange gathering at Portrush, with 500 uniformed volunteers ready to face the enemy – the British, not the Germans. Lady Charles attended a production of *Don Giovanni* on the same day. Then Beresford returned from Ireland in time for a State Ball on 17 July. Two days later he was at a Unionist garden party at Panshanger, the holiday home of the socialite Lady Desborough. On 29 July, he found himself in Lichfield, where he unveiled a statue of Commander E J Smith, the captain of the *Titanic*. Noting that 'Europe might be on the eve of one of the greatest catastrophes which the world had ever seen' he praised the mercantile marine and 'men like Captain Smith'. Britain and the Navy could count on them to show the 'same grit and pluck and devotion to duty as those who went down in the Titanic'.

Beresford (standing right) unveiling the statue to Commander Smith six days before the start of the Great War

Meanwhile, since the hour of the Archduke's assassination, the Prime Minister and the Cabinet had wrestled almost night and day with the Ulster problem. Even as late as 24 July Asquith, writing to his young lady friend, Venetia Stanley, said of the approaching war in Europe: 'Happily there seems to be no reason why we should be anything more than spectators.' On 3 August – just ten days later – Sir Edward Grey stood up in the Commons and, under the guise of surveying the European situation, made it clear that he saw war as inevitable if the German Army crossed into Belgium. The next day, Britain was at war with Germany.

Last days of peace 1914

On 3 August Beresford issued a press statement calling for Britain (or England, as he put it) to enter the war. Without explaining what he meant, he said that 'the future safety of the Empire depends upon the decision arrived at by Parliament to-day'. The sole justification that he gave for Britain entering the war was that 'if we break the *Entente Cordiale* and desert France in her dire necessity ... we shall be false to those who have placed implicit faith in our moral pledges'. What those moral pledges were, he did not say but his statement suggests that, like so many of his fellow countrymen, he thought the *Entente Cordiale* was a treaty of alliance. Had he read it, he would have discovered that it merely dealt with the colonial interests of the two countries in Egypt, Morocco, Newfoundland, Africa and Asia. There was not a word about Europe or home waters. Hardly a compact that would justify Armageddon.

Chapter 27
The arrival of war 1914

Unknown to the public and to most members of Parliament, the Committee for Imperial Defence had, for years, been preparing plans for the defence of Britain in the event of war. These were not plans to *make* war but plans to survive the consequences of an attack on land or at sea. Its pages and pages of orders were put into action in the first few days of war. Grey announced the setting up of a state insurance scheme for shipping on the day war was declared. Asquith next announced plans for a system for the distribution of food. Beresford welcomed this saying it should 'start at once' and include 'food and coal' as 'contraband of war'. The following day McKenna announced new powers to control aliens during the war. Those who contravened the regulations could be fined or imprisoned for up to six months. Showing more foresight than most of his countrymen, Beresford asked 'Is it decreed that these aliens are to come out after six months? War might not be over and they might give an immense amount of information.' This was not to be the last of Beresford's interest in aliens. Indeed he was to be obsessed by them.

Another early war requirement was money. On 7 August Parliament was asked to vote a credit of £100m for the costs of the war to 31 March 1915. The sum – which seemed large at the time – was woefully inadequate and, by 31 March 1915 the government had had to ask for a total of £362,000,000. Showing his capacity to move from grand strategy to the life of the common people, Beresford used the occasion to urge once more the better pensions for widows.

* * *

As the country mobilized for war there was no call for Beresford's services. There was not even the offer of a minor committee nor an obscure advisory post, let alone one of high strategy that he thought he deserved. But Beresford did not intend to be idle during the war. He threw himself into a flurry of voluntary work which placed a heavy toll on his health. At various times he claimed to be the chairman or president of eight to twelve committees. He acquired the first of these in the second week of the war. It was to coordinate the use of voluntary hospitals for taking in wounded soldiers. (In those days, with no National Health Service, most hospitals were independent charitable institutions, each with its own financial and admissions procedures.)

The arrival of war 1914

After years of condemning McKenna for his alleged system of espionage in the Navy, on 23 August Beresford encouraged McKenna to close down another system of espionage. Was the Home Office aware, he asked in the Commons, of the 'growing feeling of irritation against those Germans in this country who are suspected of being spies'? Was McKenna going to take action before places like Portsmouth 'take the law into their own hands'? When McKenna limited his answer to deploring such vigilante action, Beresford pressed him once more, calling for 'stringent measures' from the government. McKenna dissembled, referring to the 'unfounded rumours' and the fact that the police had produced 'no evidence of actual malpractice'. Any action would be 'premature'.

After only a month of war Beresford had begun to contemplate taking revenge on Germany after the war. Speaking at a recruiting campaign in Yorkshire on 8 September he looked forward to 'a day of reckoning' when Germany would pay 'for the brutality of her methods by land and sea'. Perhaps recalling his own intention to be chivalrous towards the Russians in 1904, he lamented that Germany 'had not even the chivalry of the old-time buccaneers and filibusters'.

* * *

In early October Beresford's memoirs were published. The *Times Literary Supplement* gave the book a gentle review and recommended it for 'the lighter side' of his life, which showed him 'as an Irishman and a sportsman'. Readers would discover 'many treasures' such as his racy stories of electioneering at Waterford and the pranks he played on London Society. The *Manchester Guardian* noted that 'for some reason Lord Charles Beresford's account of the days of sailing ships and the great men who manned them is the most interesting part of the book'. What the reviewer did not note was that, the more Beresford's career developed, the less he had to say. His great commands were reduced to a few paltry pages. His mighty clashes with Fisher and Scott went unmentioned. Nevertheless the publishers were justified in describing the book as 'long and anxiously awaited' and were not far off the mark when they claimed that it was '*the* book of the autumn'. For the *Daily Mail* Beresford's 'record [of] spirited adventure' and his 'entertaining stories' could not 'easily be surpassed'. Contemporary comment was generous. From today's perspective it is difficult not to carp over his errors, omissions and deliberate obfuscations.

The arrival of war 1914

* * *

On August 28 Beresford, in the full hearing of other members of the Carlton Club, delivered a vicious racist attack on the First Sea Lord. The members had been talking about German spies, when Beresford declared that '*all* Germans, including highly placed ones, ought to leave the country as they were in close touch with Germans abroad'. Arthur Lee, who witnessed the outrage, told Churchill that Beresford had said that Battenberg should resign since 'nothing could alter the fact that he is a *German* ... [and] keeps German servants and has his property in Germany'. This led to a strong reprimand from Churchill, but no disciplinary action was taken.

However, Beresford had not been alone in his determination to drive out Battenberg. At the end of October the newspapers announced that the Prince had resigned, citing his 'birth and parentage' as impairments to his role. But it was not Beresford whom Churchill called on to fill the gap: it was Fisher. What an irony that as one adversary walked out of Admiralty House, another, already once ejected, walked back in. It was in a sense the final verdict of the 1909 Enquiry: the country had no use for the accuser, but recalled the accused to arms. As if Fisher's appointment was not hurtful enough, the *Manchester Guardian* had the effrontery to quote Beresford's own words in support of the appointment. Citing his memoirs, the paper recalled Beresford's high praise for Fisher's work in the Mediterranean.

* * *

It was on the day of Fisher's appointment that Beresford spoke in public for the first time on the subject of aliens. He told an audience in Chesterfield that 'we must intern the lot of them'. He saw no injustice in this and declared internment 'necessary for our safety'.

Beresford's attacks on aliens were quickly followed by his appointment to two new committees. The first was the Ladies' Emergency Committee set up by the Navy League, with which Beresford was now reconciled. In a letter to *The Times* he appealed for 'warm clothing and other comforts' for men in ships in home waters. The second was the British Ambulance Committee, which was established to raise funds to send cars to France for use as ambulances.

No one could dispute the value of Beresford's committees nor his selfless pursuit of their high aims. But he had no such constructive approach to war policy and was persistently unhelpful in his attacks on the government. One of his first Commons' clashes of the war illustrates his style. The topic under discussion was the torpedoing of three old armoured cruisers – the *Aboukir, Hogue* and *Crecy* – in the North Sea on 22 September. Beresford was soon telling anyone who would listen that the ships were 'lost on account of information given from this country to the German Admiralty'. In the Commons McKenna criticised Beresford for these remarks. Beresford retorted 'I should not have said it if I did not believe it.' When McKenna enlarged on what Beresford had said, Beresford interjected 'Will the right hon. Gentleman quote my words?' McKenna quoted Beresford as having said 'That is a monstrous thing, and it should be stopped.' He went on to say that he would invite public meetings all over the country to compel the Home Office to do its duty and prevent such a thing happening again.' The truth about their sinking could not be told until after the War. The three old, slow and defenceless ships had been left on patrol in a place where they were in full view of German patrols. Churchill discovered this on 17 September and the next day he ordered their removal. The dilatory Battenberg took no action. Three days later the ships were sunk by German torpedoes.

A British Ambulance Committee vehicle

Because the East Coast was under the supervision of the military, Beresford's remarks had been referred to the Director of Public Prosecutions. The Director, said McKenna, had written to Beresford to ask him for his evidence. 'The Noble Lord's reply was that he had no information.' When Beresford challenged this, McKenna read from his reply to the Director: 'There were certain aspects of the occurrence of which I spoke which conclusively appeared to me to justify my remarks.' When asked a second time to provide details, he replied 'I have been so busy since I received your letter that I have not had an opportunity of answering it.'

There was a brief pause in Beresford's spy-mania on 21 November when he turned up at Downing Street to lecture Asquith on his conduct of the war. It was, said Asquith, 'a most boring conversation ... with all the obvious criticisms'.

On 23 November Beresford once more spoke about spies. This time he wanted the government 'to legalise vigilance committees' made up of 'older men not likely to be carried away by panic or excitement'. McKenna replied on behalf of Asquith, saying that such committees 'would tend to hamper rather than to assist their inquiries', which were necessarily secret in nature.

In a Consolidated Funds Bill debate on 26 November, Beresford harassed McKenna again over his handling of aliens and spies. He wanted McKenna to lock up (or hand over to the military authorities for internment) every alien in sight. 'That there are spies everybody knows.' McKenna was taking insufficient precautions and was 'always asking for evidence'. He then turned his attention to naturalised citizens. These, Beresford said, were 'far more dangerous' than the those not naturalised. They could 'get into a number of places in society and military, naval, and Governmental circles' and could use their position, wealth and education to collect information. McKenna refused to accept that he was failing to act over aliens and told the Commons that, in the Metropolitan area alone, 120,000 cases had been investigated – an average of over 1,000 cases a day – and '342 persons have been interned'. Even the cases of those interned lacked sufficient evidence to prosecute.

As the year drew to a close, Beresford again took up the issues of reprisals and spies. Reprisals came up at a recruiting meeting on 3 December in Darlington, where he shared a platform with the Labour Party leader Arthur Henderson MP. He spoke passionately about the 'barbarous methods' but he was against reprisals 'of a brutal character'. Rather he hoped that the British would show their 'undoubted chivalry' at the war's end.

As to spies, Beresford told Lady Londonderry on 18 December that he was planning public meetings '*of protest re spies*', who, he was convinced, were assisting the Germans in their East Coast raids. There followed a long attack on the failures of the Navy, and he concluded 'I have the *right to speak* after my warnings.' It was a sad letter, revealing his bitter resentment at not being called to some high office in a national emergency.'

The arrival of war 1914

Meanwhile Lady Beresford grumbled about the lack of an official post for her husband: 'How disgracefully they treat him' she told Lady Londonderry.

Chapter 28
Goodbye to the Commons 1915

In early January Beresford and Carson visited Hartlepool to seek evidence that the German raids on east coast ports in 1914 had been the Admiralty's fault. They do not appear to have pursued this further, but within days Beresford had switched to the loss of HMS *Formidable* on 1 January after being struck by two German torpedoes.

Without access to the details of the incident Beresford wrote to the press to denounce the loss. It was all the fault of the Admiralty for allowing heavy ships to go to sea without destroyers. 'It is unpardonable that officers and men should be thus gratuitously exposed to conditions in which they are sent to the bottom without a shot being fired' he wrote. In the Commons two days later he demanded that someone should be court-martialled for this loss: 'The country ought to know by whose authority this great Act has been abrogated.' He received no answer other than the Civil Lord to the Admiralty pointing out that there was no obligation to hold a court martial. Behind the scenes the Admiralty quietly moved Vice Admiral Bayly from the Channel Fleet. It was his neglect to take precautions against submarines that had led to the loss of the *Formidable*.

It was in January 1915 that Beresford's relentless attacks on the government and the Admiralty began to draw criticism. The *Manchester Guardian* noted that he was 'the only retired officer in either service who has held high position who thinks it proper in time of war to write a letter to a newspaper criticising the Admiralty and those in command of the fleets'. This may explain why Beresford approached Long around this time to bemoan the way the party ignored him on naval matters. Long, writing to the Tory Party leader Bonar Law, suggested that it would be a kindness 'to invite him to any discussion you may have on the Navy'. Law's reaction is not known.

* * *

Having pronounced on one of the big issues of the war Beresford spent March on the sort of minutiae that so appealed to him, when he once more pressed for reprisals against German officers. He asked the Prime Minister 'to treat as pirates all those caught in the act of sinking undefended vessels without any attempt to rescue life and publicly hang them, according to the universal practice'. A joint threat from the allied governments 'to take action against the German piratical policy' was

Goodbye to the Commons 1915

what was needed, he said. Then he turned to aliens and called for a harsher approach. In Germany, he told the Commons, 'every British subject is interned', whatever his age or state of health. Once interned, they were 'ill-used, insulted, and ill-fed'. Yet in Britain aliens were 'looked after in every possible way, and made much of'. Indeed, they were even 'allowed all over the place after they are interned'.

In the same speech he attacked the British government's treatment of dead German officers. He wanted to know how it was that the captain of the German cruiser *Blücher* had been given 'an honourable military funeral'. He had, said Beresford, been 'instrumental in killing and wounding 388 women and children'. The funeral, he added, was 'particularly offensive to those who have lost their wives and children by these piratical acts'. (Beresford had clearly forgotten that in 1899 he had complained that Kitchener had not buried the Mahdi 'in an honourable manner'.) The matter was not pursued as the debate moved back to its main subject of aliens.

* * *

One reason why Beresford was less engaged with the large issues of the war was that no one asked for his opinions. That did not stop him from offering them. Six years after his letter of 2 April 1909 to Asquith that had precipitated the 1909 Enquiry, Beresford sent the Prime Minister ten typescript pages about the war. He began by reminding Asquith of the earlier letter. This had led to the Enquiry, which had 'confirmed my statements in all important particulars'. Then, he reminded Asquith of a letter he had sent him on 27 July 1911 'after you made a speech of intense gravity in the House of Commons'. This letter, Beresford said, had included eight suggestions for immediate action. These 'weaknesses' Beresford claimed 'were at once taken in hand'. Having established the pivotal role that his advice had played in directing Admiralty policy over the last seven years, Beresford confidently plunged into a long critique of the Admiralty's recent performance. The odd thing about the letter was that everything in it had already been said by Beresford in the Commons. Why he thought criticisms and advice not accepted in that forum would be accepted now is hard to fathom. It was just the usual litany: the delay in creating a war staff, the shortage of small craft, the lack of cruisers, and so on. Only in one particular did the letter contain a piece of sound advice that Asquith was not receiving from elsewhere: the need to convoy merchant ships. The resistance of the Admiralty and many merchant seamen to convoys carried a heavy cost until convoys were started in 1917 at the insistence of Lloyd George. But Beresford had cried wolf too often. Asquith sent a brief reply and filed the letter.

Another aspect of the war that Beresford took an interest in was the naval attack on the Dardanelles. In a letter of 17 April to Leopold Maxse, Editor of the *National Review*, he said that Churchill had 'against the advice of the Admiralty (and I believe Kitchener) forced the naval attack' at the Dardanelles. Doubtless this was a common story at the time. The truth is that both Kitchener and Asquith were enthusiastic supporters of the Dardanelles operation, as the War Council minutes show. There had been no need to pressure them. Indeed it was Kitchener who had asked Churchill to initiate the naval bombardment of the forts in a letter of 2 January 1915. The myth that the operation was a hare-brained scheme of Churchill's was put around by his enemies and has stuck to this day. So, when Beresford told Maxse that 'Churchill is a serious danger to the State' he was, for once, not alone in his views. His temper was not assuaged by the fact that both Scott and Bacon had been recalled to duty: 'so we got all the old lot back at the Admiralty'. (The full evidence of the extent to which the Dardanelles operation was a War Council operation rather than a Churchill one can be found in Freeman, R. 2013.)

Warships firing on the Dardanelles

Exactly what Beresford really thought about the Dardanelles campaign is difficult to grasp. According to his wife he thoroughly approved of it since '[it] may hasten end of War'. Yet at Portsmouth on 1 May he publicly described it as 'a piece of amateur strategy'. This remark led a Mr A G Powell to write in protest to the *Observer*. He noted that Beresford had been speaking at a recruiting meeting, and asked: 'Does he hope to enlist men to fight by first telling them they will have to serve under "amateur strategists"?'

* * *

Beresford took a particular interest in the British prisoners of war held in Germany, receiving many letters about their fate from their friends and relatives. He told the Commons on 27 April that these letters were 'heart-breaking'. British prisoners were being starved and both officers and men were crying out 'For God's sake send me bread!' The men, Beresford added, were suffering 'brutalities' and their 'greatcoats, tunics, and so forth' were being taken from them. There was, he continued, 'a deliberate attempt to starve our people' and to ruin their health by putting them 'in unhealthy surroundings where they are certain to contract consumption, with the result that they will die when the summer comes'. A few days later he wrote to *The Times* complaining that prisoners received 'devilish treatment, cowardly and malicious ill-usage' and were 'forced to do filthy and disgusting jobs'. They were 'clubbed with rifles, fired at, bayoneted in the arms and legs [and] spat upon'. He added 'When prisoners die there is no inquiry.' It is hard to make any sense of this since the prisoners themselves would never have been allowed to report such maltreatment in letters home. Beresford seems to have accepted as the truth every wild rumour that reached him.

At Portsmouth two days later Beresford suggested that the British government should round up 'the rich German aliens' and take them hostage. He added 'When the war was over every responsible German, should be tried by court martial and punished if found guilty.' A few days later he took another swipe at what he saw as the government's soft treatment of aliens. He referred to the Donington Hall camp in Leicestershire, where he considered the facilities and regime too well-appointed. (They were remarkably well-appointed.) 'Do you think the Germans are grateful?' he asked the Commons. Three days later he piled the pressure on with a petition to Parliament 'to free our country from the menace of the alien in our midst', which had been signed by 250,000 women.

Beresford's despicable attitude to anyone with any connection with Germany took a new and vicious turn on 13 May. Speaking at a Mansion House meeting he asked 'Why does Haldane occupy his position?' Richard Haldane had been Lord Chancellor since 1912. Before that he had been Leader of the House of Lords and previously had been arguably the finest War Minister Britain has ever seen. So why did Beresford want him out? Solely because Haldane had studied in Germany and was a fluent German speaker. This, according to Beresford, made Haldane one of 'the most dangerous enemies in our midst'. These were, he said 'the rich, independent, naturalized Germans of high social position'. He added 'Every German throughout the whole Empire should now be considered an enemy.' Did Beresford think Haldane was a German? That is hard to credit since Haldane was a son of a wealthy Scottish family, with a seat at Cloanden. Down the years the family had played a distinguished part in British military and naval life.

The luxurious conditions of the Donington Hall Camp

It was now time for one of the war's surprises, although Beresford missed it by paying a brief visit to France, where he spent eight days in his capacity of Chairman of the British Ambulance Committee. (At that time his Committee had 120 ambulances in operation.)

On Saturday 15 May Fisher had arrived at his office at his usual early hour. He found on his desk some draft telegrams from Churchill to the naval commander at the Dardanelles. For the last few weeks Fisher had been increasingly concerned both about the ships being risked at the Dardanelles and Churchill's predilection for taking over the work of the sea lords. Fisher cracked and resigned on the spot. After penning his resignation letter he walked out of Admiralty House and disappeared. By Monday the opposition had spotted their chance to demand that Asquith form a coalition government. By Thursday 19 May the deal was done and Churchill and Fisher were both out, being replaced by Arthur Balfour and Admiral Sir Henry Jackson respectively.

When Beresford returned home at the end of May he found that his Unionist friends were in office. Bonar Law, despite being Leader of the party, had accepted the derisory post of Colonial Secretary. Walter Long had taken the Local Government Board and Carson was now Attorney-General. No one had thought of securing Beresford an office during his absence.

Goodbye to the Commons 1915

* * *

Having failed to benefit from the coalition upheavals, Beresford had to look elsewhere to bolster his diminishing influence. An obvious start would be a peerage. Off he went to lobby Balfour. He complained, Balfour told Asquith, that he had been 'extremely ill-used' by 'all persons in high place'. It was 'essential to his honour' that he be given a chance to 'explain to the public how right he has been in all the advice ... he has given to successive Governments'. Beresford asked that he be given a peerage so that he could speak in the Lords on the Admiralty's behalf. Balfour baulked at such a formal role. It would 'revive all the old Fisher-Beresford rows' but he supported the idea of a peerage. In reply Asquith acquiesced in the distasteful act of conferring a peerage on a man who had caused him so much tribulation.

* * *

Although Asquith yielded over the peerage, Beresford did not know that it had been approved, telling Law that 'My present position is foul.' After being extremely active in the first half of 1915 Beresford suddenly gave up the Commons and his public speaking. There is some evidence to show that this was deliberate. When he was invited to speak at a rally of the Central Committee for National Patriotic Organisations on 4 August, he declined, saying 'I do not intend to speak anywhere at the moment. If my advice had been taken, there would be no war.' Further evidence of his sense of rejection comes from a letter he wrote the next day to the American journalist Ralph Blumenfeld, in which he said that '[I have] only two strong supporters ... in the press.' (These were Blumenfeld at the *Daily Express* and Howell Gwynne at *The Standard*.) What is unclear was the exact reason for his withdrawal. Was it despair? Or had his bombastic self-confidence been pricked? Whatever the reason, after speaking in the Commons 136 times between January and May, he vanished from the political scene. His next speech was on 14 October and there were only three further interventions during the rest of the year.

Beresford had an attack of gout in August but was able to write to the press to demand that cotton be made contraband of war: 'had cotton been declared contraband in February the war would now be approaching the closing scenes'. There was little the government could do to fend off such attacks since they could not publicly admit the reason for their actions. The fact was that many in the United States of

America were ready to declare war on Britain if American exports were blocked in this way.

Later that same month Beresford signed a manifesto appealing for national service. In October he provided an advertising puff for a new book by William Le Queux called *The Devil's Spawn*. Le Queux was notorious for using his literary skills to create invasion and other scares, one of his most infamous books being *The Invasion of 1910*, published in 1906. Le Queux's irresponsible writings never bothered Beresford, who welcomed the new book, saying: '[It] shows how completely naturalized Germans and alien enemies have managed to work themselves into every department of the State of Italy.'

* * *

In November Beresford made his last speech in the Commons, choosing appropriately the Board of Admiralty as his topic. He looked back to 1869 when Gladstone 'did away with the collective responsibility of the Board'. He reminded the House that it was Hamilton's dictatorial powers that had led to his own resignation in 1888. While under this system Churchill was 'quite within his right' to make policy, but such power was 'altogether wrong'. There were fewer scares, he argued, under the old system. He declared that there had been five panics in his time and 'he was instrumental in getting some of them up'. (This was a rare admission. He always accused others of causing scares; he merely drew attention to facts.)

Ostracised by those in power, Beresford wrote to *The Times* on 8 December with a forthright attack on the conduct of the war. He said that the country was 'in a complex tangle of muddle and mismanagement'. There was no 'objective or plan'. The war staffs, he declared, had not been consulted 'as to whether they had the means in men and material for enforcing the different policies inaugurated by the Cabinet'.

The following day a long article by *The Times* Military Correspondent, Charles À Court Repington, appeared in which he discussed the right method to criticise in time of war. He concluded that if the Cabinet 'for a day' allowed the military chiefs to run the war 'our affairs would be retrieved'. Perhaps the article's appearance was mere coincidence. But it is more likely that Repington and Beresford were in league against their joint enemy: the Cabinet. Repington had dined with the Beresfords on 30 November, visited them on 1 December and dined with them the night after his article appeared. The two men were not in total agreement, though, since a few days later Beresford told the poet

Goodbye to the Commons 1915

Edward Blakeney that 'we shall lose this war unless we get rid of the present Cabinet and place the affairs of State under business men'.

Chapter 29
In another place 1916

The new year of 1916 saw Beresford's elevation to the peerage as baron. Lord Charles Beresford had been transformed into Baron Beresford of Metemmeh and Curraghmore, Co Waterford. In turn, Lady Charles became Lady Beresford. In sending a farewell message to his constituents Beresford recalled his 22 years in the Commons, where he had battled for 'a sufficient and efficient Navy'. (It was typical of him to have stretched an actual 17 years 10 months to 22 years.) He assured them that 'I do not for one moment intend relaxing my efforts in these directions.' The Commons, declared the *Manchester Guardian*, had lost 'its last pinch of old authentic salt'.

Baron Beresford of Metemmeh and Curraghmore, Co Waterford

Towards the end of the year Beresford explained to the journalist Leopold Maxse that he had given up the Commons because 'on four separate occasions I convened meetings of Members … to put forward written proposals to be taken to the Prime Minister and sent to the Press' but the members who turned up were reluctant to criticise ministers.

In another place 1916

'The whole thing so disgusted me that when I was offered a Peerage, though it disrated me 9 places, I accepted it.' (Had he forgotten that he had *asked* for the peerage?)

Beresford celebrated his peerage quietly with a dinner with some friends on 7 January. No one of real note was there, other than the loyal Repington, who recorded that Beresford talked 'with shrewd good sense and much to the point'. Two days later Beresford and Repington were both staying at Coombe Abbey, where his peerage was discussed. Repington noted that some guests thought Beresford had erred in accepting an honour from Asquith 'whom he attacked so severely'.

***

On 12 January Sir Edward Carson called a meeting of the Constitutional Club to discuss the foundation of a new political party. Beresford and Maxse were amongst his most zealous supporters. Carson told the meeting that the country needed 'to wipe many things off the slate and make a fresh start'. Before the war, the country was 'living in a fool's paradise', lacking the means to defend itself and allowing foreigners to live in Britain and promote its defeat. Gwynne of *The Standard* proposed the formation of a national party to govern under 'some big man who never lies to the country', by which he meant Carson, not Beresford. He then set out a ten point policy which, apart from winning the war, included banning any German commercial activity in Britain for 25 years and, hilariously, declaring elections won by lies to be 'null and void'. The party would, of course, 'only have regard for the national good'. Beresford spoke in support of all this and confided that 'of the twenty-two members of the Government only one had the faintest idea what war meant'. He and the MP Colonel Page-Croft both suggested that 'the war should be placed in the control of a small body of military and naval experts'. For all the crankiness of the meeting, it did at least anticipate the formation of a War Council with full military representation.

***

Beresford took his seat in the Lords on 26 January, but did not speak until 22 February when he made a forceful attack on the ineffectiveness of the government's blockade policy. It was just 'a paper blockade'. If total blockade had been 'turned over to the Navy to enforce' then 'the war would have been over'. He roused their Lordships with his lively account of the products still reaching Germany: 'The Army in Flanders know perfectly well that we allowed fatty compounds, cotton, and metal

In another place 1916

ore to go into Germany. The Army in Flanders know perfectly well that most of the ammunition fired at them now need not have been there provided we had stopped the commodities that made it. They also know that this is not the way to conduct a war ... All commodities going into Germany should be made absolute contraband.'

* * *

Three weeks later Beresford spoke on the topic of aviation. He began by saying that the role of aircraft in the war had not been thought out and that aircraft had been bought with no thought to their purpose. This mattered because 'this new air warfare is going to be perhaps of so tremendous a character that it may supersede armies and navies'. However, Beresford could not agree with the proposal from Lord Montagu (a member of the Aircraft Committee) for an Air Minister: 'I do not think it will help the case', he said. Perceptively, he objected to a single air service because 'An air service is needed for the Army and another for the Navy' since their needs are 'totally different'. The same point applied, he said, when it came to manufacture. Planes for the Navy needed to be specified by sailors; those for the Army by soldiers.

While still able to make occasional contributions on important issues such as aerial warfare, much of Beresford's attention was now focused on minor matters. On 14 March he made an appeal for an end to taxing the income of officers. Although the Chancellor of the Exchequer had made concessions in the previous budget, serving officers still paid just over 1s 9½d (9 per cent) in the pound income tax. This, said Beresford, was 'very unfair' since, unlike civilians, 'officers ... are risking their lives in defence of the country'. He went on at great length, but the Duke of Devonshire offered no further concessions when he replied for the government.

Then it was back to aliens on 30 March, when Viscount Templeton proposed in the Lords that 'London should be at once declared a 'Prohibited Area' for aliens. Beresford keenly supported this but the Conservative Leader in the Lords, Lord Lansdowne, pointed out that making London a prohibited area 'would impose more work upon the police than was worthwhile'. It was also easier to keep an eye on aliens in London than when they were dispersed throughout the country.

After these diversions the Lords faced the serious question of conscription on 19 April. The motion to introduce conscription exposed violent disagreements within the Cabinet. Beresford, who was fully behind national service, remarked that 'the life of the country is far more valuable than the life of the Government'. He used their

In another place 1916

indecision on the issue as an excuse to attack their prevarications in general: 'The Government say that they cannot make up their minds on the question of recruiting. I wish respectfully to tell them that they have not made up their minds on any single question material to the war.' He urged the Lords to force a division so as to show that there were some people in the country 'who know what they want and how to get it'. Indecision won the day and the debate was adjourned.

On 3 May Beresford made a long and detailed speech about the losses of mercantile ships during the war. He estimated that, allowing for losses and ships commandeered by the Admiralty, there were now only 8853 vessels to do the work of the 11,353 before the war. Lord Curzon, who replied for the government could not reveal the true figures but reassured the Lords that the situation was 'serious', but no worse than that.

* * *

Beresford's contributions to political debate in the first half of 1916 had been dominated by contrived issues. Then came a spate of external events, which gave him a chance to comment on issues that forced themselves to the fore.

The first of these was the defeat of a British army at Kut in Mesopotamia on 29 April where 13,000 men had surrendered to the Turkish army after a long siege. In the Lords, Beresford asked Lord Kitchener for more details. Kitchener had no trouble in describing General Townshend's humiliating defeat as an apparent British triumph. Beresford let the matter drop.

A much more serious issue was the recent Sinn Fein Easter Rising of 24-30 April in Dublin. (In this Irish Nationalist rebellion 1200 volunteers occupied key sites in Dublin. It took 16,000 troops and 1000 police a week to regain control of the city.) When the Lords debated the insurrection on 10 May, Beresford took the opportunity to hit out at the government on a broad front. As usual he justified his attacks by saying that their only purpose was 'to make the Government stronger'. Calling attention to the spate of bad news – the rejection of the *Military Service Bill*, the fall of Kut, and the Irish rebellion – he declared that Parliament was to blame for all these events 'because there has been little or no criticism in either House where disasters have occurred'. 'None of the Cabinet', he added, 'can get out of the doctrine laid down by the Prime Minister – the policy of "Wait and See".'

Turning to the rebellion, he accused the government of being too complacent. They were lucky things had not been worse: 'The rebels could easily have taken Dublin; there were no soldiers there; they could have cut the wires and the whole city would have been in their hands. The whole country, North, South, East, and West could have risen.' The rebellion itself was caused by the class of men whom the British Government have sent to rule Ireland in recent years' and the current administration there was 'the weakest that country has ever had'.

British troops surrendering at Kut 1916

Troo

After the government had set up a War Council to run the war, Beresford asked in the Lords on 11 May how the new arrangements differed from the old. There was a long and aimless discussion which, at the last moment, took a surprising turn when the Marquess of Lincolnshire criticised Beresford's behaviour in the Lords. Beresford, used to the rougher ways of the Commons, had changed little in the Lords. The Marquess asked whether Beresford had 'the smallest conception of how a good many people dislike and resent the tone and temper of some of the speeches'. He then listed some of the many criticisms that Beresford had made that day. Noting that Lord Cromer had recently said that, even in war, 'nobody could object to criticism if it were just and reasonable', the Marquess added that: 'with the enemy at the gate' criticism 'ought not only to be just and reasonable' but should avoid deprecating the government. In particular 'it ought not to contain one single word which would in any way give away military secrets or endanger the lives or limbs of our soldiers and sailors who are fighting abroad'. Beresford declined to defend himself against what he called an 'amusing attack'.

In another place 1916

That same day Beresford asked about the conditions under which British prisoners were kept in Germany. He (and other peers) quoted terrible stories of starvation and maltreatment that they had heard. Lord Newton, who replied for the government, emphasised the difficulties of obtaining any detailed information as to the conditions in the camps. However, 100,000 food parcels left Britain every week for Germany and the reports of the American Ambassador in Berlin, who had access to the camps, did not bear out the allegations. It was, said Lord Newton, 'cruel to the relations of our men to spread such reports'.

* * *

The one great naval battle of the war – Jutland – took place on 31 May and 1 June. The outcome was seen as inconclusive with considerable losses on both sides. A few days after the battle, Beresford issued a statement giving his own interpretation of events: 'a victory for us' even if it had been 'hard earned'. 'The grand traditions of the British Fleet have been nobly maintained' and 'our margin of safety remains'. Later he said that Jutland 'would be the turning point of the war if the authorities would enforce a strong, rigid, effective blockade now'. He repeated his victory remark in July after he had read Admiral Jellicoe's despatch and sympathised with him over the poor weather. Had it been better 'not a single German ship would have returned to port' which would have allowed the fleet 'a decisive victory'. He was indeed right about Jutland. Admiral Scheer's fleet had only avoided annihilation because it had escaped in the mist and rain; Jellicoe's fleet had so terrified the German High Seas Fleet that it never left port again to seek battle. The damage to the British ships was soon overcome, leaving the Grand Fleet stronger than ever.

On 5 June Lord Kitchener set out in HMS *Hampshire* on a diplomatic mission to Russia. The government, unable to stomach any more of his incompetence in Whitehall, had seized on the chance to get the Secretary of State for War out of the way without the opprobrium of sacking him. Not long after sailing the *Hampshire* hit a mine. Only a handful of men survived, but K of Khartoum was no more. A few days later Beresford, speaking at the Mansion House, said that 'He felt his death most acutely' and had been 'an old friend since the days [in 1885] when they marched together through the Sudan desert.'

Beresford's capacity to see military action from the viewpoint of the common people explains why Jutland is forever associated with the courage of John Cornwell. After the battle the sixteen year old gunner was found by medics at his gun, awaiting orders, his chest pierced by a shard of metal. On 26 July Beresford rose in the Lords to request that Cornwell be awarded a posthumous Victoria Cross. It was, he said, 'a special instance of heroic conduct' and hoped that 'respect will be paid to the memory of this gallant lad, who was a credit to himself, to his family, and to the whole Naval Service'. The Duke of Devonshire sympathised but said they would have to wait for a recommendation from the commander. Vice Admiral Beatty's recommendation came in due course and he echoed Beresford's words when he asked for 'special recognition' of John Cornwell's case. The medal was later approved.

Battle of Jutland 31 May – 1 June 1916

Sometime after the battle two different appeals for memorials to John Cornwell appeared. Beresford wrote to the press to explain that they did not overlap. One, an appeal by residents of East Ham, from where the boy came, was for cottage homes and a naval scholarship in the borough. The other was organized by the Navy League on behalf of the Red Cross. The funds raised were to endow a ward at the Star and Garter home in Richmond and this second appeal would be to boys and girls only.

These appeals were immensely successful. By October Beresford had been appointed treasurer to the John Cornwell memorial fund, which was collecting in schools around the country – the fund asked for one penny from each child. Balfour at the Admiralty sent a message to say that the fund 'has my warmest sympathy'. There was no better way for children to show 'their appreciation of Cornwell's gallantry' than to subscribe. Already, reported Beresford, four million children had contributed and, in the first month, £15,000 had been raised.

* * *

Although at the start of the war Beresford had argued against reprisals, he had long since changed his mind. When on 27 July a Captain Fryatt, a civilian mariner, was executed by the Germans for having used his ship to ram a German vessel Beresford suggested in the Lords that the government might confiscate German property in Britain as a retaliation. Lord Lansdowne was willing to consider such retaliation but thought the matter needed 'the utmost care and circumspection' since 'very difficult commercial questions were involved'.

Field Marshal Lord Kitchener

In a debate on the submarine menace on 15 November Beresford declared that the government thought 'they were going to win the war by some lucky chance … [but] all previous wars were won by energy, foresight, and by attack'. Demanding that the Admiralty develop a policy of attack, Beresford declared that 'Our sea supremacy was being challenged by the submarine.' What was needed at the Admiralty was 'new blood and younger men … fresh from the sea'. In a typically simplistic announcement he said he would 'supersede every officer who had made a mistake in strategy or tactics'. (Would that have left one single officer of significant rank in either the Army or the Navy?) Next he demanded that the government arm mercantile ships, build ships to replace losses, standardise ship design and deny German access to allied coaling stations for two years after the war. He ended by stretching the credulity of his peers when, as an example of the 'completeness of the German system of espionage' he declared he had seen a Royal Navy List printed in German containing information 'which nobody in this country possessed except our leading admirals and the members of the Cabinet'. Where did he see it? How did he know what it contained since he did not read German? And how did he know which information leading admirals and Cabinet members did or did or not possess? It was a sad come down for an ageing admiral to resort to transparent fairy tales to bolster an already sound case.

Towards the end of November Lady Londonderry invited the Beresfords to stay for Christmas. There was a general air of weariness in the two families: Lady Londonderry had a broken arm, Lady Beresford was 'not well at all' and Beresford was 'really oversubscribed with many Com^{ttes}'. At 70 years of age Beresford complained to Maxse that 'I am overworked on my eight different Committees, yet I do not see how I can get rid of any of them, as they all have to do with those who have been affected by the War.'

By early December Lloyd George (Minister of War) had finally lost all faith in Asquith's capacity to conduct the war. He resigned and so brought about Asquith's fall. Although the King offered the premiership to Bonar Law, he declined the task when Asquith refused to serve under him. The King then turned to Lloyd George, who accepted the post of Prime Minister. As Asquith departed, Beresford could comfort himself that one more of his enemies had been driven from the scene.

Beresford's last speech of the year was to the Women's Imperial Defence Council, which had called a meeting to protest against 'The Unseen Hand', that is 'the power of German influence and money' in Britain. The Council declared that 'the women of this country were determined to use every effort to eradicate this sinister influence'. Beresford moved a resolution which said that 'it was imperative to eliminate all trace of enemy influence from our social, political, and economic life'.

It was around this time that Lady Beresford shared with Lady Londonderry her anguish about the progress of the war. 'The country,' she wrote 'is well-punished for not putting Charlie at the Admiralty.' Her letters to Lady Londonderry at this time are full of despair with talk of the country 'in utter chaos' and 'revolution' in the air. 'We are in for an awful time with no prospect whatever of winning the war.' However, Beresford was telling her that 'even now he could save the situation.' But would he be given the chance?

Chapter 30
Sniping from the sidelines 1917

Beresford began 1917 with a bout of flu but was well enough by 15 January to attend the memorial service for Alexander Benckendorff who had been Russian ambassador to the Court of St James since 1903. Lady Beresford had also been unwell – she was suffering from gout – so the two of them went off to Brighton on 19 January and stayed there for about ten days.

In the few months since the John Cornwell memorial fund had been set up it had made astonishing progress. At Buckingham Palace, in two ceremonies in early February, the Queen first received the title deeds of the Star and Garter home and the adjacent Ancaster House in Richmond. These, together with a cheque for £13,705 were the gift of the Auctioneers' and Estate Agents' Institute in memory of the boy. Then Beresford presented a cheque for £18,000, raised entirely from children's donations. (As a result of these donations the Richmond site has hosted a Star and Garter home into the early twenty-first century; the residents moved to a new home in Surbiton in 2013.)

John Cornwell's funeral

When the Lords debated the submarine menace on 13 February Beresford was in an unusually relaxed mood. He drew attention to the losses caused by submarines and wondered why a situation that was said to be 'well in hand' in August 1915 was still leading to so many losses. For once he neither attempted to explain the losses nor accused those in high office of failure. Rather, he wished to know 'what measures have been taken' and what success they have had. In passing he heaped praise on the government in which he had 'the greatest faith'. He had 'even more faith' in the Admiralty, he added. It was a new, mellow Beresford. Perhaps the Lords were taming him at last.

On 26 February a 'Great Demonstration' was held at Kingsway Hall in London to protest against the continued holding of 4000 British civilians at the Ruhleben camp in Germany. In his speech Beresford demanded the immediate repatriation of the 4000 men and women 'on the grounds of humanity and expediency' or 'their transference to a neutral country'.

* * *

In early 1917 Germany announced that it would engage in unrestricted submarine warfare. Not surprisingly, this led Beresford to take a much greater interest in the perils to food and shipping. In Walthamstow in early March he declared that the submarine problem was being handled 'gratifyingly'. He put this down to the new government. (This remark is utterly inexplicable – sinkings by submarine peaked in April 1917 at 900,000 tons.) As for the old government, he wanted its ministers 'impeached' for their lack of preparedness. Later in the month he warned the Lords that the public needed to realise that the food situation was 'most serious'. They must 'strictly observe the regulations' otherwise they would soon be 'in a bad way'.

Although Germany had thought that the full horror of unrestricted submarine warfare would deter America from entering the war, the reverse was the case. On 6 April the United States declared war on Germany. Beresford welcomed their participation, saying it 'was impossible to over-rate' its value.

On 25 April Beresford spoke in the Lords once more about food supplies. 'Our people', he said, 'were easily-handled if they were only told the truth.' He wanted them to be told about the cereal shortage and suggested that leaflets should be 'sent to county councils, parish councils, police magistrates, and all the education authorities'. He and the government were, for once, in full agreement. From the government side there was a strong desire to urge people to cut waste and eat less.

* * *

Beresford's mellowing mood continued as he accepted an invitation to a Navy League lunch on 17 May. A few days later he was appointed to the executive committee of the newly formed Local War Museums Association. Then, on 24 May, Beresford was on fine form when he spoke at an Empire Association dinner at the Savoy Hotel. In the midst of his speech, just as he was complaining about the presence of Germans in Britain, he picked up his dinner plate and declared: 'We have actually been dining off German plates.' The guests proceeded to smash their plates, while Beresford demanded that the Association 'must see that such a state of things never occurs again'.

In late May Lady Beresford was unwell again after undergoing both a cataract operation and a tooth extraction. She is 'in agonies' Beresford told Lady Londonderry and 'I have had to sit with her night and day.' Although now on eleven committees, his wife's illness kept him out of the public eye for at least six weeks. He did, though, attend a meeting of the Kitchener Memorial Fund in early June at the Mansion House. The fund, which then stood at £400,000, was established to provide scholarships for the children of service men. It reached £500,000 sometime later and continues to function today.

Beresford's bitterness in his final years was repeatedly exacerbated by watching his fallen enemies return to power. In June he was beside himself at the rumour that Winston Churchill would soon be back in the government. He told Law that he had 'papers and proofs' that he would use to bring Churchill down, adding that he would 'stop at nothing'. He claimed he had set up 'a small Committee of well-known and influential men' who would stomp the country 'calling attention to Winston Churchill's career'. Was this a total fantasy? By 1917 Beresford does not seem to have had a single ally, all his old supporters having withdrawn to the sidelines.

Yet Beresford's status as a great figure was endlessly underlined by little events, which kept his name before the public. It had been in January 1916 that Beresford had asked the composer Sir Edward Elgar to write music for some poems in Rudyard Kipling's book *Fringes of the Fleet*. Elgar willingly agreed and his four songs had their first performance on 11 June 1917. They carried the dedication 'to my friend Admiral Lord Beresford'.

The miscellany of the great man's activities widened with the news of his appointment as a trustee of the Eagle and British Dominions Insurance company in late June and his message of support to the inaugural meeting of King George's Fund for Sailors in July.

In April 1916 Beresford had asked for details of the Army's defeat at Kut in Mesopotamia, but had received no reply. On the publication in July 1917 of the Report of the Mesopotamia Commission he now wanted to know why there was not to be a court of enquiry 'for punishing those found culpable'. In the past, he wrote in a letter to *The Times*, 'all sorts of persons have been punished ... for acts the Government thought were culpable'. In the parliamentary debates there had been 'great confusion' as to whether courts-martial could be used in these cases. Indeed they could, he argued. There was no need (as others had stated) to take evidence on oath before convening a court-martial. Nor (as had again been stated) did officers have a right to demand a court-martial. He awaited government action.

Sir Edward Elgar, composer and close friend of Beresford

Having failed to force action over Mesopotamia, Beresford sought other means to strike at ministers. The recent Cabinet changes provided the opportunity. On 17 July Churchill returned to the War Cabinet as Minister of Munitions and Sir Eric Geddes, a businessman turned wartime minister, became the new First Lord of the Admiralty. These (and other minor changes) were criticised by Beresford at the Queen's Hall in London on 25 July. They showed that the Prime Minister 'was completely out of touch with public opinion'. While saying that he did not wish to be personal, he denounced Churchill's appointment on the grounds that 'his past official career stamped him as entirely unfitted for his present or any other position in the Government'. He claimed that he had received 'hundreds of letters protesting against Mr Churchill's return to office'. As a result of Beresford's eloquence the meeting passed a resolution declaring that the appointments weakened the government's 'power and prestige' and brought it 'into disrepute'. (Churchill's highly successful period at Munitions is detailed in Freeman 2013.)

Beresford's condemnation of the appointment of Edwin Montagu as Secretary of State for India was sharply condemned by Abbas Ali Baig, an Indian member of the Council of the Secretary of State for India. 'Lord Beresford is evidently unaware' he wrote 'that Mr Montagu's appointment has already been hailed with profound gratification by Indians throughout the country'.

* * *

While in February Beresford had taken a relaxed view of the submarine danger, by October he had completely changed his mind. At a meeting in Birmingham on 12 October he declared that the submarine 'would never have attained its present position' had 'a proper War Staff' been at the Admiralty before the war started. Such a staff would have ensured adequate numbers of 'small craft and destroyers ... for protecting the trade routes'. He had clearly forgotten that, immediately before the war, he had declared that submarines were useless in attack. And, oddly, he failed to spot the real reason for the severity of the submarine menace: the Admiralty's refusal to introduce convoys – something that he had recommended to Asquith in 1915.

As the war ground on, Beresford looked forward to reprisals once peace returned. In September he spoke in the Albert Hall at a meeting organized by the National Sailors' and Firemen's Union to consider a boycott of Germany after the war in retaliation for its U-boat activities. Admission was free and the public was tempted in by the promise of a 'musical programme and choir'. He then attended a Merchant Seamen's League meeting in Cardiff on 14 October to join in their attack on Germans. A resolution was passed which demanded that British employers should not employ Germans after the war. The public should refuse to buy German goods or recognise the German flag on land or sea. Beresford joined enthusiastically in this. He was particularly concerned about the 'Hidden Hand', 'Something' he said '[was] going on in this country which has not been to our advantage'. No doubt he also cheered when the chairman said that that there were 'undoubtedly' spies in Cardiff.

A by-election in Islington in October provided Beresford with another opportunity to talk about spies. It was spies, he said, that were responsible for 'the recent loss of convoyed ships from Norway'. Although it was only three months since Beresford had said 'reprisals' were 'absolutely repugnant to our race' he now called for one thousand aeroplanes to bomb German cities: 'four towns of theirs for every town of ours'.

Beresford's isolation from the mainstream of politics was highlighted in October when he presided over the inaugural meeting of the new National Party. He explained that 'The Liberal Party was discredited and the Unionist Party defunct.' In any case, Labour was 'the great party that was coming' and the new National Party should work with it 'to make the conditions better for the workers'. The embryonic party had attracted seven MPs and seventeen peers, and was to field 25 candidates at the 1918 General Election. This resulted in two members of Parliament. From then on the party rapidly declined. Whether Beresford joined the party is not clear, but there is no record of his active participation in its events.

The following day Beresford, in a more gracious mood, supported a motion by Lord Curzon for a vote of thanks to the forces – the first occasion on which such a vote had taken place in wartime. He was in more hostile mood a week later when he put down a parliamentary question asking for detailed information about mercantile losses. In a lengthy speech he revealed many details of the situation and requested even more detail from the government. Lord Lytton, Civil Lord to the Admiralty, replied that 'I am afraid I am unable to give my noble and gallant friend any satisfaction this afternoon' since it would not be in the public interest to give the details. Then, with glee, he drew attention to a speech Beresford had made in the previous April, where he had said 'I am not going to say anything to-day about the tonnage. I have been requested not to do so, and I think the Government are wise in not publishing the tonnage.'

Beresford's last swipe at authority in 1917 came in the Lords. He asked, in a tabled question, whether 'statements made lately by His Majesty's Ministers … represent the view of the War Cabinet as a whole'. It was only when he began to speak in reply that Lord Curzon realised that Beresford intended to mention (or allude) to specific ministers and specific speeches. Curzon was dumbfounded at this 'extraordinary Motion'. Beresford's conduct was 'impossible'. Curzon continued, 'What am I to do? What am I to say? Am I called upon to defend the speeches of Lord Lytton and of Sir Leo Chiozza Money? [a Liberal MP]' Why had Beresford not asked Lord Lytton to defend his own speeches? He went on 'As regards the Prime Minister, am I called upon here to defend every utterance that has fallen from the Prime Minister?' In short, Curzon brusquely refused to answer Beresford's question. Beresford was unrepentant, saying 'I still maintain that my remarks were perfectly justified and correct.' After two years in the House, Beresford still did not appreciate that it comported itself like a gentlemen's club, and not like the bear-pit of the Commons.

Lord Curzon, Leader of the House of Lords 1916-1924

Perhaps it was guilt that caused Beresford to praise Lloyd George two days later. Speaking in Hull, he described a recent speech by the Prime Minister as 'one which was wanted'. It 'would let the German nation know what British grit was'. That was not a bad note on which to end the year.

Chapter 31
War's end 1918

At the start of 1918 Beresford took stock. He told Lady Londonderry that he was on eleven committees and was busy distributing £730,000 that he had recently raised. Equivalent to around £31m today, it was a staggering achievement. For all his hostility to government, Beresford was making a significant contribution to the war. As he looked back on the last year he drew comfort from the departure of Lord Fisher from the Board of Inventions and Research, and Reginald Bacon from his command of the Dover patrol. On the other hand, he raged against the 'criminal mistakes at Antwerp, Gallipoli & Mesopotamia' which, he said, had lengthened the war.

On 17 January Beresford moved an amendment to the *Representation of the People Bill*. He wanted to add the words 'No person who is not a natural-born British subject shall be qualified to be elected a Member of Parliament.' In justifying this, he alleged that there had been 'some very alarming cases lately of people becoming Members of Parliament'. He went on to describe in barely credible detail the cases of a man whom, he alleged was 'an Austrian spy' and a Mr Laszlo, who 'was naturalised only seven days before the war'. Viscount Harcourt, a senior Liberal peer, cleverly retaliated by noting that two men whom Beresford greatly admired would, by his amendment, be barred from being MPs: General Botha (First Prime Minister of South Africa) and General Smuts (a member of the British War Cabinet). Beresford withdrew his amendment.

In February Beresford's attacks on war policy were directed at Lloyd George's new War Council. The Council, he said, would lead to 'divided military control'. In his view the Chief of the Imperial General Staff, Sir William Robertson, 'was perfectly right to leave', which he did in that month. (Beresford could not have been more wrong. Lloyd George's masterstroke of creating a unified allied command finally put an end to the French and British armies fighting their own separate wars.)

* * *

On 3 March Beresford revealed to the Lords a series of horrifying details of the torture and maltreatment of British prisoners of war in Germany. It all sounded barbaric beyond belief. And beyond belief it was, as Lord Newton pointed out. Two of the places where the alleged cruelties had occurred were the names of people! Newton elaborated: Stiemes was not a chemical factory, but 'a German financial magnate', just as Thyssins was 'a German commercial magnate'. As to some of the real places Beresford mentioned, his accusations just did not hold up. Newton cited Recklingen, where Beresford claimed terrible things were happening. It was, said Newton, a chemical works and had been visited by the Dutch in November. Two British prisoners were employed there. Then there was Mulheim, where there were nineteen men in hospital, sixty-two working in, according to the Dutch, 'satisfactory' conditions. And so it went on as Newton assiduously worked through the reports that Beresford could have read before putting down his resolution.

Beresford followed this bizarre performance by returning to one of his favourite topics of the war: the spies who were responsible for shipping losses. On 6 March he told the Lords of 'the serious losses of vessels' in the Irish Sea. This was, he said, due to insufficient defence and spies in English docks. He called for convoys for this traffic. Losses were so great that 'soon there will be no traffic left across the Irish Sea'. He added that the weekly list of shipping movements 'is most misleading; it tells the public nothing definite'. Shipping losses were again debated in the Lords on 21 March. Once more Beresford asserted that 'there is close connection between these sinkings and spies'. As evidence he cited the captains with whom he had spoken in Swansea and Cardiff. They were, he said, 'perfectly convinced that there are too many aliens in the Swansea and Cardiff docks'. In reply the Earl of Lytton reminded the House that the government had repeatedly denied that aliens were responsible for the sinkings but he did not 'suppose that, if this assurance were repeated ever so many times, it would prevent a certain number of people from believing that this connection exists'.

Spies had been on Beresford's mind since 1914 but in 1918 he found a new set of 'agencies in this country who are serving the cause of the enemy'. By this he meant pacifists. He indulged in a long rant about the large numbers of pacifists who 'associate with spies, traitors, and sedition-mongers'. He did not mind Quakers since 'They go out to the Front and do their level best with the ambulances' but for the rest, he wanted them tried by court-martial. He also wanted them to be stopped from 'holding anti-patriotic meetings' or heckling at meetings. They were, he concluded, 'a real danger to the State'.

In June Beresford spoke twice on Ireland. He forecast that the decision to apply the *Defence of the Realm Regulations* to Ireland would prove pointless: 'Regulations have all been sent over, but they

War's end 1918

have never been enforced.' He added 'nothing whatever will be done'. He was similarly negative about the proposal to recruit 50,000 men from Ireland, promising them land as a reward, Beresford declared this 'impossible'. It would only be 'another broken pledge' to Ireland. (Around 200,000 Irishmen fought for Britain during the war.)

Meanwhile, in compensation for this negativity, Beresford opened a fair in Trafalgar Square in aid of his Ambulance Committee. Speaking to reporters, he said they had now sent 300 cars to France and transported 300,000 wounded French.

It is hard to credit that after nearly four years of war, Beresford still thought it worth his while to criticise the government's treatment of aliens, but on 8 July he took up the topic once more. He proceeded to deliver a lengthy and vicious attack on the 6,600 German aliens resident in Britain, accusing them of all manner of illegal and evil activities. When Lord Buckmaster replied for the government, he swept aside the whole of Beresford's argument with a tirade of ridicule:

> 'If ... it were true that the action of our Foreign Office is, or ever had been, dictated or influenced in anyway by German influence; if it were true that our Civil Service was the home for a number of justly suspected people; if it were true that our gallant merchant seamen went to sea with their fate foredoomed by the operation of German spies – if these things were true, there certainly would be grave reason for uneasiness and apprehension among the people of this country.'

But, Buckmaster continued, 'I could not find one of the cases that he quoted which in the least degree justified any such statements being made.' He concluded that Beresford's sole objection to these people was 'their names and their associations'.

* * *

The war ended on 11 November 1918. What Beresford's thoughts were we do not know. Was he embarrassed that Cabinets and Admiralty Boards, which in his view had never done one right thing, had nevertheless brought victory? Perhaps. One thing we can be sure of is that his four years as an outcast from official action had left him more bitter than ever. Others had fared so much better. McKenna had been Home Secretary and Chancellor of the Exchequer until Lloyd George became Prime Minister; Churchill had been First Lord of the Admiralty and Minister of Munitions; Fisher had been First Lord and Chairman of the Board of Inventions and Research; Bacon had been in charge of the Dover patrol. So much success for so many enemies.

War's end 1918

* * *

Beresford's war had been a humiliation. True, he could look back with pride on his eleven committees, which had raised £800,000 during the war. (In today's terms that is over £34 million.) It was a great achievement and says much both for his energy and the faith that the public had in his name. But it was not the recognition that he had sought. In his private correspondence with Lady Londonderry and Maxse we find a deeply unhappy man. Embittered by his failure to gain an appointment after his abrupt removal from the Channel Fleet and the adamant refusal of the Admiralty to promote him to Admiral of the Fleet, the war had only emphasized his redundant status. It was more than he could bear. Resentful and hurt he had turned to one hate campaign after another. Asquith, Churchill and McKenna had been his favourite targets. He had dragged in names from the past as soon as they were called to arms – Scott and Bacon being the most notable. For a man who made such high claims for himself, his conduct in the war was, to say the least, reprehensible.

Chapter 32
Last days 1919

As 1919 opened Beresford was ageing and his wife was still suffering from the effects of her cataract operation. They had been unable to visit the Londonderrys at Christmas because 'Dot cannot see to write yet', Beresford told Lady Londonderry. At 72, Beresford was also in failing health with spells of heart trouble, phlebitis and gout.

On 10 January he attended the funeral of the merchant banker Lord Michelham. A few days later he was at an exhibition of art work produced by prisoners in the Ruhleben camp. On 18 January he was at a dinner for the American Ambassador. February began with a memorial service in Westminster Abbey for President Roosevelt. Then on 10 February Beresford fell ill and his doctor ordered 'no visitors for ten days'. Bennett says that he had had a heart attack, but the source for this is unclear. Two months later, recuperating at Brighton, Beresford told the naval journalist Archibald Hurd that 'I have been seriously ill' so it seems likely that he was out of action for all this time – certainly he does not seem to have attended any public functions. His illness kept him away from the funeral of Lady Londonderry, who died on 5 March. He was, though, well enough to indulge in his old hatreds when writing to Hurd: there was McKenna, whom he blamed for his being kept out of naval affairs ever since his flag came down; then there were Churchill and Fisher who were responsible for 'my gallant dead shipmates'.

His first public appearance after Roosevelt's memorial service was at the Royal Academy dinner on 3 May. Three weeks later he was able to attend the Empire Day service at Westminster Abbey on 24 May.

On 29 May Beresford spoke in the Lords for the first time that year. It was to be his penultimate appearance there and a typical Beresfordian performance at that. A Miss Violet Douglas-Pennant had been dismissed from the Royal Air Force following a critical report on her work as Commander of the Women's Royal Air Force. It seemed unlikely that Beresford would have had anything to say, but he did because 'my case is very similar'. Being more than economical with the truth, he told the Lords that:

> 'I represented to the Admiralty when I was Commander-in-Chief that the trade routes were not protected, and that a number of other things were wanting, such as a war staff, and that our food supply was insecure. I did not agree with the views of the Admiralty, in fact, I said that the Admiralty did not appear to

understand anything about war. The Admiralty put me on the beach. They made me haul down my flag, and discharged me from the Service.'

He added 'I never complained.' which is odd since he never stopped complaining. Indeed only in April he had raised the issue once more with Hurd.

Although Beresford now felt that he had not long to live, wealth still came to him. In June his nephew William Warren de la Poer Beresford, who had died aged 21, left him £1000 a year from an estate of £432,533. On 13 June Beresford was well enough to attend the thanksgiving service for the Navy's role in the war. This was followed by Ascot on 19 June and the Royal Tournament on 25 June.

On 9 July Beresford spoke in the Lords for the last time. Fittingly the debate was about the inadequate facilities for training ex-servicemen. He wondered how this could be after 'a war which lasted nearly five years' and reminded his fellow peers that 'we are bound to keep our promises to these men'. Few admirals, if any, ever showed such genuine concern for the common soldier and seaman as did Beresford. Had he known that it was to be his last speech, he would doubtless have been content that it were so.

In the same month Beresford also wrote to *The Times* to protest against the proposal to put the Kaiser on trial. At the time, Britain did not even have a mandate from its allies to take charge of the Kaiser. And, predicted Beresford, such a trial would only inflame opinion in Germany. 'A trial in this country would land us in countless difficulties.' Then, on 13 August a meeting at Claridges Hotel to recognise the role of British merchant seaman in the war listened to a message from Beresford – his last intervention in a public occasion.

On 22 August Beresford went to Scotland to stay with his friend the Duke of Portland. On 5 September he was in fine form and went out fishing, returning in good spirits. The following day, feeling unwell, he abandoned his plan to go shooting and remained indoors. At dinner nothing seemed amiss but not long after, he felt indisposed and, just before going to bed, collapsed. He died the same night of 'apoplexy'. He was just 73 years 6 months old.

The Times obituary was confined largely to a factual account of Beresford's life. *The Daily Mail* letter of 1901 was slid over, noting that 'the blame fell mainly on his correspondent [White]'. Only the *cognoscenti* would have understood the paper's cryptic allusion to the Scott incidents, which were described as events that brought his name 'rather painfully before the public'. As to the quarrels with Fisher the paper noted that Beresford was 'imperfectly in sympathy' with his reforms and relations 'were at times exceedingly strained' with 'faults on both sides'. Referring to the 'punitive termination' of his command in 1909 and his consignment to half-pay, the paper conjectured that Beresford might have been made commander-in-chief of the Home Fleet 'had he been more submissive and his interpretation of the requirements of naval discipline less eccentric'.

Although the obituary was remarkably sympathetic to an admiral whom the paper had criticised so much, there was one sting towards the end. Having remarked on the equivocal report of the 1909 Enquiry and Fisher's resignation, the paper noted that his replacement (Wilson) had made 'no conspicuous changes of policy'. This 'may perhaps be taken to show that the criticisms were, in the judgement of so distinguished an officer ... either exaggerated or ill-founded'.

Correspondents wrote to *The Times* with their personal tributes. One praised 'his efforts to help every possible war work', which had undermined his health. The same correspondent praised his 'unstinting labour' in aiding the wounded French and the Belgian casualties. 'He was fearless, determined, and bursting with humour.' Another commented on his role as Chairman of the British Ambulance Committee where, 'with unflagging energy ... [he] read through mountains of correspondence, directed operations, and gave advice'. The German papers, meanwhile, described Beresford as 'one of Germany's most inexorable enemies' but, despite their 'shattered' fleet, it was impossible to 'refuse its respect for a dead adversary'.

Beresford, so often a pallbearer at the funerals of so many great men, was honoured at his funeral by one admiral of the fleet (Meux), four admirals (Custance, Bridgeman, Startin and Sturdee), one vice admiral (Browning), one rear admiral (Brock) and one major-general (Mercer). Six of the seven had served under him, but only Custance had been a true acolyte. In addition to the pallbearers, Beresford's coffin was accompanied by 50 royal marines (with a band), 70 seamen, 50 engine-room ratings and 30 other ratings.

The chief mourners were naturally the family, led by Beresford's only surviving brother, Lord Marcus, and the seventh Marquis, John Charles. There were also cousins and nieces, but Lady Beresford does not appear to have attended. Nor did Lord Fisher. St Paul's Cathedral was almost full on 14 September when eight bluejackets carried the coffin down the aisle to the strains of Chopin's funeral march. Draped in a Union Jack, surmounted by Beresford's cap and sword, the coffin stopped at the chancel step. There, between tall white candles it remained as the service began with Psalm 90 (Lord, thou hast been our dwelling place in all generations). The *Manchester Guardian* found the service 'impressive' and 'a fitting climax to a life given to the service of his country'. After a brief ceremony the coffin was carried out to the sound of the Dead March from *Saul*. Later in the day he was buried at Putney Vale cemetery.

On the day that Beresford died he had written his last appeal – indeed it is the last known Beresford document. It was sent to *The Times* but not published until nearly three weeks later and was for a fund to convert a building in the Commercial Road, London, into accommodation for sailors. The fund needed £30,000 for the site, £90,000 for the building and £50,000 for an endowment. It was, said Beresford 'a fine conception and deserves the utmost support of a grateful nation'. It was fitting that a man whose life was largely devoted to belligerent antagonisms should, at the end, express one of his finest qualities: his devotion to the welfare of the common seaman.

Most of Beresford's wealth went to his wife. His younger daughter, Eileen, received an oil-painting of the action of *El Safieh*, together with all his medals and decorations. To his nephew went his hunting and sporting trophies. The main bequests of money were £2000 for Lord Marcus, £200 to his dead brother Lord Delaval and annuities of £50 to his butler and his nurse. (The bequest to his dead brother Delaval is an indication that Beresford had not revised his will in over thirteen years.)

A memorial fund was set up for a bas relief of Beresford in the crypt of St Paul's Cathedral. Later the fund's trustees decided to endow a Beresford Memorial Wing at the Sailors' Rest at Devonport. Part of the fund went to erect a tablet in St Paul's, with wording chosen by Lord Crewe:

Charles William de la Poer Beresford

Admiral Lord Beresford of Metemmeh GCB, GCVO, DCL, LLD

Born February 10th 1846, died September 6th 1919

At Alexandria 1882, on the Nile 1885

Three times Commander in Chief at sea

A member of the House of Commons for more than twenty years

A skilful and gallant sailor, a devoted public servant.

And the genial comrade of many illustrious and humble friends.

It can be seen there today.

Epilogue

People found it hard to dislike Beresford. He had the easy charm of an aristocrat and the self-confidence that enabled him to treat everyone as his equal. He feared no one nor bowed to any man.

His virtues were noble. He was courageous, whether when riding, hunting or saving lives. Like Winston Churchill, he was oblivious to danger. He had dash and determination. Whether it was a race to be run, a pig to be stuck or a man to be pulled from the sea, Beresford threw himself at the task,

He was charitable, too. He never refused a gift or a loan to someone in distress and he worked tirelessly for the underpaid seamen of the fleet. Every widow or invalided seaman who sought his aid received his support. He took up cases in Parliament and incessantly battled for better pay and pensions for the men and their widows.

Beresford was resourceful too. No man showed more determination or initiative in a crisis. Collisions at sea, grounded ships or street accidents always brought out the best in him. He took decisions, he organized, he drove men to do the impossible.

But despite rising to the rank of admiral and being three times commander-in-chief, Beresford's naval career was undistinguished. It was not that he lacked talent. Rather he lacked dedication. For all his grand claims in his memoirs, Beresford rarely applied his whole mind to a command. Whether on the *Condor* or *Undaunted* or *Ramillies*, Beresford was too often in his cabin writing to leading politicians at home or stirring up trouble with the aid of his wife and the likes of Bellairs. Even if there were times when he genuinely looked forward to a command, no sooner had Beresford got to sea than he began to feel withdrawal symptoms at leaving the political fray.

Then there was his darker side. Beresford was widely recognized as having been the most insubordinate admiral of all time. His long battles with the Board and governments were partly over matters of principle and professional practice. But they were almost always motivated by jealousy or resentment. He could not bear to be wrong nor accept being overlooked. If he lost an argument or was passed over for a post, the matter soon became personal. Fundamentally Beresford could never accept a subordinate position. Whether in the Navy or in politics, he hated taking orders and resented authority. His pathetic quarrel with Lord George Hamilton over the NID salaries came down to no more than his objection to Hamilton having the power to rule on the issue.

Epilogue

In politics Beresford truly deserved his reputation as a windbag. Had he worked with others or shown more moderation his wide naval knowledge would have richly informed Commons debates. As it was, MPs adored him for his entertainment value but had little time for his opinions. For all his nearly 18 years in the Commons Beresford's high professional knowledge had delivered few results. Once in the more gentlemanly Lords, his methods became ever more counter-productive.

For no good or worthy reason, Beresford turned differences of opinion with Hamilton, Fisher, McKenna, Churchill and Asquith (amongst others) into personal vendettas. He sought out every scrap of gossip or scandal that he could throw at them and he plotted with the likes of Bellairs and Maxse to drive his victims from office. Nor did he limit his quarry to those with whom he differed on policy. He also sought to ruin the careers of those who had sided with his enemies. Scott was his victim solely because he refused to attack Fisher. And, for even lower motives, Beresford turned on Battenberg merely because he was of German birth.

It was this petty and vindictive side that denied Beresford the greatness that could have been his. His legacy was and remains notoriety.

Chronology

S=start; E=end

1846 Birth: 10 Feb
1859 *Britannia*: 13 Dec (S); Naval cadet
1861 *Britannia*: 21 March (E); Marlborough: 22 March (S)
1862 Midshipman: 21 June
1863 *Marlborough*: 25 June (E); *Defence*: 24 July (S)
1864 *Defence*: 14 July (E); *Clio*: 15 July (S)
1865 *Clio*: 28 Oct (E); *Sutlej*: 29 Oct (S) + few days in Clio again
1866 Sub-Lieut: 2 Jan; *Sutlej*: 30 June (E); *Excellent*: 1 July (S)
1867 *Excellent*: 17 Aug (E)
1868 *Victoria & Albert*: 16 Jul (S); Lieut: 21 Sept; *Victoria & Albert*: 30 Sept (E);
Galatea: 17 Oct (S);
1871 *Galatea*: 2 June (E)
1872 *Royal Adelaide*: 1 Nov (S)
1874 MP for Waterford: 5 Mar (S); *Royal Adelaide*: 13 Aug (E); *Bellerophon*: 14 Aug
(S)
1875 *Bellerophon*: 10 Jan (E); Commander: 2 Nov
1876 *Vernon*: 12 Dec (S)
1877 *Vernon*: 22 Mar (E); *Thunderer*: 1 May (S)
1878 *Thunderer*: 22 June (E)
1879 RY *Osborne*: 18 June (S)
1880 MP for Waterford: 24 Mar (E)
1881 *Osborne*: 2 Nov (E); *Condor*: 31 Dec (S)
1882 *Condor*: 31 Aug (E); Captain: 11 July
1885 MP for Marylebone: 24 Nov (S)
1886 Junior Naval Lord: 9 Aug (S)
1888 Junior Naval Lord: 29 Jan (E)
1889 MP for Marylebone: 11 Jul (E); *Undaunted*: 19 Dec (S)
1893 *Undaunted*: 20 June (E); Steam Reserve: 15 July (S)
1896 Steam Reserve: 15 Mar (E)
1897 Rear-Adm: 16 Sept 1897
1898 MP for York: 13 Jan (S)
1900 MP for York: 26 Jan (E); *Ramillies*: 12 Jan (S)
1902 *Ramillies*: 8 Feb (E); Vice Adm: 3 Oct 1902
1903 *Majestic/Caesar*:17 Apr (S)
1905 *Majestic/Caesar*: 5 Mar (E); *Bulwark*: 1 May (S)
1907 *Bulwark*: 26 Jan (E); K Edward VII: 4 Mar (S)
1909 K Edward VII: 24 Mar (E)
1910 MP for Portsmouth; 15 Jan 1910 (S)
1911 Retired: 10 Feb 1911
1916 Peerage: 1 Jan; MP for Portsmouth: 8 Jan 1916 (E)
1919 Died: 6 Sept 1919

End notes

Abbreviations in end notes
BL: British Library; CCA: Churchill College Archives; CUL: Cambridge University Library; D: Durham County Archives; HC Deb: House of Commons Debates; HL Deb: House of Lords Debates; HSP Hatfield Salisbury Papers; NMM: National Maritime Museum; ODNB: Oxford Dictionary of National Biography; PA: Parliamentary Archives; TNA: The National Archives.

Chapter 1 The wild youth from Curraghmore 1846-65

'wild Irish' Leslie S., 1938, p. 74. 'fox-hunting thug' Leslie, A., p. 110. 'meet an army' Leslie S., 1938, p. 74. 'the biggest bully' *Reynolds's Newspaper*, 25 March 1877. 'no Beresford ever' *New York Times*, 30 Apr 1882. 'a more unruly' *Times*, 4 Feb 1888. 'more flogged than' *HC Deb* 09 March 1915 Vol 70 cc1356-9. 'did not interest' Beresford, 1914, p. 7. 'gave any clear' De Crespigny, 1896, p. 66. 'smartest and happiest' Beresford, 1914, p. 34. 'could neither read' *Times*, 21 March 1898. 'ridiculous ... a very' *Times*, 4 Apr 1898 'severely reprimanded' Beresford, 1914, pp. 26-7. 'Marlborough Star of' Beresford, 1914, p. 30. 'We used to' Beresford, 1914, p. 20. 'Each British sailor' Beresford, 1914, p. 34. 'a slovenly, unhandy' Beresford, 1914, p. 41. 'I hit a lady' Beresford, 1914, p. 45. 'sowing their wild' *Liverpool Mercury*, 23 Nov 1863. 'The days are' Beresford, 1914, pp. 45-6. 'I ... tell you' Waterford to Beresford, 6 Dec 1863. NMM MRF/61. 'What can be' Beresford, 1914, pp. 51-2. 'for every penny' Beresford, 1914, p. 52. 'dropping lighted tallow' Beresford, 1914, p. 52. 'the usual ceremony' TNA ADM 53/9146. 'being ducked and' Beresford, 1914, p. 53. 'a most repulsive' Beresford, 1914, p. 55. 'totally naked ... beat' Beresford, 1914, p. 55. 'become the centre' Beresford, 1914, pp. 59-60. 'all the courage' *Times*, 16 Oct 1865.

Chapter 2 First steps 1865-72

'I took up' Beresford, 1914, p. 64. 'sobriety, diligence, attention' Beresford, 1914, p. 64. 'the British naval' *Times*, 19 Mar 1866. 'retching of the' *Times*, 8 Nov 1866. 'most strongly recommended' TNA ADM 196/83/86. 'hunted a good' Beresford, 1914, p. 71. 'a rollicking disregard' *Times*, 10 Feb 1869. 'a small cheque' Beresford, 1914, p. 75. 'the most timid' Beresford, 1914, p. 108. 'which ... was the' Beresford, 1914, pp. 79-80. 'never seemed to' Beresford, 1914, p. 87. 'in Japan none' Beresford, 1914, p. 101. 'dim figure' Beresford, 1914, p. 101. 'extraordinary prevalence of' Beresford, 1914, p. 102. 'with much difficulty' *North Otago Times*, 5 Sept 1871.

Chapter 3 Sailor or politician? 1872-76

'We used to' Beresford, 1914, p. 115. 'a good deal' Beresford, 1914, p. 119. 'my first independent' Beresford, 1914, p. 120. 'The first thing' Beresford, 1914, p. 120. 'with considerable difficulty' *Pall Mall Gazette*, 25 Aug 1873. 'the Prince led' *Jackson's Oxford Journal*, 13 Dec 1873. 'My boy, don't' Beresford, 1914, p. 139. 'would lay in' *HC Deb* 08 May 1874 Vol 218 cc1991-2022. 'exceedingly easy style' *Graphic*, 16 May 1874. 'Oh, I'll give' *Freeman's Journal and Daily Commercial Advertiser*, 20 Aug

End notes

1874. 'camping out, and' Beresford, 1914, p. 539. 'my old messmate' Beresford, 1914, p. 539. 'a curious illustration' Beresford, 1914, p. 539. 'launches of ironclads' *Times*, 8 Apr 1875. 'The men in' *HC Deb* 09 April 1875 Vol 223 cc639-43. 'merchants would naturally' *HC Deb* 13 April 1875 Vol 223 cc822-64. 'not met the' *HC Deb* 01 June 1875 Vol 224 cc1256-93. 'had been excellent' *HC Deb* 01 June 1875 Vol 224 cc1256-93. 'a fortnight ... The' *HC Deb* 03 August 1875 Vol 226 cc477-508. 'half a dozen' Cowles, 1956, p. 145. 'somewhat monotonous' *Times*, 18 Oct 1875. 'he came down' Suffield, 1913, p. 169. 'covered with debris' Gay, 1876, p. 138-9. 'was happily not Suffield, 1913, p. 204-5. 'doomed to misadventure' Suffield, 1913, p. 169. 'it was a good' *HC Deb* 20 June 1876 Vol 230 cc147-78.

Chapter 4 Marking time 1876-81

'no economical consideration' *HC Deb* 19 March 1877 Vol 233 cc128-33 'Took great exception' Beresford, 1914, p. 142. 'sailor-like' *Graphic*, 24 Mar 1877. 'the Prince of Wales' Beresford, 1914, p. 150. 'derived the greatest' *Times*, 24 May 1877. 'she is likely' *Freeman's Journal and Daily Commercial Advertiser*, 29 May 29, 1877. 'behaved admirably' *Times*, 18 June 1877. 'which was very' Buckle, 1926, pp. 562-3. 'electric broadside' *Times*, 14 Aug 1877. ''Don't think me' Bolitho 1934, p. 302. 'no stability' *HC Deb* 11 March 1878 Vol 238 cc1057-125. 'benefit ... the men' *HC Deb* 18 March 1878 Vol 238 cc1495-505. 'a very pretty' Blathwayt, 1917, pp. 274-5. 'a good musician' *New York Times*, 23 Aug 1903. 'to inquire into' *HC Deb* 04 June 1878 Vol 240 cc1216-36. 'a most beautiful' Beresford, 1914, p. 169. 'the Red Admiral' Leslie, 1938, pp. 83-4. 'four hundred and' Suffield, 1913, p 157. 'excepting under conditions' *Times*, 7 Jan 1879. 'would go even' *HC Deb* 15 May 1879 Vol 246 cc475-506. 'a strange blending' *New York Times*, 26 Aug 1894 'Had it struck' Beresford, 1914, p. 153. 'the claims of his' *Times*, 16 Mar 1880. 'What I want' BL Add mss 63116. 'the plate is' BL Add mss 63116. 'Scullery Maid &'. BL Add mss 63116. 'a thousand brethren' *Times*, 26 May 1881.

Chapter 5 Triumph in Alexandria 1882

'Egypt is in' *Times*, 11 May 1882. 'in justice to' Magnus, 1964, p. 174. 'During the ensuing' Beresford, 1914, p. 186. 'The officer in' *Times*, 7 July 1882. 'Now my lads' Beresford, 1914, p. 187. 'Commenced action with' TNA ADM 53/11912. 'are treated with' *Times*, 12 July 1882. 'Silenced 3 of' TNA ADM 53/11912. 'Well done, Condor!' TNA ADM 53/11912. 'the admiral's ship's' Beresford, 1914, p. 189. 'I never saw' Beresford, 1914, p. 191. 'ably executed' *Times*, 15 July 1882. 'the Greek and' *Times*, 17 July 1882. 'The work of' *Times*, 19 July 1882. 'a town in' *Times*, 20 July 1882. 'unless the admiral' Beresford, 1914, p. 193. 'an Englishman like' *Times*, 22 July 1882. 'the humane means' *Times*, 24 July 1882. 'the absolute necessity' *Times*, 24 July 1882. 'much to raise' *Times*, 29 July 1882. 'it would be' TNA ADM 196/83-86. 'It was after' Beresford, 1914, p. 76.

Chapter 6 Between wars 1882-84

'fought most gallantly' *Times*, 19 Oct 1882. 'four or five' *Times*, 1 Nov 1882. 'In the Navy' Scott, 1919, p. 202, fn 1. 'danger to the' *Times*, 16 June 1883. 'my Lords cannot' TNA ADM 196/83/86. 'my old friend' Beresford, 1914, p. 210. 'I may have' BL Add

End notes

mss 63116. 'protest against the' *Times*, 7 May 1884. 'all very fast' *Times*, 4 July 1884. 'there is to' BL Add mss 63116. 'I shall have' BL Add mss 63116.

Chapter 7 His finest hour 1884-85

'the manners of' NMM MRF/61. 'Fancy 9 officers' NMM MRF/61. 'never was so' NMM MRF/61. 'The cataract is' NMM MRF/61. 'rendered invaluable services' *Times*, 13 Jan 1885. 'all the valuable' NMM MRF/61. 'On arrival at' Colvile, Vol II, 1889, pp. 9-10. 'a beautiful spectacle' *Times*, 9 Jan 1885. 'one pond of dirty' Wilson, 1886, p. 8. 'capital dinner' Wilson, 1886, p. 14. 'At first' Wilson, 1886, p. 21. 'our skirmishers had' Wilson, 1886, p. 27. 'By Jove, they' Wilson, 1886, pp. 28-9. 'dropping like ninepins' Beresford, 1914, p. 263. 'and one recent' Asher, 2005, p. 228. 'the consistency of' Beresford, 1914, p. 270. 'The men breakfasted' Beresford, 1914, p. 273. 'hardly able to' Beresford, 1914, p. 280. 'if I were' *Times*, 21 May 1885. 'a more disreputable' Marling, 1931, p. 140. 'if he took' Beresford, 1914, p. 296. 'heavy rifle fire' *Times*, 29 Apr 1885. 'driven away without' Colvile, 1889, Vol II, p. 70. 'excellent conduct' *Times* 29 Apr 1885. 'there are none' *HC Deb* 12 August 1885 Vol 300 cc1872-87. 'Possibly there is' *HC Deb* 12 August 1885 Vol 300 cc1859-68. 'statement of reasons' TNA 196/83-86.

Chapter 8 Fall from grace 1885-88

'if war was' *Times*, 30 July 1885. 'the first person' *HL Deb* 16 May 1893 Vol 12 cc1018-38. 'the cheapness of' *HC Deb* 15 March 1886 Vol 303 cc827-905. 'a majority of' *Times*, 1 July 1886. 'the weak spot' Hamilton, 1922, pp. 88-90. 'The perilous absence' TNA ADM 116/3106. 'the Board have' CUL Add Ms 9248/16/1888. 'rough copy into' Hamilton, 1922, p. 88. 'It became public' *HC Deb* 03 March 1887 Vol 311 cc1083-4. 'It was stolen' Beresford, 1914, pp. 348-9. 'without delay' TNA ADM 116/3106. 'very kindly read' Beresford, 1914, p. 347. 'purely advisory' *Times* 28, Feb 1887. 'We are getting' Beresford to Randolph Churchill, 12 Mar 1887. CUL Add. MS 9248/19/2412. 'much cheering' *Times*, 6 Jan 1887. 'Some further change' *Times*, 25 July 1887. 'tremendous breach of' NMM MRF/61. 'but I am' BL Ad mss 63117. 'you have always' NMM MRF/61. 'still unreconciled to' TNA ADM 116/3106. 'on the ground' NMM MRF/61. 'great ability afloat' Bennett, 1968, pp. 145-6. 'outside the Admiralty' *Times*, 27 Jan 1888. 'the formation of' NMM MRF/61. 'on question of' TNA CAB 16/9B. 'I will show' *Times*, 4 Feb 1888.

Chapter 9 Beached on the back benches 1888-89

'the civil and' *HC Deb* 04 May 1888 Vol 325 cc1370-3. 'had fallen flat' *Times*, 9 Apr 1890. 'You all sit' *Times*, 21 Jan 1929. 'the unsettled state' *Times*, 24 May 1888. 'did not ask' *HC Deb* 04 June 1888 Vol 326 cc1033-143. 'did not ask' *HC Deb* 04 June 1888 Vol 326 cc1033-143. 'the minimum required' *HC Deb* 04 June 1888 Vol 326 cc1033-143. 'Does anyone believe' *HC Deb* 04 June 1888 Vol 326 cc1033-143. 'I was then' *HC Deb* 04 June 1888 Vol 326 cc1033-143. 'The First Lord' *Times*, 6 June 1888. 'Great Britain ... is' TNA CAB 37/22/24. 'a necessary part' *Times*, 11 June 1888. 'put a definite' *HC Deb* 13 December 1888 Vol 332 cc124-225. 'Does the noble' *HC Deb* 13 December 1888 Vol 332 cc124-225. 'my noble and gallant' *HC Deb* 13 December 1888 Vol 332 cc124-225. 'I do not remember' *Times*, 7 Feb 1889. 'our duty to' *HC Deb* 07 March 1889 Vol 333 cc1164-212. 'a full survey' *HC Deb* 07 March 1889 Vol

End notes

333 cc1164-212. 'a phantom' *HC Deb* 07 March 1889 Vol 333 cc1164-212. 'eminently satisfactory' *Times*, 8 Mar 1889. 'how extremely difficult' *Times*, 9 Mar 1889. 'we agree entirely' *HC Deb* 01 April 1889 Vol 334 cc1253-346. 'When news went' Lucy, 1892, pp. 512-3. 'how empty the' NMM MRF/61. 'distinguished naval officer' *HC Deb* 12 April 1889 Vol 335 cc363-4. 'watch and destroy' *HC Deb* 07 May 1889 Vol 335 cc1368-416. 'offensive' NMM MRF/61. 'I have been' NMM FTN/8/5.

Chapter 10 Back to sea 1890-93

'worked splendidly' *Times*, 1 Mar 1890. 'whenever you like' CUL Add. MS 9248/26/3648. 'I am so innocent' BL Add MSS 49713. 'could form a' CUL Add.MS 9248/26/3649. 'the politicians would' King-Hall's diary, 14 Nov 1890. 'found her captain' Beresford, 1914, p. 379. 'come off with' King-Hall's diary 1 May 1891. 'you have instituted' *HSP*. 'openly slighting and' *HSP*. 'a loss to' *HSP*. 'I regret to find' Magnus, 1964, p. 235. 'I had a model' Beresford, 1914, p. 399. 'I can never forget' *HSP*. 'Whatever his parliamentary' BL Add MSS 49713. 'of a disciplinary' BL Add MSS 49713. 'not justifiable in' NMM MRF/61. 'A boy with' 7 Feb 1893. *HSP*. 'honourably acquitted' *Times*, 4 and 7 Apr 1893. 'a ship that' 28 May 1893. NMM MRF/61. 'he was confident that' *Times*, 26 June 1893.

Chapter 11 To be an admiral 1893-96

'so cleverly studded' *Times* and *Manchester Guardian*, 14 July 1893. 'I commanded more' Enquiry Proceedings, p. 98. TNA CAB 16/9A. 'a permanent "Navy League"' *Times*, 22 Jan 1894. 'impossible to overestimate' *North American Review*, Nov 1894. 'only refer him' TNA ADM 196/8386. 'the First Lord asks' *HC Deb* 07 March 1895 Vol 31 cc546-9. 'so able, zealous' *Times*, 24 Oct 1895.

Chapter 12 Tub thumping 1896-98

'the system' *Times* 20 Mar 1896. 'past work' *Times*, 24 Apr 1896. 'not enough men *Times*, 20 Apr 1896. 'irresponsible' *Times*, 9 May 1896. 'useless' *Times*, 21 July1896. 'without division' *Times*, 30 July 1896. 'a myth' *Times*, 31 July 1896. 'fine personal character' *Times*, 18 Aug 1896. 'who chatted pleasantly' *Times*, 13 June 1896. 'vogue' *Times*, 15 June 1896. 'there was no' *Manchester Guardian*, 19 Oct 1896. 'was not a nice' *Manchester Guardian*, 19 Oct 1896. 'be disposed to' *Times*, 22 Mar 1897 'for three or' Bennett, 1968, p. 199. 'Either the ships' *Times*, 10 Apr 1897. 'the life, pay, and' *Times*, 3 May 1897. 'said he had' Anand, 2008, p. 80. 'to set the' *Times*, 9 June 1897. 'Lord Charles Beresford came in' *Times*, 21 and 23 June 1897. 'It is very bad form' TNA ADM 116/3108. 'his many medals' *Times*, 11 Dec 1897. 'independent-minded man' *Times*, 31 Dec 1897. 'growing popularity' *Times*, 5 Jan 1898.

Chapter 13 MP for York 1898

'a critic and' *Times*, 27 Jan 1898; 'a mere question' *Times*, 23 Feb 1898; 'a very serious' *HC Deb* 10 March 1898 Vol 54 cc1252-342. 'shrink from being' *HC Deb* 18 March 1898 Vol 55 cc251-364. 'there are some' *HC Deb* 10 March 1898 Vol 54 c1211. 'six good fighting' *HC Deb* 22 July 1898 Vol 62 cc854-967. 'about the only' *HC Deb* 22 July 1898 Vol 62 cc854-967. 'control the "belly"' *Times*, 29 Mar 1898. 'leased or ceded' *HC Deb* 25 February 1898 Vol 54 cc30-1. 'to obtain accurate' Beresford, 1899,

End notes

pp. 447-8. 'pour into the' Bennett, 1968, p. 215. 'The only power' Salisbury to Beresford, 18 Aug 1898. NMM MRF/61. 'great Russian commercial' *Times*, 10 Nov 1898. 'to place a body' *Times*, 11 Nov 1898. 'there was no' *Times*, 4 Jan 1899.

Chapter 14 MP for York 1899

'as good a naval' *HC Deb* 14 April 1899 Vol 69 cc1141-237. 'employed with great' *HC Deb* 21 April 1899 Vol 70 cc223-315. 'I shall oppose the' *HC Deb* 21 June 1899 Vol 73 cc163-221. 'no security at' Beresford, 1899, p. 6. 'so elaborate and' *Times*, 15 May 1899. 'light reading' *Manchester Guardian*, 15 May 1890. 'Very big words' *HC Deb* 09 June 1899 Vol 72 cc777-876. 'upon which we' *Times*, 23 June 1899. 'the conditions under' *HC Deb* 04 July 1899 Vol 73 c1408. 'it is now' *New York Times*, 19 Nov 1899. 'no truth in' *Observer*, 19 Nov 1899. 'The very fact' *Times*, 6 Nov 1899. 'I most emphatically' Beresford, 1914, p. 461.

Chapter 15 Giants at bay 1900-1902

'say what he' *Times*, 10 Jan 1900. 'had to take' Beresford's Notebook, p. O5. NMM GBK/1. 'linked together with' Beresford, 1914, p. 465. 'anxious to stir' King-Hall's diary, 19 Mar 1900. 'in the interest' Beresford to Balfour, 8 Apr 1900. BL Add Mss 49713. 'sending home strong' Beresford to Sandars, 8 Apr 1900. BL Add Mss 49713. 'from 5th February' Beresford's Notebook, p. O5. NMM GBK/1. 'if anything were' Beresford's Notebook, p, S8. nd. NMM GBK/1. 'the Custom of' Beresford to Balfour, 8 Apr 1900. BL Add Mss 49713. 'an official letter' Beresford to Fisher, 15 June 1900. NMM WHI/1. 'strong Mediterranean flavour' Marder, 1952, pp. 169-70. 'uncommonly well' Marder, 1952, pp. 161-2. 'learnt more in' Marder, 1952, p. 161-2. 'I have never' Beresford's Notebook, p. P4., nd. NMM GBK/1. 'I regret that' Bennett, 1968, p. 235. 'did not employ' *Times*, 31 Dec 1900. 'in tragic circumstances' *Manchester Guardian*, 18 Dec 1900. 'see both sides' Beresford to Bellairs, 27 Dec 1900. McGill Bellairs archive. 'I get on' Beresford to Bellairs, Dec? 1900. McGill Bellairs archive. '[I] was told' Beresford's Notebook, p. O5, nd, but before 18 March 1901. NMM GBK/1. 'severe reprimand' Beresford to Bellairs, 9 Dec 1900. McGill Bellairs archive. 'a complete innovation' *New York Times*, 24 Sept 1901. 'Lord C. is not' Lady Charles to White, 9 April [1901]. NMM WHI/7. 'more urgent than' Boyce, 1990, pp. 115-8. 'very strong … on' King-Hall's diary, 9 June 1901. 'have made efficiency' *Daily Mail*, 11 June 1901. 'we no longer' National Review, July 1901. 'It would be' *Daily Mail*, 21 June 1901. 'Before it is' *Daily Mail*, 24 June 1901. 'there is nothing' *HC Deb* 24 June 1901 Vol 95 cc1200-1. 'Wilson in A fleet' King-Hall's diary, 6 Sept 1901. 'had decidedly the' King-Hall's diary, 10 Sept 1901. 'Both Wilson and' Marder, 1952, pp. 207-8. 'in the best' Lady Charles to White. NMM WHI/7. 'Your flagship is' Chatfield, 1942, p. 41. 'a free hand' *Times*, 2 July 1901. 'I feel confident' Beresford to Bellairs, 26 Oct 1901. McGill Bellairs archive. 'C.B. abusing Fisher' King-Hall, 1935, p. 313. 'I have a' Beresford to Fisher, nd. CCA FISR 1/2. 'the lasting gratitude' Beresford's Notebook, 14 Nov 1901. NMM GBK/1. 'it is quite' Beresford to Fisher, 4 June 1901. TNA ADM 1/7450B. 'the proper position' Beresford's Notebook, Nov 1901. NMM GBK/1. 'He is a first-rate' Fisher to Spencer, 28 Mar 1902 in Marder, 1952, pp. 237-8.

End notes

Chapter 16 Hammering on the Parliamentary anvil 1902-03

'to call for' Fisher to Beresford, 27 Feb 1902. NMM THU/1. 'head straight' Fisher to Thursfield, 27 Feb 1902. NMM THU/1. 'prolonged cheers' *Times*, 15 Mar 1902. 'a most respectful letter' LLC pamphlet. BL Add Mss 50288. 'remonstrated with his' *Manchester Guardian*, 17 Mar 1902. 'I cannot allow' Noel to Admiralty, 17 March 1902. NMM NOE/5. 'for the particular' *Times*, 9 Apr 1902. 'imparted to you' Arnold-Forster to Beresford, 25 Apr 1902. BL Add MSS 50288. 'it is possible' Beresford to Arnold-Forster, 27 Apr 1902. BL Add MSS 50288. 'a very grave' *Times*, 29 April 1902. 'grave displeasure' TNA ADM 196/83/86. 'The constituted authorities' *HC Deb* 05 May 1902 Vol 107 cc613-5. 'physical and military' *HC Deb* 09 June 1902 Vol 109 cc97-8. 'during the late' *Manchester Guardian*, 26 Dec 1902. 'in order to' *HC Deb* 20 June 1902 Vol 109 cc1257-326. 'deny that the' *HC Deb* 20 June 1902 Vol 109 cc1257-326. 'on the occasion' White to Scott, 16 July 1902. NMM WHI/2. 'in low state' King-Hall's Diary, 21 Aug 1902. 'pure and simple' *Times*, 2 Oct 1902. 'until they shall' Cmd. 1385, December 1902. 'satisfied with their' *HC Deb* 10 June 1902 Vol 109 c236. 'a brilliant and' Western Morning News, 1 Jan 1903.

Chapter 17 The Channel Fleet 1903-05

'Lord Charles Beresford' *Times*, 2 May 1903. 'it was difficult' James, 1956, pp. 100-2. 'a marvellous man' Pelly, 1938, p. 85. 'A lady asked' Richmond's diary, 26 Oct 1903. NMM RIC 1/6. 'scurvily treated' James, 1956, pp. 101-2. 'had caused no' *Observer*, 24 May 1903. 'unprecedented in magnitude' *Manchester Guardian*, 6 Aug 1903. 'I have always' Beresford to Balfour, 30 Aug 1903. BL Add MSS 49713. 'The officers recognized' *Manchester Guardian*, 14 Sept 1903. 'bitter disappointment' *Manchester Guardian*, 14 Sept 1903. 'honourably acquitted' *Times*, 28 Oct 1903. 'it will be' *Manchester Guardian*, 12 Dec 1903. 'he sustained concussion' *Times*, 19 Jan 1904. 'Every boat burned' Beresford, 1914, pp. 493-4. 'neither called' TNA ADM 196/83-86. 'improved turret sights' Adm to Beresford, 11 Apr 1904. TNA ADM 116/3108. 'evidently much annoyed' *Times*, 23 Apr 1904. 'who perfectly appreciated' *Times*, 26 April 1904. 'judicious and appropriate' Knollys to Beresford, 3 May 1904. NMM MRF/61. 'a genius' Beresford to Balfour, 25 May 1904. BL Add MSS 49713. 'would only be' Marder, 1940, p. 440. 'If this statement' Hough, 1969, p. 208. 'their Lordships would' Marder, 1940, p. 441, fn10. 'he did not intend' King-Hall's Diary, 3 March 1905. 'It made him' Beresford to Bellairs, 12 Dec 1905. McGill Bellairs Archive. 'all sorts of' Pelly, 1938, pp. 85-8. 'He will be' Pakenham to Sykes, 21 Feb 1905. NMM PKM/2/20.

Chapter 18 The Mediterranean command 1905-07

'more cordial, spontaneous' *Times*, 1 July 1905. 'Lady Charles' disappointment' Crease to Bacon 9 July 1928. CCA FISR 15/3/1/2. 'one of T H R E A T' Beresford to Bellairs, 12 Dec 1905. McGill Bellairs archive. '[Battenberg] may be a' Beresford to Bellairs, 4 Feb 1906. McGill Bellairs archive. 'refused the billet' Wemyss to his wife, 22 July 1906. CCA WMYS 7/6. 'any means of' Beresford to Sykes NMM PKM/2/21. 'Sir John see' Bacon, 1940, pp. 126-32. 'I am more' Bacon to Fisher, 31 March 1906. CCA FISR 15/3/1/1 Pt 4. 'not being consulted' Bacon to Fisher, 15 April 1906. CCA FISR 8/17. 'Beresford's insulting and' Magnus, 1964, p. 363. 'no sooner was' *Times*, 18 Aug 1906. 'Just finished the' Bennett, 1968, p. 278. 'a properly fitted' TNA CAB

End notes

16/9 B, p. 78. 'the policy was' TNA CAB 16/9B, p. 78. 'a new Home' Marder, 1956, pp. 98-9. 'France and Russia' Admiralty. The Home Fleet. Dec 1906, p. 2. 'The pamphlet is' Beresford to Admiralty, 8 Dec 1906. TNA ADM 116/3108. 'an outside point' Fisher minute 9 Dec 1906 TNA ADM 116/3108. 'I could not' Beresford to Tweedmouth, 22 Jan 1907. TNA CAB 16/9B. 'My conviction is' Marder, 1956, p. 117. 'exercise and manoeuvres' Points agreed minute, 28 Jan 1907. TNA ADM 116/3108. 'Three cheers for' *Observer*, 27 Jan 1907. 'I am very fit' Beresford to Jessica Sykes 11 Feb 1906. NMM PKM/2/21. 'anybody look so' Wemyss to his wife, 17 June 1906. CCA WMYS 7/6. 'Admirals' Frewen, 1961, p. 117. 'the Admiral is' Wemyss to his wife, late 1905. CCA WMYS 7/4. 'Everything and' Wemyss to his wife, 19 June 1906. CCA WMYS 7/6. 'the nine Battleships' Beresford to Pakenham, 12 Nov 1905. NMM PKM/2/21. 'development of gunnery' TNA ADM 196/83/86. 'Vice Admiral Commanding' Memorandum on relations. 1907 TNA ADM 116/3108. 'Certainly he holds' Hay to Fisher, 8 Jan 1906. TNA ADM 116/3108.

Chapter 19 The Channel Fleet 1907-08

'narrow, dogmatic, and' ODNB. '[He] insisted on' Chatfield, 1942, pp. 56-67. 'ammunition for you' Beresford to Fisher, 22 Apr 1907. CCA FISR 15/3/1/1 Pt 4. 'eight different ideas' Fisher to Beresford, 30 Apr 1907. TNA CAB 16/9 B, p. 121. 'loath to appear' Beresford to Fisher, 2 May 1907. CCA FISR 1/5 FP 242. 'I don't want' Fisher to Beresford, 4 May 1907 TNA ADM 116/3108. 'to rearrange the' Admiralty to Beresford, 13 May 1907. TNA ADM 116/3108. 'employed more battleships' War arrangements, June 1907 TNA ADM 116/3108. 'The Fleet which' Admiralty to Beresford, 14 June 1907. TNA ADM 116/3108. 'Admiral in Command' Fisher to White, nd 1907? NMM WHI/75. 'the most gigantic' *Times*, 29 June 1907. 'Carry on, please' Dawson, 1936, p. 55. 'catchers' Dawson, 1936, p. 56. 'cosy rather than' *Daily Despatch*, 7 Aug 1907. 'a breezy talk' Ponsonby to Fisher, 8 Oct 1907. CCA FISR 1/5 FP 259. 'unless I know' Beresford to Admiralty, 27 June 1907. TNA ADM 116/1037. 'a fraud and' Minutes of 5 July meeting. TNA ADM 116/3108. 'If you will' Minutes of 5 July meeting. TNA ADM 116/3108. 'I cannot see' Minutes of 5 July meeting. TNA ADM 116/3108. 'allow the present' Thomas to Beresford, 5 July 1908. TNA ADM 116/3108. 'liars trying to' Hough, 1969, p. 220. 'disposition of the' Admiralty to Beresford, 30 July 1907. TNA CAB 16/9 B, p. 32-33. 'There's Charlie Beresford' *Times*, 7 Aug 1907. 'a breezy speech' *Manchester Guardian*, 7 Aug 1907. 'take immediate steps' Beresford to Blumenfeld nd c 8 Aug 1907. PA BLU/1/2/BERE.3. 'unfair conditions' Ponsonby, 1951, p. 132. 'I never enjoyed' Beresford to Lady Londonderry, 25 Sept 1907. D/Lo/C645(2). 'remained in a' Scott's record of the incidents Feb 1909. CCA FISR 5/16 FP 4265. 'Paint work appears' Scott's record of the incidents Feb 1909. CCA FISR 5/16 FP 4265. 'The ships are' Beresford paintwork memo, 1 Nov 1907. TNA ADM 1/7924. 'That was a' Dawson, 1936, p. 60. 'The staffs were' *New York Times*, 12 Nov 1907. 'a changed Sir' (Dawson 1933), p. 61. 'after such a' Beresford to the Admiralty, 8 Nov 1907. TNA ADM 116/3108. 'inexcusable' Admiralty to Beresford, 13 Nov 1907. TNA ADM 116/3108. 'on the competence' Admiralty to Beresford, 17 Jan 1908. T NA ADM 116/3108. 'shamming illness' Esher to Fisher, 19 Jan 1908. CCA FISR 1/6 FP 276. 'it has come' TNA CAB 16/9B, p. 174-5. 'a very serious' Admiralty to Beresford 30 July 1907 TNA ADM 116/1037.

End notes

Chapter 20 The Channel Fleet 1908-09

'sick of the' Beresford to White, 3 Mar 1908. NMM WHI/2. 'the author of' Beresford to Bellairs, 6 Mar 1908. McGill Bellairs archive. 'the Navy has' Beresford to Balfour, 7 Mar 1908. BL Add MSS 49713, ff 177-83. 'It is their' Beresford to Fleet, 27 Feb 1908. TNA ADM 116/3108. 'grave disapprobation' *HC Deb* 09 March 1908 Vol 185 c1098. 'a mining vessel' Beresford to Admiralty 11 Apr 1908. TNA CAB 16/9 A, p. 188. 'at present the' Admiralty to Beresford, 16 Apr 1904. TNA CAB 16/9 A, p. 188. '[Beresford] will not' Morris, 1981, p. 61. 'It is unprecedented' Fisher to McKenna, 16 April 1908. CCA FISR 6/1 FP 306. 'a pack of' Magnus, 1964, p. 370. 'marked antagonism' Memorandum, May? 1908 TNA ADM 116/3108. 'the gallantry of' *Times*, 25 May 1908. 'the wide community' *Manchester Guardian* 29 May 1908. 'officers who will' Memorandum, early June 1908. TNA ADM 116/3108. 'study alternative plans' Admiralty to Beresford, c 10 June 1908 (draft). TNA ADM 116/3108. 'is a terrible' Beresford to de Robeck, 23 May 1908. CCA DRBK 3/26. 'provide some little' Scott, 1919, p. 209. 'a very false' Beresford to the Secretary of the Admiralty, 11 Aug 1908. TNA ADM 116/3108. 'in a loud' Scott's record of the incidents (1909) CCA FISR 5/16 (FP 4365). 'he shoved the' Scott to White, 23 June 1908. NMM WHI/2. 'not to report' Crease to White, 23 June 1908. NMM WHI/76. '7.4 Ordered by Flag' Good Hope log book. TNA ADM 53/21377. 'Had the signal' *Times*, 7 July 1908. 'the Commander-in-Chief' *Times*, 6 July 1908. 'We say frankly' *Times*, 8 July 1908. 'Were the rules' *HC Deb* 9 July 1908 Vol 192, cols 53-54. 'recognise their special' *HC Deb* 28 July 1908 Vol 193 cc1211-2. 'are satisfied that' *HC Deb* 30 July 1908 Vol 193 cc1741-2. 'address myself to' Beresford to de Robeck, 6 Aug 1908. CCA DRBK 3/26. 'never forget the' Magnus, 1964, p. 371 'great pleasure and' Lee, 1927, p. 600. 'let me repeat' Queen Alexandra to Beresford, 20 Aug 1908. NMM MRF/61. 'vacate the command' *Times*, 6 Aug 1908. 'contains much information' McKenna to Beresford, 11 Aug 1908. CCA FISR 1/7 (FP 326). 'would do its' *Manchester Guardian*, 26 Sept 1908. 'no tactical training' Beresford to Admiralty, 7 Oct 1908. TNA ADM 116/1037. 'false economies' Beresford to Bellairs, 11 Oct 1908. McGill Bellairs archive. 'to shake up' Beresford to Lady Londonderry, c 2 Dec 1908. D/Lo/C645(10). 'fulfil my duty' Beresford to Admiralty, 3 Dec 1908. TNA ADM 116/1037. 'would not remain' Beresford to Long, 5 Dec 1908. BL Add MSS 62407. 'have heard something' Beresford to Lady Londonderry, early Dec 1908. D/Lo/C645(9). 'These Landing Parties' Beresford to Admiralty, 31 Dec 1908. TNA ADM 1/7811. 'Altogether it was' Beresford to Queen of Norway, 11 Dec 1908. NMM MRF/61. 'B.B.B.B. – the Beresford' Beresford to Queen of Norway, 11 Dec 1908. NMM MRF/61. 'Some Time' *New York Times*, 10 Jan 1909 'a trifle stout' Lucy, 1920, pp. 250-1. 'this decision will' McKenna to Beresford, 19 Dec 1908. BL Add MSS 62407. 'Walter Long hopes' Marder, 1956, pp. 204-5. 'not either convenient Beresford on King Ed VII to McKenna, 23 Dec 1908. CCA MCKN 3/8, f 20. 'sit still and' Beresford to Long, 14 Jan 1909. BL Add MSS 62407. 'knew that the' Beresford to Noel, 17 Jan 1909. NMM NOE/5. 'a long talk' Beresford to Noel, 11 Feb 1909. NMM NOE/5. 'cashier' Marder, 1961, p. 161. 'In the ordinary' Fisher to McKenna, 27 Feb 1909. CCA MCKN 6/2 f37. 'parting gift on' *Times*, 13 Mar 1909. 'good-bye, good luck and' *Manchester Guardian*, 24 Mar 1909. 'boatswain's ball and chain' Beresford to Lady Londonderry, nd. D/Lo/C645(40). 'For he's a' *Times*, 25 Mar 1909.

End notes

Chapter 21 Career's end 1909-10

'During the whole' Beresford to Asquith, 2 Apr 1909. BL Add MSS 49713, ff 195-202. 'I do not intend' Beresford to Asquith, 2 Apr 1909 (2nd letter). TNA CAB 17/7. 'surest way to' McKenna to Asquith, nd. In McKenna, 1948, pp. 86-7. 'the absolute incompetence' Marder, 1961, p. 192. 'It is plain' Report – early draft, nd. TNA CAB 17/7. 'arrangements [were] quite' *Times*, 14 Aug 1909. 'no words of' Esher to Balfour, 15 Aug 1909. (Esher, 1934), pp. 399-400. 'cowardly document' Fisher to McKenna, 19 Aug 1909. CCA FISR 1/8 (FP 406). 'in ecstasies' Balfour to Esher, 16 Aug 1909. CCA ESHR 5/31. 'canvass the electors' *Times*, 24 Nov 1909. 'to address open-air' *Times*, 26 Nov 1909. '[a] disenfranchisement of' *Times*, 1 Dec 1909. 'the question of' *Manchester Guardian*, 18 Jan 1910.

Chapter 22 Return to the back benches 1910

'give us credit' *HC Deb* 02 March 1910 Vol 14 cc906-39. 'about nothing but' *HC Deb* 14 March 1910 Vol 15 cc38-147. 'I investigated the' *HC Deb* 14 March 1910 Vol 15 cc38-147 'the kindness, generosity' Bennett, 1968, Chpt 12. 'was always excellent' *HC Deb* 08 June 1910 Vol 17 cc830-7. 'who get killed' *HC Deb* 08 June 1910 Vol 17 cc878-83. 'the Government are' *HC Deb* 14 July 1910 Vol 19 cc621-737. 'he wished to' *Manchester Guardian*, 12 Oct 1910. 'created by the' *Times*, 28 Oct 1910. 'a keen controversialist' *Times*, 24 Nov 1910. 'disquieted' *Manchester Guardian*, 29 Nov 1910. 'no personal objections' Asquith to McKenna, 26 Dec 1910, McKenna, 1948, p. 90. 'to be heard' Beresford to Long, 19 Dec 1910. BL Add Mss 62407. 'indispensable' McKenna to Asquith. CCA MCKN 3/18.

Chapter 23 Member for the Navy 1911

'officially', *HC Deb* 08 February 1911 Vol 21 cc264-6. 'Parliament will have' *HC Deb* 09 February 1911 Vol 21 cc416-8. 'No one knows' *Times*, 10 Feb 1911. 'I maintain that' *HC Deb* 18 May 1911 Vol 25 cc2157-63. 'one of the' *HC Deb* 25 May 1911 Vol 26 cc451-571. 'a secretly organized' *Times*, 20 June 1911. 'grave concern' *Times*, 26 June 1911. 'the teeth and' *Times*, 27 June 1911. 'a grave emergency' *Times*, 28 June 1911. 'if the Declaration' *HC Deb* 29 June 1911 Vol 27 cc574-696. 'no communication will be' Beresford to Asquith, 27 July 1911. CCA MCKN 3/22.

Chapter 24 Home Rule 1912

'corrections of detail' *Times* 5 Nov 1911. 'in part due' *Times*, 7 Nov 1911. 'deceived' Beresford, 1912. 'much reduced dimensions' *Observer*, 4 Feb 1912. 'all that emphasis' *Times*, 29 Jan 1912. 'particularly piquant' *New York Times*, 7 Feb 1912. 'Surely the foundation of' *HC Deb* 18 March 1912 Vol 35 cc1549-618. 'prevent a good' *HC Deb* 20 March 1912 Vol 35 cc1964-93. 'interfering in a' *Times*, 23 Mar 1912. 'the dauntless heroism' *Times*, 22 Apr 1912. 'determined virtually' *Times*, 18 June 1912. 'The Mediterranean has' *Manchester Guardian*, 22 Jul 1912. 'Who is more' *HC Deb* 24 July 1912 Vol 41 cc1197-265. 'most eccentric individual' *Times*, 08 August 1912. 'using all means' Hyde, 1979, p. 111. 'the ship was' *HC Deb* 07 October 1912 Vol 42 cc32-148. 'the full circumstances' *Times*, *HC Deb* 11 December 1912 Vol 45 cc433-4. 'ever since he' *HC Deb* 20 December 1912 Vol 45 cc1875-907 'Since the First' *HC Deb* 20 December 1912 Vol 45 cc1875-907. 'it will be' *Manchester Guardian*, 21 Dec 1912.

End notes

Chapter 25 Slowing down 1913

'if you go' *HC Deb* 27 March 1913 Vol 50 cc1889-974. 'of being 20,000' *HC Deb* 31 March 1913 Vol 51 cc58-171. '[the mastery] of the' *Manchester Guardian*, 6 May 1913. 'robbed' *HC Deb* 04 June 1913 Vol 53 cc934-47. 'subsidising personal habits' *HC Deb* 04 June 1913 Vol 53 cc907-30. 'I am an' *HC Deb* 10 June 1913 Vol 53 cc1463-589. 'zeal and enthusiasm' *Times*, 5 July 1913. 'I cannot understand' Midleton to Law, 17 July 1913. PA BL/29/6/24. 'we have up' *HC Deb* 17 July 1913 Vol 55 cc1465-583. 'The authority of the' *Times*, 21 July 1913. 'a prominent figure' *Times*, 5 Sept 1913. 'but the date' *Times*, 10 Oct 1913. 'great regret' *Times*, 18 Oct 1913. 'Ulster was terribly' *Manchester Guardian*, 27 Oct 1913. 'the English would' *Observer*, 2 Nov 1913. 'I am told' Beresford to Lady Londonderry, 10 Nov 1913. D/Lo/C645(22).

Chapter 26 Last days of peace 1914

'disturbed in his' Paget to Law, 14 Jan 1914. PA BL/31/2/38. 'there will be' Beresford to Vesey, 29 Jan 1914. PA BL/31/2/68. 'As long as' *Times*, 12 Feb 1914. 'seriously ill with' Beresford to Law, 2 Mar 1914. PA BL/31/4/1. 'for a fact' *Manchester Guardian*, 23 Mar 1914. 'Whether a battle' *HC Deb* 25 March 1914 Vol 60 cc375-81. 'would be in' *HC Deb* 25 March 1914 Vol 60 cc375-81. 'outrageous' *HC Deb* 26 March 1914 Vol 60 cc529-34. 'we have broken' *HC Deb* 28 April 1914 Vol 61 cc1550-661. 'cheered so much' *Observer*, 5 Apr 1914; *Manchester Guardian*, 6 Apr 1914. 'an Irishman, a' *Manchester Guardian*, 10 May 1914. 'The political effects' *Times*, 29 June 1914. 'appalling catastrophe towards' Beresford to Times 28 June 1914. 'gambling transaction' *HC Deb* 07 July 1914 Vol 64 cc1032-55. 'defence rather than' *Times*, 11 July 1914. 'Europe might be' *Manchester Guardian*, 30 July 1914. 'Happily there seems' Asquith, 1982, p. 123. 'the future safety' *Manchester Guardian*, 3 Aug 1914.

Chapter 27 The arrival of war 1914

'start at once' *HC Deb* 04 August 1914 Vol 65 cc1941-52. 'Is it decreed' *HC Deb* 05 August 1914 Vol 65 cc1987-90. 'growing feeling of' *HC Deb* 28 August 1914 Vol 66 cc266-8. 'a day of reckoning' *Manchester Guardian*, 9 Sept 1914. 'the lighter side' TLS, 8 Oct 1914. 'for some reason' *Manchester Guardian*, 8 Oct 1914. 'long and anxiously' *Times*, 16 Oct 1914. 'record [of] spirited' *Daily Mail*. 'all Germans, including' Lee to WSC, 29 Aug 1914 in Gilbert, 1972, p 66-8. 'we must intern' *Manchester Guardian*, 31 Oct 1914. 'warm clothing and' *Times*, 31 Oct 1914. 'lost on account' *HC Deb* 12 Nov 1914 Vol 68 cc79-123. 'The Noble Lord's' *HC Deb* 12 Nov 1914 Vol 68 cc79-123. 'a most boring' Asquith, 1982, p. 318. 'to legalise vigilance' *HC Deb* 23 Nov 1914 Vol 68 cc773-4. 'That there are' *HC Deb* 26 Nov 1914 Vol 68 cc1361-457. 'barbarous methods' *Manchester Guardian*, 4 Dec 1914. 'of protest re' Beresford to Lady Londonderry, 18 Dec 1914. D/Lo/C645(25). 'How disgracefully they' Lady Charles to Lady Londonderry, 10 Dec 1914. D/Lo/C646(44).

Chapter 28 Goodbye to the Commons 1915

'It is unpardonable' *New York Times* 13 Jan 1915. 'The country ought' *HC Deb* 15 February 1915 Vol 69 cc919-79. 'the only retired' *Manchester Guardian*, 14 Jan 1915. 'to invite him' Long to Law, 30 Jan 1915. PA BL/36/2/55. 'to treat as' *HC Deb* 01 March 1915 Vol 70 cc573-4. 'every British subject' *HC Deb* 03 March 1915 Vol 70

End notes

cc833-916. 'an honourable military' *HC Deb* 03 March 1915 Vol 70 cc833-916. 'confirmed my statements' Beresford to Asquith, 15 Apr 1915 MAXSE/470, f 150. 'against the advice' Beresford to Maxse, 17 Apr 1915. WSRO MAXSE/470, f 148-9 '[it] may hasten' Lady Charles to Lady Londonderry, 17 Mar 1915. D/Lo/C646(48). 'a piece of' *Observer*, 2 May 1915. 'Does he hope' Powell in *Observer*, 9 May 1915. 'heart-breaking' *HC Deb* 27 April 1915 Vol 71 cc623-92. 'devilish treatment, cowardly' *Times*, 1 May 1915. 'the rich German' *Observer*, 2 May 1915. 'Do you think' *HC Deb* 11 May 1915 Vol 71 cc1606-16. 'to free our' *Times*, 15 May1915. 'Why does Haldane' *Times*, 14 May 1915. 'Every German throughout' *Times*, 14 May 1915. 'extremely ill-used' Bennett, 1968. 'My present position' Beresford to Law, 31 May 1915. PA BL/50/3/71. 'I do not' Lincolnshire County Archives. '[I have] only' Morris, 1984, p. 131. 'had cotton been' *Manchester Guardian*, 12 Aug 1915. '[It] shows how' *Times*, 8 Oct 1915. 'did away with' *Times*, 19 Nov 1915. 'in a complex' Beresford to *Times*, 8 Dec 1915. 'for a day' *Times* 9 Dec 1915. 'we shall lose' Beresford to Blakeney, 11 Dec 1915. CUL Add.MS7509/45.

Chapter 29 In another place 1916

'a sufficient and' *Observer*, 2 Jan 1916. 'its last pinch' *Manchester Guardian*, 4 Jan 1916. 'on four separate' Beresford to Maxse, 10 Oct 1916. WSRO MAXSE/473, f 809 'with shrewd good' Repington 1920, p. 102. 'whom he attacked' Repington 1920, p. 103. 'to wipe many' *Manchester Guardian*, 13 Jan 1916. 'a paper blockade' *HL Deb* 22 February 1916 Vol 21 cc72-128. 'this new air' *HL Deb* 09 March 1916 Vol 21 cc318-63. 'very unfair' *HL Deb* 14 March 1916 Vol 21 cc377-86. 'London should be' *HL Deb* 30 March 1916 Vol 21 cc580-6. 'the life of' *HL Deb* 19 April 1916 Vol 21 cc791-808. 'to make the' *HL Deb* 11 May 1916 Vol 21 cc1002-36 'The rebels could' *HL Deb* 11 May 1916 Vol 21 cc1002-36. 'the smallest conception' *HL Deb* 31 May 1916 Vol 22 cc222-49. 'cruel to the' *HL Deb* 31 May 1916 Vol 22 cc249-68. 'a victory for us' *Times*, 5 June 1916. 'would be the' *Times*, 10 June 1916. 'not a single' Beresford to Jellicoe, 9 July 1916 in Jellicoe, Vol. 1, 1966-68. 'He felt his' *Times*, 10 June 1916. 'a special instance' *HL Deb* 26 July 1916 Vol 22 cc920-1. 'has my warmest' *Times*, 23 Oct 1916. 'very difficult commercial' *Manchester Guardian* 10 Aug 1916. 'they were going' *Manchester Guardian*, 16 Nov 1916. 'not well at' Beresford to Lady Londonderry, 24 Nov 1916. D/Lo/C645(29). 'I am overworked' Beresford to Maxse, 10 Oct 1916. WSRO MAXSE/473, f 809. 'The Unseen Hand' *Manchester Guardian*, 16 Dec 1916. 'The country' Mina Beresford to Lady Londonderry, 1916. D/Lo/C646(52). 'in utter chaos' Mina Beresford to Lady Londonderry, 12 Dec 1916. D/Lo/C646(58). 'even now he' Mina Beresford to Lady Londonderry, 4 Dec 1916. D/Lo/C646(55).

Chapter 30 Sniping from the sidelines 1917

'well in hand' *Times*, 14 Feb 1917. 'on the grounds' *Times*, 27 Feb 1917. 'gratifyingly' *Times*, 3 Mar 1917. 'strictly observe the' *Times*, 23 Mar 1917. was impossible to' *Times*, 20 Apr 1917. 'Our people' *Times*, 26 Apr 1917. 'We have actually' *Times*, 25 May 1917. 'in agonies' Beresford to Lady Londonderry, 27 May 1917. D/Lo/C645(31). 'papers and proofs' Beresford to Law, 2 June 1917. PA BL/82/1/3. 'to my friend' Wikipedia. 'for punishing those' *Times*, 17 July 1917. 'was completely out' *Times*, 26 July 1917. 'Lord Beresford is' *Times*, 30 July 1917. 'would never have' *Times*, 12 Oct 1917. 'musical programme and' *Times*, 17 Sept 1917. 'Something [was] going' *Times*, 15 Oct 1917. 'the recent loss' *Times*, 13 July 1917. 'four towns of' *Times*, 23 Oct 1917.

End notes

'The Liberal Party' *Times*, 26 Oct 1917. 'I am afraid' *HL Deb* 01 Nov 1917 Vol 26 cc887-98. 'statements made lately' *HL Deb* 13 December 1917 Vol 27 cc151-62. 'one which was' *Observer*, 16 Dec 1917.

Chapter 31 War's end 1918

'criminal mistakes at' Beresford to Lady Londonderry, 12 Jan 1918. D/Lo/C645(32). 'No person who' *HL Deb* 17 January 1918 Vol 27 cc739-816. 'divided military control' *HL Deb* 19 February 1918 Vol 29 cc38-72. 'a German financial' *HL Deb* 05 March 1918 Vol 29 cc229-39. 'the serious losses' *HL Deb* 06 March 1918 Vol 29 cc307-24. 'there is close' *HL Deb* 21 March 1918 Vol 29 cc571-81. 'agencies in this' *HL Deb* 08 May 1918 Vol 29 cc1009-51. 'Regulations have all' *HL Deb* 11 June 1918 Vol 30 cc165-88. 'impossible' *HL Deb* 27 June 1918 Vol 30 cc431-93. 'If … it were' *HL Deb* 08 July 1918 Vol 30 cc649-94

Chapter 32 Last days 1919

'Dot cannot see' Beresford to Lady Londonderry, 28 Dec 1918. D/Lo/C645(33). 'no visitors for' *Times*, 11 Feb 1919. 'I have been' Beresford to Hurd, 5 Apr 1919. CCA HURD 1/5. 'my gallant dead' Beresford to Hurd, 5 Apr 1919. CCA HURD 1/5. 'my case is very' *HL Deb* 29 May 1919 Vol 34 cc921-59. 'a war which' *HL Deb* 09 July 1919 Vol 35 cc408-21. 'A trial in' *Times*, 9 Jul 1919. 'apoplexy' *Manchester Guardian*, 9 Sept 1919. 'the blame fell' *Times*, 8 Sept 1919. 'no conspicuous changes' *Times*, 8 Sept 1919. 'his efforts to' *Times*, 9 Sept 1919. 'one of Germany's' *Times*, 10 Sept 1919. 'impressive' *Manchester Guardian*, 15 Sept 1919. 'a fine conception' *Manchester Guardian*, 24 Sept 1919. 'Charles William de' CUL Crewe C.34.1.27.

Bibliography

Anand, S. 2008. Daisy. *The Life and Loves of the Countess of Warwick*. London: Piaktus.

Asher, M. 2005. *Khartoum: The Ultimate Imperial Adventure*. London: Viking.

Asquith, H. H. (Ed M, & E. Brock) 1982. *Letters to Venetia Stanley*. Oxford: Oxford University Press.

Bacon, R. H. S. 1940. *From 1900 Onwards*. London: Hutchinson.

Bayly, S. L. 1939. *Pull Together!* London: George G Harrap & Co Ltd.

Bennett, G. 1968. *Charlie B*. London: Dawnay.

Beresford, Lord C. 1899. *The Break-Up of China*. London: Harper & Bros.

Beresford, Lord C. 1914. *The Memoirs of Admiral Lord Charles Beresford*. London: Methuen and Co.

Beresford, Lord C. 1912. *The Betrayal*. London: P. S. King & Son.

Blathwayt, R. 1917. *Through Life and Round the World*. London: George Allen & Unwin.

Blumenfeld, R. D. 1930. *R D.B.'s Diary, 1887-1914*. London : Heinemann.

Bolitho, H. 1934. *Victoria, the Widow and Her Son*. London: Cobden-Sanderson.

Boyce, (Ed) 1990. *The crisis of British power: the imperial and naval papers of the second earl of Selborne 1895–1910*. London: Historians' Press.

Bradford, A. S. 1923. *Life of Admiral of the Fleet Sir Arthur Knyvet Wilson*. London: John Murray.

Buckle, G. (Ed) 1926. *The Letters of Queen Victoria*. London: J. Murray.

Chalmers, W. S. 1951. *The Life and Letters of David, Earl Beatty*. London: Hodder and Stoughton.

Chatfield, L. 1942. *The Navy and Defence*. London: William Heinemann Ltd.

Churchill, P. and Mitchell, J. 1974. *Jennie Lady Randolph Churchill*. London: Collins.

Clowes, E. L. 1903. *The Royal Navy, Vol VII*. London: Sampson Low.

Colvile, H. E. 1889. *History of the Sudan Campaign*. London: Stationery Office.

Cowles, V. 1956. *Edward VII and his Circle*. London: Hamish Hamilton.

Cunningham A. B. 1951. *A Sailor's Odyssey*. London: Hutchinson.

Bibliography

Curteis, G. 1889. *Bishop Selwyn of New Zealand and Litchfield*. London: Kegan Paul.

Dark, S. 1923. *W. S. Gilbert: His Life and Letters*. London: Methuen.

Dawson, L. 1933. *Flotillas: A Hard-Lying Story*. London: Rich & Cowan Ltd.

Dawson, L. 1936. *Gone for a Sailor*. London: Rich & Cowan Ltd.

De Crespigny, C. (Ed Dewar) 1896. *Memoirs of Sir Claude Champion de Crespigny*. London: Lawrence & Bullen.

Deacon, E. W. L. 1978. *The Silent War: A History of Western Naval Intelligence*. London: Muller.

Lyall, Sir A. C. 1905. *The Life of the Marquis of Dufferin and Ava*. London: John Murray.

Elliot, A. D. 1911. *The life of George Joachim Goschen, first Viscount Goschen, 1831–1907*. London: Longmans, Green & Co.

Esher, R. B. 1934. *Journals and Letters 1903-1910*. London: Ivor Nicholson and Watson.

Fortesque, Sir S. 1920. *Looking Back*. London: Longmans, Green & Co.

Freeman, R. 2009. *The Great Edwardian Naval Feud*. Barnsley: Pen and Sword.

Freeman, R. 2013. *'Unsinkable': Churchill and the First World War*. London: The History Press.

Frewen, O. 1961. *Sailor's Soliloquy*. London: Hutchinson.

Gay, J. D. 1876. *From Pall Mall to the Punjab*. London: Chatto & Windus.

Gilbert, M. 1972 *Winston Churchill, Vol III, Companion Volume 1*. London: Heinemann.

Gretton, Sir P. 1968. *Former Naval Person*. London: Cassell.

Hamilton, Lord G. 1922. *Parliamentary Reminiscences and Reflections. Vol 2: 1886-1906*. London: John Murray.

Hough, R. 1969. *First Sea Lord: An Authorised Biography of Admiral Lord Fisher*. London: George Allen and Unwin.

Hyde, H. M. 1979. *The Londonderys*. London: Hamish Hamilton.

James, A. S. 1956. *A Great Seaman: The Life of Admiral of the Fleet Sir Henry F Oliver*. London: Witherby Ltd.

James, Sir W. *The Eyes of the Navy*. London: Methuen & Co Ltd.

Jameson, W. 1962. *The Fleet that Jack Built*. London: Rupert Hart-Davies.

Jellicoe, J. (Ed Patterson) 1966-68. *Jellicoe Papers*. Navy Records Society.

Keppel, H. 1899. *A Sailor's Life Under Four Sovereigns*. London: Macmillan.

Bibliography

Kerr, M. 193). *Prince Louis of Battenberg Admiral of the Fleet.* London: Longmans.

King-Hall, L. (Ed) 1935. *Sea Saga: Being the Naval Diaries of Four Generations of the King-Hall Family.* London: Victor Gollanz Ltd.

Lambert, A. 2008. *Admirals. The Naval Commanders who Made Britain Great.* London: Faber and Faber.

Lee, S. S. 1927. *King Edward VII: A Biography.* London: Macmillan and Co., Limited.

Leslie, A. 1972. *Edwardians in Love.* London: Hutchinson & Co.

Leslie, S. 1938. *The Film of Memory.* London: Michael Joseph.

Lucy, H. W. 1892. *A Diary of the Salisbury Parliament 1886-1892.* London: Cassell and Company Ltd.

Lucy, H. W. 1920. *The Diary of a Journalist 1890-1910.* London: Murray.

Mackay, R. F. 1973. *Fisher of Kilverstone.* Oxford: Oxford University Press.

Magnus, P. M. 1958. *Kitchener: Portrait of an Imperialist.* London: John Murray.

Magnus, P. M. 1964. *King Edward The Seventh.* London: John Murray.

Marder, A. J. 1940. *British Naval Policy, 1880-1905: The Anatomy of British Sea Power.* London: Cassell.

Marder, A. J. 1952. *Fear God and Dread Nought, Vol I.* London: Jonathan Cape.

Marder, A. J. 1956. *Fear God and Dread Nought, Vol II.* London: Jonathan Cape.

Marder, A. J. 1961. *From Dreadnought to Scapa Flow, Vol 1.* London: Oxford University Press.

Marling, Col Sir P. 1931. *Rifleman and Hussar.* London: John Murray.

McKenna, S. 1948. *Reginald McKenna 1863-1943.* London: Eyre and Spottiswoode.

Morris, A. J. 1981. *A Not So Silent Service.* Moira (University of Ulster Polytechnic).

Morris, A. J. 1984. *The Scaremongers: The Advocacy of War and Rearmament, 1896-1914.* London: Routledge & Kegan Paul.

Naylor, L. E. 1965. *The Irrepressible Victorian.* London: Macdonald.

Pelly, H. B. 1938. *300,000 Sea Miles. An Autobiography.* London: Chatto and Windus.

Ponsonby, S. F. 1951. *Recollections of Three Reigns.* London: Eyre and Spottiswoode.

Repington, C. 1920. *The First World War, 1914-1918.* London: Constable.

Bibliography

Royle, C. 1900. *The Egyptian Campaigns 1882 to 1885. New and Revised Edition Continued to December, 1899.* London: Hurst and Blackett Ltd.

Schurman, D. M. 1981. *Julian S. Corbett, 1854-1922.* London: Royal Historical Society.

Scott, S. P. 1919. *Fifty Years in the Royal Navy.* London: John Murray.

Stuart, V. 1967. *The Beloved Little Admiral.* London: Hale.

Suffield, C. 1913. *My Memories, 1830-1913.* London: H. Jenkins.

Villiers, F. 1920. *Villiers: His Five Decades of Adventure.* Harper & Bros.

Wilson, Sir C. W. 1886. *From Korti to Khartum.* Edinburgh: William Blackwood and Sons.

Wolseley, G. J. (Ed Arthur) 1922. *The Letters of Lord and Lady Wolseley 1870-1911.* London: William Heinemann.

Index

Aberdeen, 161

Aberystwyth, 161, 166

Ahmad, Muhammad, 46

Alcester, Lord, 74

Alexandra, Queen, 181, 192

Alexandria, 5, 37, 38, 39, 41, 42, 43, 45, 48, 49, 78, 83, 85, 88, 89, 142, 260, 265

Algiers, 145

Arabi, 37, 44, 46

Archer-Shee, Major, 204, 205

Armagh, Archbishop of, 32

Armstrong, Sir George, 192

Arnold-Forster, Hugh, 120, 129

Arthur Lee, 179

Ascension Island, 11

Asquith, Herbert Henry, 173, 184, 187, 188, 189, 195, 196, 197, 199, 200, 213, 215, 218, 220, 222, 226, 229, 230, 232, 233, 237, 244, 250, 256, 262

Association of Chambers of Commerce, 97, 106

Aylesford, Earl of, 17, 23

Aylesford, Lady, 25

Bacon, Reginald, 144, 148, 149, 202, 230, 253, 255, 256, 276

Baird, Mr, 213

Balfour, Arthur, 82, 105, 114, 115, 116, 123, 135, 139, 150, 173, 187, 189, 232, 233, 242

Baring, Sir Evelyn, 48

Battenberg, Prince Louis of, 25, 124, 146, 147, 148, 152, 156, 201, 224, 225, 262

Bayly, Lewis, 170, 216

Beatrice, Princess, 28

Beck, Arthur, 208

Belfast, 134, 135, 218

Bell, Moberly, 39, 41, 42, 43

Bellairs, Carlyon, 117, 118, 122, 141, 146, 147, 148, 164, 173, 180, 182, 261, 262

Benbow, Henry, 59, 60

Bentinck, Lord Henry, 63

Berehaven, 132, 134, 135

Beresford, Charles

    Assessment of, 261–62

    Bulldogs, 183

    Death, 258–60

    Early life, 6

    Freemasonry, **15**, **36**

    Guns and gunnery, 45

    Honours, 46, 137, 199, **213**

    Houses, 32, 35, 86

    Lieutenant, 14

    Life-saving, 16

Index

Marriage, 32

Memoirs, 223

Money, 35, 46

Social life, 19, 20, 32

Sports, 34, 210, 213

Sub-lieutenant, 12

Beresford, Charles - Accidents

Boar hunting, 15

Bolting horse, 15

Goat-hunting, **11**

India tour accidents, 24

Marabout shell 1882, 45

Rotten Row, 76

Sail furling, 8

Thrown from horse, 137

Yacht grounding, 19

Beresford, Charles - Attacks on people

Battenberg, 146–48, 224

Curzon, Lord, 251

Fisher. *See* Key events 'Relationship with Fisher'

Winston Churchill, 206, 208–9, 234, 248, 249–50

Beresford, Charles - Career

Admiral, 152

Brtiannia 1859-61, 7–8

Channel Fleet 1903-05, 130, 132–43

Channel Fleet 1907-09, 158–86

C-in-C Channel Fleet 1903-05. *See* Chapter 17

C-in-C Channel Fleet 1907-09. *See* Chapters 19 & 20

C-in-C Mediterranean Fleet 1905-07. *See* Chapter 18

Commander 1875, 24

Dismissal, 181, 185–86

Early life, 6–7

Flag-lieutenant appointment, 17

Fourth Naval Lord 1886-88, 65–72

Half-pay 1875, 21

HMS Bellerophon 1874-75, 21

HMS Clio 1864-65, 10–11

HMS Galatea 1868-71, 14–17

HMS Marlborough 1861-63, 8–9

HMS Research 1868, 13–14

HMS Sutlej & Tribune 1865-66, 12–13

HMS Thunderer, 28

HMS Thunderer 1877-78, 27–31

HMS Undaunted 1889-93, 82–89

Key dates, 263

Mediterranean Fleet 1900-02, 113–23

Mediterranean Fleet 1905-07, 144–57

Midshipman promotion, 9

MP for Marylebone East, 63

MP for Portsmouth, 190, 189–90, 191–234

MP for Waterford, 19, 33, 35

MP for Woolwich 1902-03, 126

MP for York 1898-1900, 100–101, 102–7, 108–12

Naval cadet, 7

Plymouth 1872-74, 20

Rear admiral 1897, 99

Royal Naval College 1897, 99

RY Osborne 1879-81, 32, 34–36

Steam Reserve 1893-96, 90–93

Sub-lieutenant promotion, **12**

Summary, 5

Beresford, Charles - Disputes

Admiral of the Fleet, 195–96

Corradino Heights 1900, 114

Dog cart hire, 15

Letters to Ministers 1900, 116

Officers victimised, 171–72, 189

Peace Party, 166

Scott incidents, 167–70, 173

Similarity to Douglas-Pennant case, 257–58

The Truth About the Navy 1906, 153

Theseus incident 1900, 117

War plans, 159–60, 164–65, 176–77

Beresford, Charles - Honours, 233, 236–37

Beresford, Charles - Key events

Absence from fleet 1907-08, 170–71

Alexandria 1882, 37–43

Arnold White visit 1901, 120

Bacon letters 1906, 148–49

Blandford affair 1876, 25

China visit 1898-99, 105–7

Daily Mail letter 1901, 126–27

Dogger Bank 1904, 139–41

Enquiry 1909, 187–89

India tour 1875-76, 23–25

John Cornwell appeal, 242–43, 246

Lady Brooke, 84–86

Levee incident 1908, 175

Portsmouth MP visits, 29, 65, 76

Relationship with Fisher, 116–17, 118, 122–23, 131, 139, 145–46, 148, 175–76

Royal Academy 1908, 175

Index

Scott incidents, 177–80

Sudan 1884-85, 48–62

Beresford, Charles - Pranks

Broken leg, 18

Chisel throwing, 12

Beresford, Charles - Reprimands

Bridgeman incident, 170

Britannia, 7

Coal stocks, 126

Daily Mail letter 1901, **126**

HMS Thunderer gun explosion, 32

Modes of address, 160

Pea-shooting, 10

Prince George collision 1903, 136–37

Sail competition, 9

Beresford, Charles - Speeches & campaigns

Aircraft, 238

Alcohol, 19

Aliens, 231–32, 238, 255

Barracks, 21

Blockade, 237–38

Boer War, 110

China, 108

Conduct of war, 229–30, 234–35, 239–40, 240

Conscription, 238–39

Critism of speeches, 228

Cruisers, 224–26

Curragh incident, 215–17

Dardanelles, 230

Declaration of London, 198–99

Declaration of Paris, 22

Easter Rising 1916, 239–40

Flogging, 25

Food supply, 247

Germany, 223, 228–29, 230–31, 234, 250, 253

Guns, 98, 104

HMS Formidable, 228

Home Rule, 213–14, 215, 218

Ireland, 254–55

Last speech, 258

LCC speech 1902, 124–25

Manning, 22, 210

Mediterranean, 205–6

National Insurance, 198

Naval (misc), 193, 198, 243–44

Oil, 212–13, 219

Pay and promotion 1897, 98

Pensions, 30, 211

Prisoners of war, 241, 247, 253–54

Railway Bill, 31

Reprisals, 243

Rum, 211–12

283

Index

Shipbuilding, 63, 64–65, 74–76, 76–77, 94–96, 102–4, 104–5, 193–94, 203, 204

Shipping losses, 239, 254

Ships and shipbuilding, 22, 29, 80

Spies, 223, 226, 244, 250, 254

Stopped speaking 1915, 233

Submarines, 219, 246–47, 250

Taxation, 238

Titanic, 204–5, 207–8

Torpedoes, 27

War, 221

Beresford, Charles - War work, 253, 256

    Committees, 224

    No offers made, 222

Beresford, Christiana, 6, 100, 141

Beresford, Delaval, **7**, 156

Beresford, Henry, 6

Beresford, John, 6, **13**

Beresford, John Henry, 6, 13, 64, 93

Beresford, Lady Charles, 31, 32, 36, 47, 49, 51, 69, 82, 84, 85, 86, 91, 100, 113, 115, 118, 121, 137, 144, 146, 154, 185, 214, 219, 236

Beresford, Marcus, 7, 98, 113, 141, 157, 259, 260

Beresford, William, 6, 25, 113, 117

Beresford, William Warren de la Poer, 258

Berlin, 77, 96, 203, 241

Birmingham Conservative Club, 94

Blackpool, 166

Blandford, Lord, 25

Blathwayt, Raymond, 30

Blumenfeld, Ralph, 166, 233

Boardman, Captain, 49, 93

Boer War, 111

Bombay, 24

Bordein (steamer), 58

Bowden-Smith, Admiral, 97

Bowles, Thomas, 92

Boyes, Admiral, 97

Brassey, Thomas, 29

Bridgeman, Sir Francis, 144, 152, 170, 184, 201, 208, 209, 259

Brindisi, 23, 24

Brock, Osmond, 145

Brodrick , St John. *See* Midleton

Brodrick, William, 109

Brooke, Lady, 2, 84, 85, 86, 98

Brooke, Lord, 84

Brooke, Marjorie, 84

Brownlow, Lady, 73

Buller, Redvers, 51, 52, 61, 65

Burnaby, Colonel, 55

Index

Butcher, Sir John, 199

Cambridge, Duke of, 45, 48

Campbell, Mrs Patrick, 31

Campbell-Bannerman, Sir Henry, 150, 173

Canada, 11, 156, 157, 202

Cape St Vincent, 20

Carrington, Lord, 23

Carson, Sir Edward, 207

Castlereagh, Lord, 207

Ceylon, 16

Chambers, James, 207

Channel Fleet, 76, 120, 130, 131, 132, 140, 141, 142, 150, 152, 154, 158, 161, 167, 168, 171, 173, 174, 176, 179, 180, 181, 182, 185, 187, 188, 228, 256, 269, 270, 271

Channel Squadron, 9, 27, 96, 119, 132

Chatfield, Ernle, 158

Chatfield, Lieutenant, 121

Chelmsford, Lord, 11, 34

Chicago, 157

Chief Commissioner of the London Police, 65

Childers, Hugh, 22, 65

China, 15, 16, 48, 105, 106, 108, 109, 276

Christiania, 177, 179

Churchill, Lord Randolph, 25, 67, 69, 74, 82

Churchill, Winston, 175, 200, 202, 203, 206, 208, 209, 210,

212, 213, 215, 216, 217, 248, 261

Cleethorpes, 161

Cochrane, Baillie, 22

Colomb, Vice Admiral Phillip, 96

Colvile, Captain, 52

Committee for Imperial Defence, 188, 194, 200, 222

Connaught, Duke of, 135

Connor, Charles, 33

Copenhagen, 34

Corradino Heights, 114

Cowes, 28, 31, 34

Crease, Thomas, 146, 179

Crewe, Lord, 188, 260

Cromarty, 161, 167, 169

Culme-Seymour, Michael, 133

Curragh incident, 215, 217

Curraghmore, 6, 11, 236, 264

Curzon, George, 105

Curzon, Lord, 192, 218, 239, 251

Curzon-Howe, Hon A G, 133, 134

Custance, Reginald, 158, 161, 166, 171, 176, 177, 259

Cutlers' Company, 44, 194

Daily Mail - letter of 21 June 1901, 120

Darling, C J, 92

Dawson, Lionel, 162, 169

de Robeck, 177, 180

Index

Declaration of London, 197, 198

Declaration of Paris, 22, 199

Defence of the Realm Regulations, 254

Desborough, Lady, 73

Devonport, 19, 160, 260

Devonshire, Duke of, 127, 238, 242

Dilke, Charles, 98, 102, 103

Disraeli, Benjamin, 19, 27, 35

Dogger Bank incident, 139, 140

Domvile, Admiral, 135

Douglas-Pennant, Miss Violet, 257

Dover, 48, 167, 176, 253, 255

Dowell, Sir William, 76

Doyle, Sir Hastings, 27

Dufferin, Lord, 46

Eagle and British Dominions Insurance, 248

Eddystone Lighthouse, 34

Edinburgh, Duke of, **14, 167**

Edward VII, 139, 180, 192

Edward, Prince of Wales, 7, 13, 17, 18, 19, 20, 23, 27, 28, 29, 32, 34, 38, 45, 65, 69, 70, 73, 80, 81, 84, 85, 86, 98

Egypt, 25, 35, 37, 38, 44, 46, 47, 48, 58, 88, 91, 93, 206, 221

El Safieh, steamer, 59, 60, 61, 260

Elgar, Edward, 192

Empire Association, 248

Esher, Viscount, 170, 187, 189

Evan-Thomas, Hugh, 133, 134

Falklands Islands, 11

Fanshawe, Sir Edward, 74

Ferguson, Sir James, **15**

Fifth Cruiser Squadron, 154, 167

Firth of Forth, 161, 165

Fisher, John, 17, 41, 42, 44, 65, 113, 116, 117, 118, 120, 122, 125, 130, 141, 144, 145, 146, 148, 151, 152, 153, 154, 159, 160, 163, 164, 165, 173, 175, 176, 184, 188, 189, 192, 200, 202

Fisher, Pamela, 150

Fitzgerald, Admiral Penrose, 98

Fiume, 151

Flamsteed (ship), 20

Foster, Montague, 212

Foster, Rev William, 7

Frewen, Oswald, 155, 277

Furness, Sir Christopher, 101

Furse RA, Charles, 133

Galatea, HMS, **16, 263**

Gardner, Ellen. *See* Beresford, Lady Charles

Gardner, Richard, 30

Genoa, 113, 144

George V, 192, 195

George, Prince of Wales, 148, 175, 181, 192

Gibraltar, 90, 115, 137, 140, 145, 206

Index

Gillett, Rear admiral, 8, 104

Gillford, Captain, 12

Gladstone, W E, 44, 48, 63, 64, 65, 234

Gladstone, William Ewart, 35

Glyn, H Carr, 23

Goltz, Vice Admiral Baron von der, 78

Gordon, General, 5, 46, 48, 52, 106

Goschen, George, 95, 96, 97, 102, 104, 105, 116, 277

Government of Ireland Bill, 212

Graham, Sir William, 66

Grainger, Mrs, 36

Grantham, 69

Granville, Lord, 38

Grey, Sir Edward, 188, 206, 220

Grey, Sir George, **15**

Grimsby, 161

Gun Licence Act 1870, 19

Haldane, Richard, 188, 194, 203, 231

Halifax, 20

Hamilton, Lord George, 7, 66, 67, 69, 70, 71, 72, 75, 76, 77, 78, 79, 80, 81, 261

Hamilton, Sir Richard Vesey, 76

Hammill, Commander, 52

Hardinge, Sir Charles, 149

Harrow School, 8, 104

Hartington, Lord, 48, 73

Hastings, 27, 29

Hay, Lord John, 22, 156

Hemmerde, Edward, 195

Hertford , Marquis of, 18

Heusner, Rear Admiral, 78

Hewett, Sir William, 46

Hicks Beach, Sir Michael, 62

Hicks, William, 46

HMS *Alexandra*, 21

HMS *Beacon*, 40

HMS *Bellerophon*, 20, 32, 263

HMS Bittern, 40

HMS *Britannia*, 8, 17, 263

HMS Bulwark, 144, 145, 149, 154, 156, 263

HMS Caesar, 137, 138, 263

HMS Camperdown, 89, 179

HMS *Clio*, 10, 11, 14, 263

HMS *Clio*, 263

HMS Colossus, 65

HMS Condor, 5, 17, 36, 37, 39, 40, 44, 45, 61, 208, 261, 263

HMS *Cygnet*, 39, 40

HMS *Decoy*, 40

HMS *Defence*, 9

HMS *Dominion*, 177

HMS Dreadnought, 88, 144, 148, 278

HMS *Excellent*, 65

HMS *Galatea*, **14**, **15**, **16**

HMS Good Hope, 167, 168, 169, 177, 178, 179

HMS Goshawk, 18

Index

HMS Hannibal, 136, 142

HMS Helicon, 39

HMS *Hero*, 132, 170

HMS *Hibernia*, 9, 181

HMS *Implacable*, 145

HMS *Inflexible*, 29

HMS King Edward VII, 145, 158, 162, 176, 184, 216

HMS Majestic, 132, 134, 136, 158

HMS *Marlborough*, 8, 9, 18, 19, 20, 104, 263

HMS Melita, 83, 84

HMS *Monarch*, 40

HMS Prince George, 136, 142

HMS *Ramillies*, 113, 115, 116, 121, 261, 263

HMS Renown, 121

HMS *Research*, **13**

HMS Revenge, 111

HMS Roxburgh, 167, 168, 169

HMS Royal Oak, 116

HMS Royal Sovereign, 116

HMS Sapphire, 168

HMS Serapis, 23, 24, 25

HMS *Suffolk*, 148

HMS Surprise, 154, 177, 185

HMS *Sutlej*, 12, 13, 263

HMS Téméraire, 39

HMS *Terrible*, 130

HMS *Thunderer*, 17, 27, 28, 29, 31, 32, 263

HMS Trafalgar, 9

HMS *Tribune*, 12

HMS *Undaunted*, 81, 82, 83, 84, 85, 88, 90, 113

HMS *Vernon*, 27, 263

HMS Victoria, 89

HMS Victory, 76

Holland, Swinton, 20, 32

Holyhead, 13, 18

Home Fleet, 125, 135, 152, 153, 154, 156, 160, 164, 165, 167, 170, 176, 179, 184, 187, 188, 202, 259

Home Rule, 65, 100, 126, 202, 212, 213, 215, 217, 218, 219, 272

Hong Kong, 106, 107, 108

Hood, Sir Arthur, 66

Hornby, Sir Phipps, 74, 75, 76, 93

Horsey, Algernon de, 74

Horton-Smith, Lionel, 186

Hoskins, Sir Anthony, 66, 87

Hughes, Colonel, 126

Hulbert, A R, 158, 189

Hull, 139, 161, 181, 218, 252

Humber, 161

Hunt, Rowland, 197

Imperial Scout Exhibition, 212

India, 16, 32, 117, 188, 192, 250

Ingram, Mr, 57

Institute of Naval Architects, 96, 97, 104

Index

Invergordon, 161

Inverness, 161

Ireland Club, 137

Isle of Man, 161, 166

Iveagh, Viscount, 210

Iveagh, Viscountess, 210

Japan, 5, 15, 16, 142, 148

Jellicoe, John, 65

Juan Fernández Islands, 11

Kelly, Mr, 72

Keppel, Sir Henry, **15**, **17**, 18, 19, 20, **61**, 137

Keppel, Sub-lieutenant, 61

Kerr, Walter, 81, 119

Khedive, the, 37, 41, 48, 88

King Alfonso of Spain, 138

King George's Fund for Sailors, 248

King of Greece, 24, 149

King of Norway, 177

King of Portugal, 145

King-Hall, George, 18, 83, 84, 114, 119, 120, 130

Kitchener, Herbert, 53, 192

Knollys, Lord, 154

Labour Party, 126, 195, 226

Lagos, 135, 142, 145

Lambton, Hon Hedworth, 133, 144, 149

Lamlash, 134

Law, Bonar, 212, 215, 228, 244

Lea, H C, 180

Lee, Arthur, 197, 211, 215, 224

Leslie, Shane, 32

Lewis, George, 84

Liberal Party, 65, 126, 150, 251

Liddell, Dean, 19

Lincoln, 29

Liverpool, 95, 141, 161, 166

Liverpool Chamber of Commerce, 95

Lloyd George, 175, 195, 244, 252, 253, 255

London Chamber of Commerce, 90, 113, 124, 125, 126

Londonderry, Lady, 167, 182, 185, 214, 226, 227, 244, 248, 253, 256, 257

Londonderry, Lord, 127, 157

Long, Walter, 182, 184, 195, 232

Lord Provost of Edinburgh, 161, 165

Lucy, Henry, 79, 183

Lutin - French submarine, 151

Macdonald, R H, 117

Madeira, 135

Majorca, 138

Malta, 9, 41, 49, 89, 113, 114, 115, 119, 121, 123, 126, 129, 154, 206

Mandesloh, Lucy, 30

Manila, 16

Manners, Lord John, 72

Index

Marlborough Club, 17

Marlborough House Set, 21, 23

Marling, Percival, 59

Mauritius, 16

May, Sir William, 150

McGregor, Sir Evan, 67

McKenna, Reginald, 5, 173, 174, 176, 180, 181, 184, 185, 187, 188, 189, 191, 192, 195, 196, 197, 200, 202, 206, 222, 223, 225, 226, 255, 256, 257, 262, 278

Mediterranean Fleet, 82, 89, 111, 113, 119, 122, 124, 131, 135, 141, 144, 152, 154

Melton, 34, 72

Mendez Nundez (Spanish ship), 13

Meux, Lady, 197

Mexico, 7, 156, 157, 173, 213

Michelham, Lord, 257

Midleton, Lord, 212

Mikado, 16

Milne, Sir Berkeley, 177, 178, 181, 182

Mitford, Algernon, **16**

Montgomerie, Robert, 171

Morley, Lord, 188

Morrison, Captain, 42

Nako, Count, 151

National Insurance Bill, 198

National Party, 237, 251

National Review, 119

National Sailors' and Firemen's Union, 250

Naval Defence Act 1889, 103, 104

Naval Intelligence Department (NID), 67, 68, 69, 70, 71, 73, 94, 261

Naval Prize Bill, 197

Navy League, 91, 93, 94, 99, 116, 119, 210, 224, 242, 247

Nelson, Horatio, 76, 197

New Vagabonds' Club, 100

New Zealand, 15, 171, 277

Noel, Vice Admiral Gerald, 125, 184

North East Coast Institution of Engineers and Shipbuilders, 219

Northbrook, Lord, 38, 63

Northcote, Henry, 106

Nova Scotia - ship, 20

Oliver, Henry, 133, 134

Ontario, 157

Ottley, Charles, 187, 188

Paget, Almeric, 215

Paget, Lady, 210

Paget, Lord Alfred, 24

Paget, Mrs, 47

Pakenham, Sir William, 142, 148, 155, 201

Parkes, Sir Harry, **16**

Pasha, Arabi, 37

Peace Society, 166

Pelly, Henry, 133, 141, 158

Phillimore, Augustus, 9

Index

Piraeus, 24

Plymouth, 10, 16, 17, 18, 19, 20, 82, 89

Ponsonby, Frederick, 163, 167

Port Arthur, 108

Portland, 142, 168, 182, 185, 258

Portsmouth, 19, 20, 29, 36, 132, 154, 158, 170, 181, 182, 185, 189, 190, 195, 210, 215, 223, 230, 231, 263

Powers, Frank, 49

Primrose League, 74, 206, 215

Prince of Wales, 44, 45, 81

Queen of Norway, 178, 183, 218

Queensferry, 161

Queenstown, 28, 141

Representation of the People Bill, 253

Richards. Sir Frederick, 76

Richmond, Herbert, 133

RMS *Titanic*, 204, 207, 220

Robert Yerburg,, 119

Roberts, Field Marshal Lord, 210

Robertson, Edmund, 92

Rollit, Sir Albert, 125

Roosevelt, President, 192, 257

Roper, Charles, 133, 158

Rosebery, Lord, 7

Royal Academy, 133, 175, 218, 257

Royal Commission on War Office, 73

Royal Humane Society, 16

Royal Naval Benevolent Society, 104

Royal Naval College, 99

Royal Sailors' Home, 185

Royal Thames Yacht Club, 215

RY *Osborne*, 32

RY *Victoria and Albert*, **13**

Salisbury, Lord, 5, 23, 62, 63, 65, 68, 70, 71, 85, 86, 88, 97, 106, 126, 135

Salters' Company, 170

San Francisco, 157

Sandars, John, 114, 115

Savage Club, 170

Scarborough, 135, 181

Scott, Captain R F, 185

Scott, Sir Percy, 45, 130, 167, 168, 169, 170, 171, 173, 176, 177, 178, 180, 212, 223, 230, 256, 258, 262

Seely, Sir Charles, 29

Seignelay - French ship, 83, 84

Selborne Scheme, 130

Selborne, Lord, 119, 121, 130, 133, 139, 141, 149, 202

Seymour, Sir Beauchamp, 37, 41, 43

Seymour, Sir Edward, 211

Shah of Persia, 18

Slade, Edmond, 174

Index

Smith, W H, 29, 30, 73

Somerset, Lady Blanche, 20

Souls, The, 73

South Africa, 14, 180, 218, 253

Southampton, 157

Spithead, 8, 18, 28, 69, 170

Stead, W T, 63

Stewart, Colonel Hamill, 49

Stewart, Sir Herbert, 48, 50, 52, 61

Stewart, Sir William Houston, 8

Straits of Magellan, 11

Sturdee, Frederick, 144, 158, 171, 189, 259

Suez Canal, 24

Suffield, Lord, 18, 24, 25, 32

Sunderland, 112

Sutherland, Duke of, 23, 24

Sykes, Lady Jessica, 148, 155

Symonds, Sir Thomas, 74

Tahiti, 15

Talahawiyeh, steamer, 58

Taylor, Mr, 25

Terry, Sir Joseph, 101

The Betrayal (book), 202–3, 276

The Break-up of China, 109–10

Thunderer, HMS, 28

Thursfield, James, 124

Tierra del Fuego, 11

Tom, Fat, **16**, **18**

Transvaal, 110

Tryon, Vice Admiral George, 82, 87, 88, 89, 179

Tweedmouth, Lord, 150, 154, 160, 162, 164, 165, 173, 174

Ulster, 65, 207, 212, 213, 215, 216, 217, 218, 219, 220

Unionist Aerial Defence Committee, 211

United Empire Club, 215

United Irish League, 126

USA, 8, 130, 157, 234, 247

Valparaiso, 12, 13

Venice, 151

Verne Citadel, 182

Victoria, Queen, 13, 14, **17**, 23, 28, 29, 44, 48, 70, 82, 92, 113, 179, 181, 242, 263, 276

Volo, 87, 89

Waldersee, Count, 77

Ward Hunt, George, 20, 27

Warhurst, Mr, 35

Watson, Rear Admiral Burges, 123

Wei-hai-wei, 108

Welbeck Abbey, 74

Wemyss, Rosslyn, 148, 155

Weymouth, 159, 160, 170, 185, 213, 215, 218

Wheeler, Lieutenant, 39

White, Arnold, 116, 118, 119, 126, 130, 179

White, Sir William, 96

Whitehead torpedo works, 170

Index

Wilhelm II, Emperor, 71, 77, 80, 96, 137, 168, 169, 170, 203, 258

Wilson, A K, 87, 120, 132, 135, 160, 187, 201

Wilson, John Crawford, 27

Wilson, Sir Charles, 53

Wolf, Flora, 157

Wolseley, General, 48, 49, 50, 51, 52, 61, 210

Women's Enfranchisement Bill, 198

Women's Imperial Defence Council, 244

Women's Royal Air Force, 257

Wyatt, Harold, 186

Wynyard, 167

Yangtse Valley, 106

Yarmouth, 28, 161

Yokohama, 15

York, Duke of, 98

Yuan Shik Kai, 107

Printed in Great Britain
by Amazon